Liberating the Politics of Jesus

T&T CLARK STUDIES IN ANABAPTIST
THEOLOGY AND ETHICS

Series editors:

Malinda Berry
Paul Martens

Liberating the Politics of Jesus

Renewing Peace Theology through the Wisdom of Women

Edited by
Elizabeth Soto Albrecht and
Darryl W. Stephens

t&tclark
LONDON • NEW YORK • OXFORD • NEW DELHI • SYDNEY

T&T CLARK

Bloomsbury Publishing Plc

50 Bedford Square, London, WC1B 3DP, UK

1385 Broadway, New York, NY 10018, USA

BLOOMSBURY, T&T CLARK and the T&T Clark logo are trademarks of Bloomsbury Publishing Plc

First published in Great Britain 2020

Reprinted 2020

Copyright © Elizabeth Soto Albrecht, Darryl W. Stephens and contributors, 2020

Elizabeth Soto Albrecht and Darryl W. Stephens have asserted their rights under the Copyright, Designs and Patents Act, 1988, to be identified as Editors of this work.

For legal purposes the Acknowledgments on p. xvii constitute an extension of this copyright page.

Cover design: Terry Woodley
Cover image © Teresa Pankratz

All rights reserved. No part of this publication may be reproduced or transmitted in any form or by any means, electronic or mechanical, including photocopying, recording, or any information storage or retrieval system, without prior permission in writing from the publishers.

Bloomsbury Publishing Plc does not have any control over, or responsibility for, any third-party websites referred to or in this book. All internet addresses given in this book were correct at the time of going to press. The author and publisher regret any inconvenience caused if addresses have changed or sites have ceased to exist, but can accept no responsibility for any such changes.

A catalogue record for this book is available from the British Library.

A catalog record for this book is available from the Library of Congress.

ISBN: HB: 978-0-5676-9279-5
PB: 978-0-5676-9278-8
ePDF: 978-0-5676-9281-8
eBook: 978-0-5676-9280-1

Series: T&T Clark Studies in Anabaptist Theology and Ethics

Typeset by Deanta Global Publishing Services, Chennai, India
Printed and bound in Great Britain

To find out more about our authors and books visit www.bloomsbury.com and sign up for our newsletters.

CONTENTS

Foreword vii
Series Preface xii
Preface xiii
Acknowledgments xvii
List of Abbreviations xviii

Introduction *Darryl W. Stephens* 1

PART ONE Retrieval, Remembering, and Re-envisioning 15

1. The Retrieval of a Liberating Christology *Nancy E. Bedford* 17
2. Jesus and the Stories of Our Lives *Carol Penner* 33
3. The Politics of Suffering and JustPraxis *Elizabeth Soto Albrecht* 53

PART TWO Living the Politics of Jesus in Context 67

4. Hospitality as Revolutionary In-Subordination in South Africa *Karen Suderman* 69
5. Women of Faith Advocating Peace in Colombia *Alix Lozano* 82
6. Nonviolence and the Assault on Marginalized Bodies *Regina Shands Stoltzfus* 96

PART THREE Salvation, Redemption, and Witness 113

7   Salvation for the Sinned Against *Linda Gehman Peachey* 115
8   Never Merely Victims *Erin Dufault-Hunter* 132
9   Bearing Witness to Jesus, Resurrected Survivor of Sexual Violence *Hilary Jerome Scarsella* 151

PART FOUR Responding to and Learning from John Howard Yoder's Sexual Violence 167

10   Repairing the Moral Canopy after Institutional Betrayal *Sara Wenger Shenk* 169
11   Adopting the 2015 MC USA Churchwide Statement on Sexual Abuse *Linda Gehman Peachey* 188
12   Lessons from Anabaptist Women's Responses to John Howard Yoder's Sexual Violence *Karen V. Guth* 199

Appendix: Churchwide Statement on Sexual Abuse 213
Bibliography 232
Notes on Contributors 249
Author Index 251
Subject Index 254

FOREWORD

Mennonite peace theology developed in the twentieth century largely as a discourse about war and its alternatives. If war and (violent) revolution are to be avoided, then what other options are available to those who care about making peace between antagonistic social groups? What do those options require of the church community and how does the church articulate these requirements in relation to war-making states? Given that, until very recently, the vast majority of decision-makers in churches and states, as well as the vast majority of soldiers, have been men, it is unsurprising that a focus on church, war, and peace has yielded a field dominated by men. Even the historiography of Mennonite peace witness—with its plot moving from "quietism to activism" or from "nonresistance to active nonviolence"—had tended to focus on the words and deeds of men.[1]

This masculine domination of the field of Mennonite peace studies has been challenged over the years. As Malinda Elizabeth Berry argues, Doris Janzen Longacre's bestselling *More-With-Less Cookbook* represents a major entry by a woman into the field already in 1976.[2] Longacre, according to Berry, transforms the Mennonite theology of nonconformity to the world—one of the traditional pillars of Mennonite peace theology—into a concern for joyous freedom from and prophetic resistance to "patterns of overconsumption and the imperialist mentality that equates affluence with wisdom."[3] Around the same time, a less visible but no less important contribution by women to Mennonite peace theology emerged in the form of the Mennonite Central Committee

---

[1] Leo Driedger and Donald B. Kraybill, *Mennonite Peacemaking: From Quietism to Activism* (Scottdale, PA: Herald, 1994); Ervin R. Stutzman, *From Nonresistance to Justice: The Transformation of Mennonite Church Peace Rhetoric, 1908–2008* (Scottdale, PA: Herald, 2011). See also Perry Bush, *Two Kingdoms, Two Loyalties: Mennonite Pacifism in Modern America* (Baltimore: Johns Hopkins University Press, 1998); Andrew P. Klager, ed., *From Suffering to Solidarity: The Historical Seeds of Mennonite Interreligious, Interethnic, and International Peacebuilding* (Eugene, OR: Pickwick, 2015).
[2] Malinda Elizabeth Berry, "Shalom Political Theology: A New Type of Mennonite Peace Theology for a New Era of Discipleship," *Conrad Grebel Review* 34, no. 1 (Winter 2016): 49–73; Doris Janzen Longacre, *More-With-Less Cookbook* (Scottdale, PA: Herald, 1976).
[3] Berry, "Shalom Political Theology," 69.

Women's Concerns Report. Carol Penner details the history of this vital resource in her chapter in the present volume.

Since the 1990s, a vibrant feminist strand has arisen within Mennonite peace theology. Wilma Bailey, Lydia Neufeld Harder, Mary Schertz, and others have probed the Bible as Mennonite feminists committed to peacemaking.[4] Gayle Gerber Koontz, Carol Penner, and Susanne Guenther Loewen, among others, have raised critical feminist questions about Mennonite systematic theology and ethics.[5] Marlene Epp, Rachel Waltner Goossen, Anita Hooley Yoder, and other historians have demonstrated the decisive role of women in Anabaptist and Mennonite history.[6]

---

[4]Citations in this and the following footnotes are indicative, not comprehensive. See Wilma Ann Bailey, *"You Shall Not Kill" or "You Shall Not Murder"?: The Assault on a Biblical Text* (Collegeville, MN: Liturgical, 2005); Bailey and Christina Bucher, *Lamentations, Song of Songs* (Harrisonburg, VA: Herald, 2015); Lydia Neufeld Harder, *Obedience, Suspicion, and the Gospel of Mark: A Mennonite-Feminist Exploration of Biblical Authority* (Waterloo, ON: Wilfrid Laurier University Press, 1998); Harder, *The Challenge Is in the Naming: A Theological Journey* (Winnipeg: Canadian Mennonite University Press, 2018); Mary H. Schertz and Perry B. Yoder, *Seeing the Text: Exegesis for Students of Greek and Hebrew* (Nashville: Abingdon, 2001).

[5]See Gayle Gerber Koontz, "As We Forgive Others: Christian Forgiveness and Feminist Pain," *Mennonite Quarterly Review* 68, no. 2 (April 1994): 170–93; Gayle Gerber Koontz, "Seventy Times Seven: Abuse and the Frustratingly Extravagant Call to Forgive," *Mennonite Quarterly Review* 89, no. 1 (January 2015): 129–52; Carol Penner, "Content to Suffer: An Exploration of Mennonite Theology from the Context of Violence against Women," in *Peace Theology and Violence against Women*, ed. Elizabeth G. Yoder (Elkhart, IN: Institute of Mennonite Studies, 1992); Carol Penner, "Violence against Women in the Mennonite Brethren Church: Abuse Policies are Not Enough," *Direction* 45, no. 2 (Fall 2016): 192–208; Susanne Guenther Loewen, "Can the Cross Be 'Good News' for Women? Peace Theology and the Suffering of Women," *Anabaptist Witness* 3, no. 2 (December 2016): 109–21.

[6]See Marlene Epp, *Women without Men: Mennonite Refugees of the Second World War* (Toronto: University of Toronto Press, 1999); Marlene Epp, *Mennonite Women in Canada: A History* (Winnipeg: University of Manitoba Press, 2011); Rachel Waltner Goossen, *Women against the War: Conscientious Objection and Gender on the American Home Front, 1941–1947* (Chapel Hill, NC: University of North Carolina Press, 1997); Rachel Waltner Goossen, "'Defanging the Beast': Mennonite Responses to John Howard Yoder's Sexual Abuse," *Mennonite Quarterly Review* 89, no. 1 (January 2015): 7–80; Anita Hooley Yoder, *Circles of Sisterhood: A History of Mission, Service and Fellowship in Mennonite Women's Organizations* (Harrisonburg, VA: Herald, 2017).

Beyond individual scholarly work, beginning in 1992 the Women Doing Theology conferences gathered North American Mennonite women theologians and church leaders for collective revisioning of Mennonite thought.[7] Similarly, Mennonite women in Africa, Asia, and Latin America created organizations for lay and academic theological inquiry.[8] Mennonite women in institutional leadership positions, such as Iris de León-Hartshorn and Michelle Armster in the United States, also began to agitate for a peace theology that addressed issues of sexism and racism.[9]

The Institute of Mennonite Studies (IMS), the research and publishing arm of Anabaptist Mennonite Biblical Seminary (AMBS), has endeavored for several decades to empower feminist voices in moving beyond male-dominated Mennonite peace theology. This support is reflected in IMS's publication list, which includes *Perspectives on Feminist Hermeneutics*, *Peace Theology and Violence against Women*, and *According to the Grace Given to Her: The Ministry of Emma Sommers Richards*.[10] Women have

---

[7] See Carol Penner, "Mennonite Women Doing Theology: A Methodological Reflection on Twenty-Five Years of Conferences," in *Recovering from the Anabaptist Vision: New Essays in Anabaptist Identity and Theological Method*, ed. Laura Schmidt Roberts, Paul Martens, and Myron A. Penner (New York: T&T Clark, 2020), 53–76.

[8] "Anabaptist Women Theologians," *Mennonite World Conference*, accessed December 6, 2019, https://mwc-cmm.org/article/anabaptist-women-theologians.

[9] For an in-depth case study of Latina women's leadership in Mennonite institutions, see Felipe Hinojosa, "Mujeres Evangélicas: Negotiating the Borderlands of Faith and Feminism," in *Latino Mennonites: Civil Rights, Faith, and Evangelical Culture* (Baltimore: Johns Hopkins University Press, 2014), 149–73.

[10] Gayle Gerber Koontz and Willard Swartley, eds., *Perspectives on Feminist Hermeneutics* (Elkhart, IN: Institute of Mennonite Studies, 1987); Elizabeth G. Yoder, ed., *Peace Theology and Violence against Women* (Elkhart, IN: Institute of Mennonite Studies, 1992); James E. Horsch, John D. Rempel, and Eldon D. Nafziger, *According to the Grace Given to Her: The Ministry of Emma Sommers Richards* (Elkhart, IN: Institute of Mennonite Studies, 2013). The first two volumes were developed out of IMS-hosted conferences. The "Peace Theology and Violence against Women" conference involved lay and academic women articulating a peace theology with a wider compass than war. Emma Sommers Richards was the first woman to be ordained to a Mennonite pastorate in the United States.

also long been involved in IMS leadership, including Mary Schertz's almost twenty-year directorship.[11]

When I became the IMS director after Schertz's retirement, I immediately became aware of Elizabeth Soto's "Liberating the Politics of Jesus" project. It seemed to me that IMS had a special calling to accompany Soto in bringing this project to fruition. Founding IMS director Cornelius J. Dyck played a major role in developing John Howard Yoder's early scholarship, including *The Politics of Jesus*, for publication. In the wake of recent publications detailing Yoder's sexual violence,[12] it was time for IMS to contribute to a feminist rethinking of his theological legacy. It also seemed to me that I had a personal calling to support Soto's work. In 2011 I graduated with a PhD from the University of Edinburgh with a thesis on Yoder's theology of the principalities and powers. It was time—well past time, in fact—for male Mennonite theologians, especially specialists on Yoder's work, to support women's "revisioning" of Anabaptist theology.[13]

It was thus a privilege for IMS to host the "Liberating the Politics of Jesus" writers' gathering on AMBS's campus in spring 2019, and it is a delight to see this book emerge from the creativity of these women writers. Our hope is that the chapters included here will gain a wide reading and prove influential in the development of Mennonite peace theology.

Jamie Pitts
Director, Institute of Mennonite Studies
Anabaptist Mennonite Biblical Seminary
Elkhart, Indiana

---

[11]For institutional history, see Jamie Pitts, "Institute of Mennonite Studies (Elkhart, Indiana, USA)," *Global Anabaptist Mennonite Encyclopedia Online*, 2019, accessed December 6, 2019, https://gameo.org/index.php?title=Institute_of_Mennonite_Studies_(Elkhart,_Indiana,_USA).

[12]Ruth Elizabeth Krall, *The Elephants in God's Living Room, volume 3, The Mennonite Church and John Howard Yoder, Collected Essays* (N.P.: Enduring Space, 2013); Waltner Goossen, "'Defanging the Beast.'"

[13]Cf. Dorothy Yoder Nyce, "The Anabaptist Vision: Was It Visionary Enough for Women?" *Conrad Grebel Review* 12, no. 3 (Fall 1994): 312.

SERIES PREFACE

T&T Clark Studies in Anabaptist Theology and Ethics is dedicated to displaying the vibrant global resurgence of theological reflection and praxis in and adjacent to the Anabaptist tradition. In a world that is fraught with overt and covert forms of violence, this series provides a platform for new ways of seeing, understanding, and living what it means to love one's enemy and one's neighbor with the peace of God that surpasses much of the wisdom of the day.

With debts to the New Testament, the early church, and late-medieval reformers, Anabaptism emerged as a loosely organized Christian movement in sixteenth-century Europe. Today the heirs of this continually evolving and sometimes highly contested tradition—whether called Mennonite, Brethren, Hutterite, Amish, or any number of other designations—are scattered around the world and especially the Global South. Therefore, while recognizing that the preponderance of academic theology in the peace church tradition still occurs in North America and Europe, this series is committed to publishing voices that represent the theological imaginations, concerns, heartbreaks, and convictions of the entire global Anabaptist family. To that end, volumes draw from established and emerging voices and take a variety of forms, including but not limited to monographs, case studies, and edited collections.

T&T Clark Studies in Anabaptist Theology and Ethics is published under the editorial direction of the Institute of Mennonite Studies, the research and publication agency of Anabaptist Mennonite Biblical Seminary in Elkhart, Indiana. The Institute of Mennonite Studies was founded in 1958 to promote and create opportunities for research, conversation, and publication on topics and issues vital to the Anabaptist faith tradition. For more information or to submit a proposal to the series, please visit www.ambs.edu/ims.

Malinda Berry, Anabaptist Mennonite Biblical Seminary
Paul Martens, Baylor University

PREFACE

The idea for this project began over a decade ago. In the beginning, it was just a dream, a flying thought, maybe a crazy idea—but one that took hold of me, not letting go. That is the way the Spirit works. The dream developed into a thought, then into a more concrete idea. It was like a new child given to me; I needed to care and nurture it until it grew and matured. It became my brainchild.

I remember approaching the Women's Concerns program of Mennonite Central Committee (MCC) in Akron, Pennsylvania, asking whether they would support a theological project to rewrite the influential book *The Politics of Jesus* by JHY. (As an act of resistance and liberation, I prefer to use the author's initials and not his full name.) I met with Linda Gehman Peachey, MCC staff person at the time, showing her the list of Mennonite women writers I had compiled on a sticky note on top of JHY's book. However, the project could not move ahead at that time because MCC decided to eliminate the staff position of the Women's Concerns desk, leaving women with fewer spaces to connect.

I knew from the start that I could not and should not take on this project alone. I had a vision of gifted and diverse women working together: global voices, women of diverse colors and theological backgrounds and ages, who were all passionate to work on justice and peace. Around this time, I started having a recurring dream. The scene was often the same: I was pregnant, and I could not believe it because I was too old. I received an infant I was told to care for, to hold and nurture, but I kept losing this child. Those nightmares repeated for several years. Several times I almost let go of the project, but the desire became an urgent calling I needed to follow.

I shared this crazy idea once with my colleague Darryl Stephens, as he was offering feedback on our Mennonite Church USA Sexual Abuse Statement. Seeing potential, he gave me courage to proceed. I remember a phone call with Sara Wenger Shenk, who was then president of AMBS. I told her about the project and my dream: "I feel I am pregnant carrying this child for a long time, and it is time to give birth to it. Will AMBS support me in this journey?" I had graduated from AMBS, and it was important for me to have the support of my *alma mater*. It was a low time for me, too. After concluding my role as Moderator of MC USA in the summer of 2015, I was falling into a deep depression. In the middle of my emotional ups and downs, I was still doubting the project, wondering whether I should turn the page, move on, and leave behind anything related to JHY. Sara kindly heard me and understood, as a woman of kindred spirit, and promised to process it with the faculty. The project emerged; embedded in it was the need to heal myself through writing and not allow myself to drown in my own brokenness.

We knew that meeting together as writers was as important as the task of writing our individual chapters. Therefore, we planned a consultation for the women authors on March 14–17, 2019, at AMBS in Elkhart, Indiana. We invited fifteen writers from various walks of life, many of whom had never met or even heard of each other. Each writer was instructed to bring their chapter in draft for feedback, and together we would jointly develop a constructive theological path. We prayed and worshiped together, learning from each other and allowing the Sofia of God to move among us. Each writer had opportunity to present her chapter twice, once in a designated group and again in an affinity group. We offered collegial, constructive feedback. Three group facilitators who were not contributing written pieces were assigned to listen carefully in each group: Linda Shelly, Marissa Smucker, and Kay Bontrager-Singer. We shared how our chapters addressed the politics of Jesus (present in our ministries of teaching and walking with those in pain and found in the Bible, not the JHY thesis) from our perspectives as Anabaptist women of distinct backgrounds and even some from outside the peace church traditions. The facilitators summarized what they heard as we aimed to unify the focus while keeping each voice unique. Like voices in a choir, each one of us sang our part. As we came together, we achieved four-part harmony. We shared common themes, such as healing, resistance, integration, witness-bearing, margins, regeneration, repairing, power, well-being, *colaboración*, jubilee, and authority. I had prayed that CristoSofia would bind us together in one spirit as we shared the value of this project; and so, it happened.

Liberating the politics of Jesus was (and still is) a pressing issue for us as women living in a highly patriarchal and sexist society. At the time of our gathering, the United States was facing a political crisis in the White House, and society was rocked by the #MeToo movement and revelations of sexual abuse by powerful men. Sports heroes, entertainment stars, religious leaders, and politicians were finally being exposed by valiant survivors. This climate demanded a religious response, and so liberating the politics of Jesus became an exercise of our political voices.

As we spent time together, we envisioned, refocused, and rewrote our chapters in the spirit of constructive theology, weaving our souls and minds into it. We understood that the project would be stronger through this engagement with a community of writers. We heard the whispers of the Divine One who desires healing for the wounded from all forms of abuse. It was a time of hope for the church we believe in—not the four walls but the true nature of the body of Christ.

In these pages we offer a distinct way of reinterpreting the politics of Jesus. If readers are looking to read about JHY, this is not what *Liberating the Politics of Jesus* is about. A few chapters touch on JHY's theological propositions but just enough to impart our own ideas. Today a group of passionate women writers can simply get on with the reconstruction work and produce new material. Contrary to interpreting an apolitical Jesus, we as women have been living our political lives infused by Jesus's political ways of existing and his ethics of being. These chapters are new pieces about how we conceive the politics of Jesus that are present in how we work for justice and peace in our respective worlds. In other words, this book renews peace theology through the wisdom of women *en la lucha*—in our everyday struggles.

I would like to close with a word of thanks to Darryl, who greatly facilitated this project with his gifted writing and editing. The IMS at AMBS also helped shape the project, and I'm particularly grateful for the support of Sara Wenger Shenk, Mary Schertz, David Cramer, and Jamie Pitts throughout the process. Finally, I would like to thank the Schowalter Foundation and JustPax Funds, whose generous grants allowed my dream to become a reality.

Elizabeth Soto Albrecht
Lancaster Theological Seminary
Lancaster, Pennsylvania

ACKNOWLEDGMENTS

Pen and ink images by Teresa Pankratz (www.teresapankratz.com). Used with permission of the artist. Do not reprint without express written permission.

Unless indicated otherwise, Scripture quotations are from New Revised Standard Version Bible, copyright © 1989 National Council of the Churches of Christ in the United States of America. Used by permission. All rights reserved worldwide.

ABBREVIATIONS

AMBS	Anabaptist Mennonite Biblical Seminary
ANC	African National Congress
ANiSA	Anabaptist Network in South Africa
FARC–EP	Revolutionary Armed Forces of Colombia–People's Army
GemPaz	Ecumenical Group of Women Builders of Peace
IMS	Institute of Mennonite Studies
LGBTQ	lesbian, gay, bisexual, transgender, questioning (or queer)
MC USA	Mennonite Church USA
MCC	Mennonite Central Committee
MQR	*Mennonite Quarterly Review*
NIV	New International Version
PTSD	Post-Traumatic Stress Disorder
Report	*MCC Women's Concerns Report*
SCE	Society of Christian Ethics
TLB	The Living Bible
UMC	The United Methodist Church
USA	United States of America

Introduction

Darryl W. Stephens

Liberating the Politics of Jesus comes at a critical time, a *kairos* moment, for both church and society. The Roman Catholic Church is reeling from scandal: parishes in Australia, Ireland, Chile, and the United States have demanded accountability and truth-telling about decades of child sexual abuse and cover-up by priests, bishops, and cardinals—the very leaders entrusted with conveying the message of the gospel.[1] Protestants in the United States are reckoning with name-brand evangelists who have wielded their charismatic powers of persuasion, not for spreading the good news of Christ but as a means to sexually harass and assault women.[2] Societies across the world are also dealing with a newfound awareness of sexualized violence as the #MeToo movement holds the powerful to account at a rate unseen in previous eras.[3] In a moment such as this, when church and world desperately need to hear the liberating politics of Jesus again, this book offers a renewal of Anabaptist peace theology through the wisdom of women.

For those outside this tradition (named for its insistence on believer's baptism), mention of the Anabaptists may elicit an array of images, from the Radical Reformation and its European martyrs[4] to the horse-drawn buggies of the Amish and "Old Order" Mennonites prominent in rural parts of Pennsylvania, Indiana, and Ohio,[5] to the worldwide relief efforts of the Mennonite Central Committee, headquartered in the United States and Canada.[6] All of these expressions of Anabaptist tradition hold in common a commitment to peace, nonviolence, forgiveness, and reconciliation as central to the gospel message. Amish and Anabaptists understand

---

[1] Dan Stockman, "Amid Abuse Crisis, Sisters Call for Healing, Changes to Church Structure," *National Catholic Reporter*, September 10, 2018, https://www.globalsistersreport.org/news/ministry-trends/amid-abuse-crisis-sisters-call-healing-changes-church-structure-55366.
[2] David Crary, "Evangelicals Confront Sex Abuse Problems in #MeToo Era," *Associated Press*, August 17, 2018, https://www.apnews.com/b768d035ed8443ad97d193a5c36e240c.
[3] See https://metoomvmt.org.
[4] David L. Weaver-Zercher, *Martyrs Mirror: A Social History* (Baltimore: Johns Hopkins University Press, 2016).
[5] Donald B. Kraybill, *Simply Amish: An Essential Guide from the Foremost Expert on Amish Life* (Harrisonburg, VA: Herald, 2018); Steven M. Nolt, *The Amish: A Concise Introduction* (Baltimore: Johns Hopkins University Press, 2016).
[6] Mennonite Central Committee (MCC), homepage, https://mcc.org.

this commitment to radical forgiveness and reconciliation as arising directly from the biblical accounts of Jesus, whose radical politics ran counter to the prevailing wisdom and political powers of his day. Anabaptist theology, then, offers a necessary ingredient of any faithful effort of the church to address the human propensity toward violence and abuse.

These same commitments to peace, nonviolence, forgiveness, and reconciliation can become abusive in themselves when practiced in ways that deny the need for truth-telling, accountability, restitution, and the protection of the vulnerable—all necessary ingredients of justice-making.[7] When peace demands secrecy, when radical forgiveness requires forgetfulness, when nonviolence eschews accountability—the most vulnerable of the community are put at increased and further risk.[8] Patriarchal structures have exacerbated these tendencies to deny the radical politics of Jesus, resulting in practices that fail to witness to the gospel. Anabaptist theology has long been the domain of male scholars and male pastoral leaders. For many years—indeed for most of the history of Anabaptist tradition—the politics of peacemaking has been developed through male experiences and worldviews. The exclusion of women's experiences and voices from Anabaptist peace theology has impoverished this tradition, resulting in a distorted understanding of the politics of Jesus and collusion with abuse.

The international Mennonite community continues to grapple with the abusive legacy of John Howard Yoder, its most famous modern-day theologian, whose work became synonymous with nonviolent theology.[9] Anabaptist women theologians, having been targeted for abuse by Yoder, provide a critical viewpoint for this task of liberating the politics of Jesus as found in the gospels. Politics is no longer confined to statecraft, and peacemaking is no longer restricted to the battlefield. Through the eyes of women,

---

[7]Marie M. Fortune, *Is Nothing Sacred? When Sex Invades the Pastoral Relationship* (San Francisco: Harper and Row, 1989), 114–18.

[8]See, for example, Shelly Bradbury and Peter Smith, "In the Shadow of Forgiveness," *Pittsburgh-Post-Gazette,* June 1, 2019, https://www.apnews.com/3000fa23351b4d28b1e49c439d0063e9.

[9]Rachel Waltner Goossen, "'Defanging the Beast': Mennonite Responses to John Howard Yoder's Sexual Abuse," *Mennonite Quarterly Review* 89, no. 1 (January 2015): 7–80.

we are reminded that the personal is political, that peacemaking pertains to the home as well as the war, and that the good news of Jesus Christ proclaims not suffering and docility but liberation and justice. Anabaptist women—and Anabaptist theology and practice itself—are emerging from Yoder's shadow with a critical assessment and renewed understanding of this tradition. This book seeks to liberate the politics of Jesus from a male-centered account by developing a constructive peace theology from the lived experiences and viewpoints of women theologians and practitioners.

Themes and Convictions

It is my privilege and responsibility, as co-editor of this volume, to introduce its themes and indicate something of its wider relevance for Christian theology and ethics. I do so with the hope that this constructive work of theology and ethics will benefit not only women but all persons, not only Anabaptists but all Christians, and not only Christians but all who work for peace and justice in the world. Written for a new generation that is aware that gender justice and peace theology are inseparable, this book claims the authority of women to interpret and reconstruct the peace church tradition on issues such as subordination, suffering, atonement, peacemaking, trauma, and discipleship. This renewed vision of Anabaptist peace theology has the potential to transform the work of theology and ministry in all Christian traditions.

Liberating the Politics of Jesus offers a fresh interpretation of the social and political implications of the gospel message, drawing on the rich tradition of Anabaptist theology and practice through the perspective and wisdom of women. This book includes new, unpublished writings from diverse contributors, many of whom are internationally known Anabaptist scholars and leaders. Each writer brings a commitment to furthering the development of Anabaptist theology in conversation with the best insights from scholarship and practice. Contributors speak from a wide range of scholarly disciplines and positions of leadership within the Mennonite tradition and beyond, drawing on years of experience in pastoral ministry with Mennonites around the world. Perhaps what is most distinctive about the methodology is its collaborative nature, bringing scholars and practitioners together for four days to work through theological reflection together, as described by Elizabeth Soto Albrecht in the preface.

This project of liberation draws wisdom from *mujerista*, feminist, and womanist discourse. This work of theological reflection and construction requires sustained attention to praxis. For example, the *mujerista* theology of Ada María Isasi-Díaz asserts that liberation is found in *la lucha*—the everyday struggle of women to survive, to live, and to claim their own moral agency—and is itself "the struggle to be self-determining within the context of community and in view of the common good."[10] Indeed, the renewal of Anabaptist tradition is embodied by the women contributing to this volume through the shared conviction that the church should hold no distinctions: "There is no longer Jew or Greek, there is no longer slave or free, there is no longer male and female; for all of you are one in Christ Jesus" (Gal. 3:28). Thus, this book operates on several levels: an exercise of theology by women claiming their own critical and constructive voices; an attempt to free Anabaptist theology from patriarchal distortions, particularly those of John Howard Yoder's life and work; and an effort to unleash the radical, political implications of the life and message of Jesus of Nazareth for a suffering world today.

The book challenges readers, Anabaptist and non-Anabaptist alike, to consider the lived reality of women in the world and the practical import and implications of Jesus's life and teachings. The authors recognize a complex understanding of "politics" extending far beyond the male-dominated domains traditionally associated with this word. There is no tidy differentiation between church and world. Where the gospel meets everyday communities, we find systems and structures of power exposed, revealing interrelations between persons, families, groups, and communities in need of the redemptive, radical, and liberating politics of Jesus. Thus, each contributor to this book, in her own way, examines systems of human relationships, those principalities and powers that order our common life in community, in order to reveal how things are in light of the kin-dom of God, the reign of God today, as inaugurated and

---

[10]Ada María Isasi-Díaz, *En La Lucha/ In the Struggle: Elaborating a Mujerista Theology*, 10th anniversary ed. (Minneapolis: Fortress, 2004), x.

lived by Jesus Christ. Out of pain and wrestling comes a renewed peace theology attuned to issues of power, privilege, and abuse.

Giving voice to the full range of the reality of women's lived experience, this book informs a wide range of issues, including sexual violence, immigration, terrorism, racism, and war. Each chapter offers liberative resources within the tradition in order to access that which allows the created order to thrive. When the church and its members are called to make decisions, we are challenged to consider the whole human, embodied self in relationship to soil, soul, and society. As a result, this work offers hope in the midst of the profound suffering that has wounded the lives of many persons. When asked to put forth one word to encapsulate the themes of this book, the contributors offered the following array of images: healing, integration, witness-bearing, margins, the congregation, resistance, *colaboración* (co-laboring), well-being, remaking, repairing, jubilation, authority, power, and regeneration. A communally based, liberative hermeneutic is evident throughout. What makes this collaborative effort distinctly Anabaptist is its ecology of discipleship and the sense of accountability within Christian community, drawing on the gospel. There is a missional principle underlying this egalitarian "church in the round."[11] This book seeks nothing less than the renewal of Anabaptist theology and practice as a witness within the Mennonite community, within the larger Christian tradition, and within the entirety of God's created, redeemed world.

Outline

This book is presented in four main parts. Part One, "Retrieval, Remembering, and Re-envisioning," sets the stage for the work of liberating the politics of Jesus and represents the wide diversity of voices and methodologies in this book. In Chapter 1, "The Retrieval of a Liberating Christology," Nancy Bedford surveys the existing landscape and clears the brush. She begins by asking whether Anabaptist Christologies help or hinder discipleship.

---

[11]Letty M. Russell, *Church in the Round: Feminist Interpretation of the Church* (Louisville: Westminster John Knox, 1993).

Writing as an Anabaptist Latina feminist systematic theologian working within the tradition of the hermeneutical spiral of deconstruction and retrieval, she argues that Christology must be liberated from normative whiteness, lethal forms of masculinity, and docetic epistemologies. Drawing on depictions of Mary by Sor Juana Inés de la Cruz, distinctive Anabaptist Christological convictions identified by Thomas Finger, and practices of her own faith community, Bedford seeks to discover what the politics of Jesus means concretely for the bodies of those who are not coded as white, straight, or male. As seen from her North American context, she concludes that the politics of Jesus, in order truly to be liberating, needs to decenter whiteness, reorient masculinity, and celebrate a holistic understanding of life.

In Chapter 2, "Jesus and the Stories of Our Lives," Carol Penner works inductively, asking what theology looks like when Anabaptist women are in charge of creating spaces to theologize. She presents the history and methodology of the Mennonite Central Committee *Women's Concerns Report* (1973–2004) as a distinct expression of peace theology. The *Report* was one of the first places where Anabaptist women controlled the agenda and format of theological writing. Through storytelling and feminist/womanist/*mujerista* analysis, this publication presented the real stories of Anabaptist women, including stories about violence and abuse, inspiring women to imagine new ways to understand Jesus, exercise power, and structure community. She suggests three important areas for continued development of Anabaptist theology: advocating for women doing theology; inclusion of personal stories; and listening to stories of the marginalized, including the stories the earth is telling us.

Chapter 3, "The Politics of Suffering and JustPraxis," complements Bedford's retrieval and Penner's remembering by re-envisioning the politics of Jesus as JustPraxis. In this chapter, Elizabeth Soto Albrecht shares her journey as a Latina practical theologian in liberating the politics of Jesus from the predominant Christian teaching of voluntary suffering. She defines suffering, refracted through Jesus's doing and being, as a political problem, recognizing it as a direct result of human actions and systems of oppression. The process of proclaiming liberation, JustPraxis, is based on truth-telling and breaking silence, giving meaning to our pain. Liberation comes when allowing justice to shine light on the truth of suffering. JustPraxis includes compassion and communal healing for those suffering from hurt and violence caused by human wrongdoing. The politics of suffering requires us to dismantle the systems of oppression that sustain sexism, classism, and racism—the root causes are shared. JustPraxis is one way to incarnate God's justice, moving us away from suffering as we address together that which produces pain. The core of JustPraxis is manifested in liberation from suffering.

Part Two, "Living the Politics of Jesus in Context," offers three concretely situated examples of Anabaptist lived theology in overtly political contexts, viewed critically and constructively through women's eyes. In Chapter 4, "Hospitality as Revolutionary In-Subordination in South Africa," Karen Suderman reflects on her experience as a missionary and examines the subversive practice of hospitality during apartheid and postapartheid South Africa. Recognizing the important role that John Howard Yoder's theology played and continues to play in South Africa, this chapter reevaluates Yoder's depiction of revolutionary subordination by reclaiming a traditionally subordinate role, that of host, as an act of revolutionary insubordination, dramatically altering power dynamics and reimagining how people of different races and socioeconomic backgrounds can engage and embrace one another. Thus, she offers a reinterpretation of the phrase "revolutionary subordination" and uses South Africa as a case study to highlight daily acts of revolution by ordinary radicals.

In Chapter 5, "Women of Faith Advocating Peace in Colombia," Alix Lozano draws on her work as a peace activist in Colombia to examine the role of women of faith in a society in crisis, amid armed conflict and both structural and social violence. She describes the role of women in the peace process and implementation of the 2016 Peace Agreement as well as theological and religious obstacles to believers' political advocacy. As a model of peacebuilding, she presents the work of the Ecumenical Group of Women Builders of Peace (GemPaz), of which she is a founding member and leader. Engaging in contextual reading of the Bible, facilitated dialogue, and other strategic methods for overcoming divisions and suspicions among Christians of different denominations, their work shows that the liberating policies of Jesus and his praxis go far beyond theoretical concepts. She also discusses ongoing challenges to ecumenical cooperation and transformation.

Chapter 6, "Nonviolence and the Assault on Marginalized Bodies," explores the potential of peace theology to address racism. Regina Shands Stoltzfus draws on critical race theory and narrative theology to identify how American racial history is a text that counters and competes with historic peace church theology. This tension is illustrated by the ambiguous history of Mennonite urban missions—white Mennonites sent to Black communities. She argues that a church committed to anti-racism work must go beyond a "racial reconciliation" model that creates the illusion of unity at the expense of particularity. To address the deep systemic roots of racism, peace theology must promote community that builds the capacity to sit together in uncomfortable places, dares to ask difficult questions, insists on holding one another accountable, and addresses power disparities. This kind of community necessitates creating a historical consciousness of American racial history.

Part Three, "Salvation, Redemption, and Witness," interrogates central theological concepts in light of the sexual violation of women, exposing the political nature of the most personal of issues. In Chapter 7, "Salvation for the Sinned Against," Linda Gehman Peachey seeks an Anabaptist theology of salvation that takes seriously women's experiences of silencing, oppression, and violation, both in the church and in the world at large. However, she observes that much of current Anabaptist atonement theology commends suffering as the way to salvation. Drawing on interviews with Anabaptist women, writings of Mennonite women over the past thirty years, and her own experience, she constructs a theology of salvation, life, and wholeness for those who have been violated and disregarded. The way to salvation is not suffering but rather God's solidarity and presence with us in creative resistance to the powers of evil. The God we meet in Jesus is always reaching out to embrace, empower, liberate, and vindicate those who have been sinned against.

In Chapter 8, "Never Merely Victims," Erin Dufault-Hunter addresses the puzzle of redemption, given the persistence of sexual violence against women: How can victims respond to violence without becoming like their victimizers? She argues that any attempt to address sexual violence must hold together two truths: the pernicious effects of sexual trauma and the reality of God's unrelenting redemption. Anabaptist theology offers hope by reminding us that victims of sexual violence are never merely victims. Because not even sexual violence overcomes God's redemptive power, victims can come to love enemies, refusing to disregard their humanity, by perceiving them truthfully, as the pitiable creatures they are. This chapter offers a glimpse of how those seemingly damned to victimization can escape the logic of violence, not through powerlessness but through the power of the wounded-yet-risen body of Christ.

Chapter 9, "Bearing Witness to Jesus, Resurrected Survivor of Sexual Violence," asks how Christian communities ought to respond to testimonies of sexual violence when a sense of certainty regarding the facts and circumstances is limited. In this chapter, Hilary Jerome Scarsella cultivates alternative ground on which to build political resistance to sexual violence and solidarity with survivors by considering Jesus's crucifixion. Given that sexual violence was a common aspect of Roman crucifixion, it is likely that Jesus was the victim of sexual assault—though we cannot be certain. The limits of our knowledge require us to restructure our politics such that solidarity with survivors is possible in the midst of uncertainty and constitutive of our witness. Bearing witness to possibility provides a concrete mode of resistance to sexual violence, enabling political action in solidarity with survivors when certainty regarding the facts of survivors' testimonies is not available.

Part Four, "Responding to and Learning from John Howard Yoder's Sexual Violence," addresses the political nature of the church and related institutions in light of its (mis)handling of Yoder's abuses. In Chapter 10, "Repairing the Moral Canopy after Institutional Betrayal," Sara Wenger Shenk narrates the journey of truth-telling at Anabaptist Mennonite Biblical Seminary (AMBS) in the wake of John Howard Yoder's case. Speaking from her perspective as its former president, she recounts the key decisions, guiding priorities, hoped for outcomes, and courageous wise collaborators (including, most importantly, victims of Yoder's sexual harassment and violence). The nonviolent politics of Jesus emboldened AMBS to listen to victims of sexual violence, call for transparency and truth-telling, adjudicate wisely when discerning next steps, confess institutional complicity in exacerbating the harm, and apologize. This work of mending the moral canopy of the AMBS community made credible again a theology of peace grounded in its tradition as a peace church, its stated convictions as a Mennonite seminary, and Jesus's life, ministry, death, and resurrection.

In Chapter 11, "Adopting the 2015 MC USA Churchwide Statement on Sexual Abuse," Linda Gehman Peachey reflects theologically on the process begun in 2013 by Mennonite Church USA to attend to the ongoing painful legacy of John Howard Yoder's sexual violence. Guided by a six-member discernment group, this process resulted in the passage of the 2015 MC USA Churchwide Statement on Sexual Abuse. From her perspective as a member of and writer for this group, she outlines the major events and concerns that led to the statement and the subsequent steps toward implementation. She discusses three ongoing challenges facing the church: sexuality and systemic violence, sexuality and hierarchical dualism, and theology and worship practices shaped with sensitivity to and informed by survivors of sexual abuse.

Chapter 12, "Lessons from Anabaptist Women's Responses to John Howard Yoder's Sexual Violence," offers a perspective from outside the Mennonite Church, making explicit the implied ecumenical impact of the conversations throughout this book. Karen V. Guth considers what scholars and teachers of theology and religion can learn from Anabaptist women's responses to John Howard Yoder's sexual violence. Concerted responses by women modeled moral repair—action that redresses the structural, cultural, and institutional scope of the problem. Key lessons include the importance of women's experience, the need to connect theory and practice, the imperative of addressing myriad forms of violence, the need to attend to misuses of power, and a reconceptualization of legitimate theological authority. The implications include a consideration of authority and moral harm in the classroom when choosing whether and how to teach Yoder's work as well as how to teach traumatic material while avoiding an unhelpful focus on redemption narratives and closure. The salience of these lessons extends beyond Yoder's case to other legacies implicated in traumatic pasts, both historical and contemporary.

As an appendix, we have included the original text, in its entirety, of the Churchwide Statement on Sexual Abuse, passed by the Mennonite Church USA Delegate Assembly at Kansas City, Missouri, July 3, 2015. The statement identifies the reality of sexual abuse in families, churches, and communities; confesses the church's failures of action and inaction; and voices repentance: "We resolve to tell the truth about sexual abuse; hold abusers accountable; acknowledge the seriousness of their sin; listen with care to those who have been wounded; protect vulnerable persons from injury; work restoratively for justice; and hold out hope that wounds will be healed, forgiveness offered, and relationships established or reestablished in healthy ways." The main statement calls for specific actions and commitments by congregations and church institutions.

Personal Reflections

As Elizabeth Soto Albrecht's colleague and fellow traveler, I share the vision and join in the struggle, though in some ways, I am an outsider. I have only a tenuous, historical connection to the Mennonite tradition through a once-excommunicated bishop that the Church of the United Brethren in Christ and, now, The United Methodist Church (UMC) claim as a founder.[12] Yet, as a male clergyperson working to end violence against women, I have found connection across denominational lines, especially through my work in a national office of the UMC dedicated to gender justice and the prevention of and response to sexual misconduct by ministerial leaders. As a staff person at the General Commission on the Status and Role of Women in the UMC, I met similarly minded leaders in other communions, including Elsie Goerzen of the Mennonite Central Committee, Canada, and utilized many of the resources and publications of the Mennonite Central Committee, USA, including those by Linda Gehman Peachey. Continuing my advocacy as a researcher at Lancaster Theological Seminary in 2014, I met my colleague Elizabeth Soto Albrecht.

Elizabeth and I immediately connected through our shared calling to address the continuing problem of sexual violence in homes, church, and society. At the time, she was serving as moderator to the Mennonite Church USA, and I was researching and writing about the aftereffects on congregations due to ministerial sexual abuse. It was during this momentous time for MC USA that Elizabeth first shared her vision with me, to liberate the politics of Jesus *from*

---

[12]Mennonites formally reversed their excommunication of Martin Boehm in 2016, more than 240 years after rejecting his evangelistic preaching of the Holy Spirit. Linda Bloom, "Mennonites Reconnect with UMC Founder," *UMNS*, June 27, 2016, https://www.umnews.org/en/news/mennonites-reconnect-with-umc-founder.

the patriarchal stranglehold of the legacy of John Howard Yoder and *for* the healing and empowerment of women. I invited her into my research, and she entrusted me with her dream. In September 2015, I convened an ecumenical consultation of church leaders to address the topic of healing congregations. Elizabeth, Linda, Elsie, and fourteen other laity and clergy leaders from across the United States and Canada, from seven different denominations in all, met in Lancaster for a day and a half of worship, fellowship, study, and strategizing.[13] I felt renewed and emboldened in our work. Our paths had converged. This project, then, became a joint effort, a work of constructive theology done *en conjunto*, together.

Elizabeth has long imagined the creation of a constructive Anabaptist theology written by women, whose voices have been historically marginalized within her peace church tradition. The innovative and ambitious nature of this approach, bringing together theologians and practitioners from several continents and multiple disciplinary perspectives, attests to the range of her vision and depth of her commitment to create a new space for this important conversation. I have served not only as editor but also midwife to Elizabeth's vision of liberating the radical political ethic of Jesus Christ from its patriarchal distortions.

We hope this work inspires liberation theologians, feminist theologians, as well as Anabaptist and ecumenical scholars and practitioners. This book would be appropriate for seminary and graduate level students, advanced undergraduates, and others studying justice and conflict, peace theology, and women and gender in religion. We also intend this book for church leaders seeking new insight into an ancient text and an eternal savior, whose politics remain ever relevant.

---

[13]The research project, "Healing Congregations: From Woundedness to Vitality," was administered through Lancaster Theological Seminary and funded in part by a grant from the Commission on Pastoral Counseling Services of the South Georgia Annual Conference of The United Methodist Church.

PART ONE

Retrieval, Remembering, and Re-envisioning

1

The Retrieval of a Liberating Christology

Nancy E. Bedford

The question I want to address is how Christology can push against the cooptation of the figure of Jesus by a racist culture. My approach is that of an Anabaptist Latina feminist systematic theologian working within the tradition of the hermeneutical spiral of deconstruction and retrieval. My working presupposition is that the gospel of Jesus is indeed good news, first and foremost for the vulnerable and ultimately for all creation. When the Christian faith functions in ways that justify violent and lethal practices, the calling of the theologian in the community of faith—and beyond—is to point out what has become off-kilter and needs to be reexamined and changed. I argue that Christology must be liberated from the normative whiteness, the lethal forms of masculinity, and the docetic epistemologies that often lurk even in well-intentioned tropes about the "politics of Jesus."[1] Put positively, in order truly to be liberating in a North American context, the "politics of Jesus" needs to decenter whiteness, reorient masculinity, and celebrate a holistic understanding of life.

Context and Culture

I write as a documented, educated, employed, white-passing Latina living in the United States. I have access to social capital and to the "benefit of the doubt" in many situations because of my Anglo-Saxon last name, my pale skin, and the cadences of my spoken English. I am coded as a "straight white lady," a "wife," a "mom," and—as I move toward the end of my fifties—increasingly as a "grandmotherly" figure. Any peculiarities I might manifest fit quite tidily and, ultimately, non-threateningly into a "professorial" typology that allows for a certain degree of eccentricity. In tension with this white-passing privilege is the fact that as a Latina I do not fully live in accordance with the assumptions and logic of normative whiteness in the United States; I'm not sure I could if I tried, as I was not born or formed in this country. My opinions and

---

[1] "Docetism" refers to the belief that Jesus Christ only *appeared* to be human and thus was only *seemingly* incarnate. A "docetic" epistemology analogously is a way of understanding that lacks attention to embodiment and detracts from the full humanity of Jesus—and by extension our own.

my choices may often be quite discordant with what is generally expected of me on the basis of how I look and sound. This can cause a ripple of cognitive dissonance that is all-too-soon dissolved back into the miasma of normative whiteness, which overrides any initial discomfort with what I say or do. It is not simple as a white or white-passing person consistently to subvert the logic of whiteness because whiteness trumps almost everything else in dominant US culture, including religious affiliation.

By "whiteness" I mean a system both symbolic and material that works in implicit and explicit ways to privilege persons coded as "white"—people who look and sound like me. It is entrenched in hegemonic common sense—in the "default setting"—about how society works, meaning that, particularly to those of us benefited by it, it can be all but invisible.[2] Those of us who are white or white-passing might imagine that racism is a personal attitude that we can choose simply to reject or even that racism is largely a problem of the past that only a recalcitrant minority continues to perpetuate. However, whiteness is not only or even primarily about individual prejudices or biases, nor is it a problem of the past. Rather, it is an enduring structural phenomenon. In the United States it is undergirded by legal, social, and economic "feedback loops" that lock in the accumulation of wealth and power by the descendants of white, Anglo-Saxon colonizers and those who can pass for such.[3] Historical amnesia about the racist principles on which this country was built up is a central component of whiteness.

---

[2]I borrow the metaphor of "default setting" from Steve Garner. He points out further that

> although it is empirically demonstrable that materially conditions for people of colour both in Europe and North America are worse than those for whites (as an average), and that this is a trend, a considerable minority of white people are convinced that this is not the case, and that the trend is actually going in the opposite direction: hence their support for projects that seem to offer mechanisms or at the very least aspirations toward turning back the clock to a time when whiteness worked more effectively as a magic cloak of privilege.

Steve Garner, "Surfing the Third Wave of Whiteness Studies: Reflections on Twine and Gallagher," *Ethnic and Racial Studies* 40, no. 9 (2017): 1590, https://doi.org/10.1080/01419870.2017.1300301.

[3]On this, see Daria Roithmayr, *Reproducing Racism: How Everyday Choices Lock in White Advantage* (New York: New York University Press, 2014).

Whiteness also traverses the logic of what is perceived as educated speech, norms for interaction and body language in the workplace, and appropriate topics of conversation.[4]

As a theologian, when I speak of whiteness, I am saying not that white or white-passing people like me are intrinsically evil or sinful but rather that, as part of our continual transformation into an ever-deeper image and likeness of God, we are called to divest ourselves of our complicities with structures that deny abundant life to those who are not coded as white. Just as the "rich young man" was asked by Jesus to sell what he had and give the proceeds to the poor (Mark 10:17-31), we who are benefited by structures of white privilege are asked to find ways to divest from them and the illusion of goodness and superiority they bestow on white people. We are called to renounce our white obliviousness, our white self-centeredness, and our white fragility. This is for our own good as well as for the good of others. In order to follow Jesus by the Spirit more deeply into newness of life, we are likewise called to discern and seek to renounce our complicities with all interlocking systems of injustice that work together with whiteness, such as sexism, heterosexism, militarism, capitalism, ableism, and disdain for nonhuman creation.[5] Awareness of these structures and our need to renounce our complicities with them is a way to contextualize our baptismal declaration of faith, in which we renounce "Satan, and all spiritual powers that rebel against God."[6]

---

[4] White racism is furthermore a complex phenomenon that does not target all persons equally; Linda Martín Alcoff helpfully describes four dimensions or "axes" that are combined in different ways: colorism, physical appearance, culture, and nativism. Linda Martín Alcoff, "Anti-Latino Racism," in *Decolonizing Epistemologies: Latina/o Theology and Philosophy*, ed. Ada María Isasi-Díaz and Eduardo Mendieta (New York: Fordham University Press, 2012): 107–26.

[5] Rather than being called to "Make America [sic] Great Again," as followers of Jesus we are called to *unmake* the racist logic, customs, and laws that undergird the idolatrous illusion of (white) "manifest destiny" and its justification of expansionism, military intervention, plutocracy, and the abuse of nonwhite people in and by the United States.

[6] This is, at least, still the language we use in baptism and in affirming membership in my own Mennonite community: Reba Place Church Membership Questions, adopted November 16, 2006, https://docs.wixstatic.com/ugd/c640b0_a44fb643feb4 471389d255f830b57bc1.pdf.

The question of how normative whiteness works is an urgent one. It is the historical pattern rather than the exception in this country for white populist politicians and vigilantes to target nonwhite people both discursively and materially.[7] There are peaks of aggressiveness, however, when events veer sharply toward ethnic cleansing, as they have done paradigmatically in the figure of Donald Trump and his enablers. One sees in their words and actions a clear "toxification" of Black and Brown immigrants in particular, which is a warning sign of genocide. Toxification means that a group begins to be referred to as a kind of vermin that needs to be removed—if necessary by extermination—in order to guarantee the health of a given group. Those belonging to the group portrayed negatively are increasingly represented "as a toxic presence that must be cauterized and destroyed. This noxiousness is regarded as irreconcilable, immutable and inextricable, and so cannot be remedied by any means other than extermination."[8] The concept helps makes sense of why Trump speaks of Central American, Haitian, and sub-Saharan African immigrants, refugees, and asylum seekers as "infesting" the United States and of their countries of origin as "shitholes."[9] It also sheds light on the reasoning behind policies at the border, such as the separation of children from their parents, the drastic reduction in the quota of refugees allowed to resettle in the United States, and severe restrictions placed on those requesting asylum. It is not an overstatement to say that segments

---

[7]On this, see Greg Grandin, *The End of the Myth: From the Frontier to the Border Wall in the Mind of America* (New York: Metropolitan, 2019); Daniel Immerwahr, *How to Hide an Empire: A Short History of the Greater United States* (New York: Farrar, Straus and Giroux, 2019).

[8]Rhiannon S. Neilsen, "'Toxification' as a More Precise Early Warning Sign for Genocide than Dehumanization? An Emerging Research Agenda," *Genocide Studies and Prevention: An International Journal* 9, no. 1 (2015): 83–95, http://dx.doi.org/10.5038/1911-9933.9.1.1277.

[9]Statements by Donald Trump, January 11, 2018, at a meeting with lawmakers and his tweet at 6:52 a.m. on June 18, 2018. Several faculty colleagues at Garrett-Evangelical and I wrote a response to his statements of May 16, 2018, in which he spoke of some immigrants as "animals": "Open Letter in Response to Donald Trump on his Chosen Language to Speak of Immigrants," June 1, 2018, https://www.garrett.edu/news/open-letter-president-donald-trump-his-chosen-language-speak-immigrants.

of the US government and citizenry are engaged in practices of ethnic cleansing in order to reinforce and preserve its whiteness.

In such a context, belonging to an Anabaptist community of faith—especially where Anabaptists are a minority—often entails a certain otherness with regard to hegemonic culture that can be helpful in developing empathy for those coded as other. Dominant values at the heart of white nationalism, such as militarism, competitiveness, individualism, and success as measured by the accumulation of wealth are very much secondary to the ethos of such faith communities. In my church, as we gather for worship and life together week by week, we seek to enact another paradigm: love your enemies; turn the other cheek; treat others as you would have them treat you; seek first the reign of God; and live out an anti-racist calling of expansive justice, peace, and love. Our stated desire to follow Jesus by the Spirit and to live in counter-hegemonic ways, however, comes up against a mighty obstacle—namely, that the Jesus whom we follow is often coded as a "white man" who not only is inoffensive to the logic of whiteness but also becomes an ideological justification for white supremacy, white nationalism, violent forms of masculinity, and a fragmented understanding of life.

Decentering Normative Whiteness

In the United States, Jesus is largely imagined as white. Langston Hughes once wrote that if Jesus were to "come back black," there would be "so many churches / Where he could not pray." He added, piercingly, that to point out that fact—alongside the way Black people, "no matter how sanctified," are treated—can get a person crucified.[10] More than half a century later, Jesus continues to be portrayed as white both in churches—in countless stained-glass windows, homiletic interpretations, and Sunday school illustrations—and in popular secular culture through movies, memes, and magazine articles.[11] A random internet search of

---

[10]Langston Hughes, "Bible Belt," in *The Panther and the Lash: Poems of Our Times* (New York: Alfred Knopf, 1969), 38.
[11]To choose just one example, the illustration for an *Atlantic* article shows a jolly, white-skinned Jesus with brown hair and a markedly aquiline nose winking at the

"Jesus" using a popular search engine requires me to scroll through forty-four images of white Jesuses before finally landing on a Blackish Jesus. I can count only about 4 or 5 nonwhite images of Jesus in the first 200, even though the search-engine algorithm surely must factor in that I have often searched for images of a Black or Brown Jesus in the past. The proportion of white to other ethnicities in the Jesus images does not mirror the demographic composition of the United States. It reflects, rather, how whiteness has seeped into and overtaken dominant Christological narratives despite decades of excellent work by Christian theologians of color deconstructing Jesus's whiteness, from Howard Thurman to James Cone, Kelly Brown Douglas, and beyond. The whiteness of Jesus continues to be presumed by the dominant narrative and is largely unquestioned, save by those who are not coded as white.

John Howard Yoder's *The Politics of Jesus* is no exception to this rule. He speaks of the "maiden Myriam" as a "Maccabean"[12] yet immediately lets the figure of Mary drop. He does not draw any kind of conclusion about what it might mean that Jesus was the son of a mother who in this culture would be coded as Brown. The problem of white racism—the original sin of the United States, a principality and power if there ever was one—is left unmentioned in the book, though other social ills do appear. Given Yoder's history of gendered abuse, the defective nature of his ideas about the dynamics of "revolutionary subordination" between men and women that appear in a later chapter of the book is perhaps the most glaring problem in looking at his "politics of Jesus" from a feminist perspective. It is worth noting, however, that by divesting Jesus of his "Brownness" or "Blackness" (and thus implicitly portraying him as white), the logic of whiteness that prevails in Euro-American theologies turns Yoder's book and theology itself into a "white space."[13] The implicitly white Jesus anchors a

---

viewer, accompanied by a blonde, hazel-eyed consort. Ariel Sabar, "The Unbelievable Tale of Jesus's Wife," *The Atlantic*, July/August 2016, https://www.theatlantic.com/magazine/archive/2016/07/the-unbelievable-tale-of-jesus-wife/485573/.

[12] John Howard Yoder, *The Politics of Jesus* (Grand Rapids: Eerdmans, 1972), 26.

[13] On this notion, see Nancy Bedford, "Theology, Violence and White Spaces," in *Envisioning the Good Life: Essays on God, Christ, and Human Flourishing in Honor of Miroslav Volf*, ed. Matthew Croasmun, Zoran Grozdanov, and Ryan McAnnally-Linz (Eugene, OR: Cascade, 2017), 149–62.

"politics" of gendered and raced "revolutionary" subordination that does not decenter the societal power and privilege of its white, male readership or challenge such readers to be renewed in the transforming of their minds in the face of the idolatries of sexism and white racism. Because these false gods are so tightly intertwined with the militarism and capitalism that the book does seek to address, Yoder's project remains curiously abstract. He does not ask the question: What do the "politics of Jesus"—of God incarnate, of the One whose crucified and resurrected body is at the center of our faith,[14] our liturgies, and our hope—mean concretely for the bodies of those who are not coded as white, or straight, or male?

What might it look like to veer down the path not taken by Yoder, the path that takes seriously the matter of Mary as what in this culture we would now call a "woman of color?" As a Latina, I look to one of my theological ancestors for some guidance: Sor Juana Inés de la Cruz. Between 1676 and 1691, the Mexican poet and theologian wrote many *villancicos*, poems in short lines (usually of six or eight syllables) used in popular liturgical celebrations. They were a way to communicate theological messages in accessible forms, through music, theater, stagecraft, and poetry. Mary often appears in Sor Juana's *villancicos*, as a student of theology (who studied *de incarnatione* in herself), a female knight-errant fighting evil, and a director of the heavenly choirs. Perhaps even more importantly, Sor Juana often portrays the mother of Jesus explicitly as a woman of color.[15] Like the beloved woman in the Song of Songs, Mary is Black and beautiful. As one exposed to the rays of the Sun—who represents God—she becomes ever Blacker and comelier even as she becomes holier:[16]

---

[14] "If any assert that he has now put off his holy flesh, and that his Godhead is stripped of the body, and deny that he is now with his body and will come again with it, let him not see the glory of his coming. For where is his body now, if not with him who assumed it?" Gregory of Nazianzus, *To Cledonius the Priest against Apollinarius* (Epistle 101), http://www.newadvent.org/fathers/3103a.htm.

[15] Sor Juana wrote her *villancicos* not only in standard Spanish (the language of the court) and Latin (the language of the church) but also in Náhuatl and in *habla de negros*, the version of Spanish spoken by many of her contemporary Afro-Mexicans, which incorporated West African vocabulary as well as its own syntax. Sor Juana Inés de la Cruz, *Obras Completas* (México: Editorial Porrúa, 2002).

[16] My own translation. For a more extensive translation and discussion of Sor Juana's *Villancico 224*, see Nicholas R. Jones, "Sor Juana's Black Atlantic: Colonial Blackness and the Poetic Subversions of *Habla de Negros*," *Hispanic Review* 86, no. 3 (Summer 2018): 265–85, doi:10.1353/hir.2018.0022.

—¡Ah, ah, ah	-Oh, Oh, Oh...
que la Reina se nos va!	The Queen is leaving us!
—¡Uh, uh, uh	-Oh, Oh, Oh...
que non blanca como tú	She's not white, as you are -
nin Paño´,	Neither is she a Spaniard!
que no sa Buena	That would not be good enough.
que Ella dici: So molena	She says: "I am Black,
con las Sole que mira´!	For the Sun shines on me!"
—¡Ah, ah, ah,	-Oh, Oh, Oh...
que la Reina se nos va!	The Queen is leaving us!

Sor Juana's Mary declares herself to be Black and holds that her Blackness makes her more beautiful.[17]

The fact that Sor Juana gives voice in her *villancicos* to Black characters who celebrate Mary's Blackness is especially significant given the enslavement of Africans and the Eurocentrism that organized social hierarchies, interactions, and access to power in seventeenth-century New Spain. It subverts the attempt by the Spaniards to use Mariology—alongside Christology and the doctrine of God—to undergird their power and privilege. It would be rare indeed to find similar materials in the Anglo-American literary and theological corpus, perhaps because of the erasure of Mary from much of Protestant theology. The tradition of the Black and Brown Madonna—in the form of the *Virgen de Guadalupe*, the *Virgen de la Caridad del Cobre*, the *Virgen de Regla*, the *Virgen de Aparecida*, and many other representations of Mary in Latin America—is ignored by Anabaptists and Protestants writ large to our peril. It is important to listen to what these representations of Mary are saying to us—namely, "I am not white, and neither is my Son."

Undoing Lethal Forms of Masculinity

Deconstructing the "whiteness" of Jesus is urgent but is not enough. In any review of his "politics" for our context, we need also to

---

[17]See, for example, Sor Juana Inés de la Cruz, "Morenica la Esposa está," *Obras Completas* (México: Porrúa, 2002), 257–8, a *villancico* of 1689 in honor of the Immaculate Conception: "Negra se confiesa/pero dice que esa negregura/es lo que le da mayor hermosura."

address the question of the construction of his masculinity since it is possible to be a Brown or Black man in the United States, or a male subaltern subject in any given power structure, who also enacts violent forms of masculinity. By "violent masculinity" I am referring to ways—tacitly approved or promoted by the dominant culture—that lead men to exercise violence on others and on themselves. Boys and men are encouraged to adopt a "tough guise" and to avoid vulnerability: "Males are not to show too much emotion, not think too much, should never back down, should only show toughness, and should be sexually aggressive with women."[18]

From a Christological perspective, the fact that Jesus was male is simply one dimension of his particularity and specificity, alongside the many others that are intrinsically part of the incarnation. The gospels also portray him as a Jew, a Galilean, the son of an articulate and courageous mother, a person who enjoyed eating and drinking in the company of friends, an astute observer of nature, an incisive speaker, a memorable teacher, and so on. His maleness is simply part of his humanity, as are all his particularities, but is not in itself the defining feature of his being nor does it limit his capacity to represent all flesh (e.g., that of non-males). In his particularities, he takes on all of our particularities, for "what has not been assumed has not been saved."[19] So how did Jesus perform masculinity?

During New Testament times, dominant forms of Graeco-Roman masculinities—at least among the elite, whose testimonies are mostly what we can access today—entailed performing a series of traits, such as avoiding "unmanliness," penetrating while remaining impenetrable, exercising power and dominance, achieving education, and exhibiting self-control.[20] Masculinity, in other words, was related to forestalling anything that might look "female" in that culture, maintaining bodily integrity by the avoidance of the penetration of the body (both in a sexual sense and as a recipient of physical violence), exhibiting courage in war and

---

[18] Melissa Bell and Nichole Bayliss, "The Tough Guise: Teaching Violent Masculinity as the Only Way to Be a Man," *Sex Roles* 72, nos. 11–12 (2015): 566–8, https://doi.org/10.1007/s11199-015-0479-8.
[19] Gregory of Nazianzus, *To Cledonius*.
[20] Eric C. Stewart, "Masculinity in the New Testament and in Early Christianity," *Biblical Theology Bulletin* 46, no. 2 (2016): 91–101, https://doi.org/10.1177/0146107916639211.

dominance in the household, and displaying classical virtues such as prudence, justice, and fortitude.[21]

If we use these lenses to look at Jesus of Nazareth as he is portrayed in the gospels, we discover a complex rendition of masculinity. It would be difficult to state that he took on ways coded as "feminine" in his culture, though some of his attitudes, such as showing emotion visibly and practicing compassion, are often means of enacting femininity in our own culture(s). Christologies that celebrate this dimension of Jesus as "feminine" often end up reifying what it means to be feminine and masculine in complementary ways rather than opening up spaces of liberation for women and men. What can be said is that Jesus treated women as serious interlocutors in ways that seemed to make some of his male disciples quite uncomfortable, as when he stayed behind to talk theology with the Samaritan woman (John 4) or insisted on finding out who had touched him and why, when he healed the woman with the flow of blood (Mark 5:25-34). He allowed himself to be corrected by the Syro-Phoenician woman (Matt. 15:21-29) and arguably even shifted his ministry emphasis as a result of his encounter with her.

It is not necessary to posit him as the only man or the only religious figure of his time who enacted his masculinity in respectful dialogue with women and allowed them to question him; Jewish feminist scholars have long pointed out that it is unfair and incorrect to use other Jewish males and religious leaders as foils to buttress his supposed exceptionalism on this matter.[22] What I think is worthwhile noting is that he engaged seriously with women, treating them as theological subjects and that such traditions were retained at the time of the writing of the gospels, even though they seem to have been somewhat bothersome to his male disciples and did not become expected or paradigmatic behavior for his male followers in the following centuries.

His status as a non-citizen of Rome and as an Aramaic-speaking Galilean (by definition "barbaric" for Roman culture) would

---

[21] Stewart, "Masculinity in the New Testament."
[22] The work of Amy-Jill Levine in particular comes to mind. See, for example, her helpful book *The Misunderstood Jew: The Church and the Scandal of the Jewish Jesus* (New York: HarperOne, 2006).

have in itself made it difficult for Jesus to exhibit classical virtues in ways amenable to elite hegemonic masculinity. As a subaltern subject, he was by definition not immune from being penetrated by blows, as seen by his condemnation to death by crucifixion, prefaced by beatings and lashings.[23] Again, what we can observe of his portrayal in the gospels is suggestive. During his ministry he consistently refused to exercise "power over" (*potestas*) those around him, freely allowing them to reject him or to choose to join him in a pneumatic community of "power for" (*potentia*) service to others, again making it clear explicitly to his male disciples that their desire to exercise power and authority in conventional ways was not in accordance with the good news (Mark 10:35-45). He also reconfigured the household, positing God as the only "Father" (Matt. 23:9), with the corollary that no mere human being was to be called "father." In this case it would seem that he used an androcentric metaphor in ways subversive of the social, political, and economic power of the *pater familias*.

It would seem that Jesus—as Eric C. Stewart says of the early Christians—"adopted, mimicked, transformed, and rejected Greek and Roman masculinities."[24] The "politics of Jesus" in a context of limitations and oppression that was anything but simple entailed improvising and crafting ways of living justly, departing from what was expected at times and doing the expected in unusual ways at other times. Following Jesus by the Spirit opens up possibilities for us to do likewise, in the face of violent variants of masculinity in our own cultures that are lethal to women, other men, and the very men that enact them.[25] As is the case for our complicities with whiteness, if we are white or white-passing people living in the United States, deconstructing and transforming complicity with

---

[23] As Stewart points out, there is no consensus among scholars about the degree to which he enacts hegemonic masculinity in his culture, though most agree that being "pierced" or "penetrated" in the crucifixion disqualifies him from elite masculine status. Stewart, "Masculinity in the New Testament," 96–7.

[24] Stewart, "Masculinity in the New Testament," 99.

[25] One place where this is painfully evident in the world of men apart from women is in the prison system, where hypermasculinity linked to violence is a key to status and often survival. See Joseph H. Michalski, "Status Hierarchies and Hegemonic Masculinity: A General Theory of Prison Violence," *British Journal of Criminology* 57, no. 1 (2017): 40–60, https://doi.org/10.1093/bjc/azv098.

violent masculinities requires of men the willingness to understand the social, cultural, and economic factors that reinforce violence, taking responsibility for their own acts of violence and exploring ways of living that do not involve or require violence.[26]

Christology, in short, need not buttress violent forms of masculinity; to the contrary, it can be a helpful paradigm in imagining and enacting alternative models of masculinity. To develop those possibilities, we need to develop a flexible epistemology with room for a pneumatic imagination to flourish—one that traps Christology neither in the norms of whiteness nor in the corset of violent masculinity.

Resisting Docetic Epistemologies

As the New Testament makes clear, our task, as Rom. 12:2 and Eph. 4:23 put it, is not to conform to the patterns of this system but to renew our collective mind.[27] As we have seen, however, what we think we "know" collectively and what seems to constitute common sense are skewed by structural injustice and sin. At first glance, in many cases Jesus looks "white," and it seems "natural" and "right" to expect men (even followers of Jesus) to act violently in love and war. In order to loosen up the binds of whiteness and violent masculinities, we need—with the help of the Spirit—to learn to understand reality anew and more deeply.

---

[26] I take these principles from the experience of the men in the "Construcción de masculinidades libres de violencia" program at the Centro Mujer Teresa de Jesús in Lima: Rhoda Mitchell, "Domestic Violence Prevention through the Constructing Violence-Free Masculinities Programme: An Experience from Perú," *Gender and Development* 21, no. 1 (2013): 97–109, https://doi.org/10.1080/13552074.2013.767516. In conjunction with Oxfam-Québec, the Center has developed "a community education approach, to challenge powerful stereotypes about gender roles, to question men's assumed dominance over women, and support men to construct new forms of masculinity, without violence. Ultimately, the programme seeks to modify and change the beliefs, values, attitudes, and behaviours of men who are aggressors" (97).

[27] Paul speaks of the renewing of your (plural) mind (singular); "mind" is thus a collective noun, the property not only of each individual but also of the community of faith.

One helpful step in shifting our understanding is to challenge docetic epistemologies—that is, the imposition of ways of knowing that implicitly or explicitly deny our reality as embodied creatures. Such epistemologies require people to strip away much of who they are in order to "know." They force people to "know" in ways divorced from their practices and their very beings. Knowing, being, and doing should be so intertwined that bodies cannot be separated from minds, faith cannot be estranged from works, and theory cannot be divorced from action. Hence, as Amardo Rodriguez puts it, "When you begin to discover that the separation between ontology, epistemology, and axiology is an illusion, then everything comes tumbling down."[28] As followers of Jesus we are to live, act, and know all in one piece, as it were.

In Christology, this intuition is embedded into the notion of the incarnation. A docetic epistemology can only lead to knowing a ghostly, docetic Jesus. To truly know Jesus, the incarnate one, we need to engage our whole, embodied selves. Thus, we *know* Jesus by *doing*—namely, by walking in the way of Jesus by the Spirit and by God's grace *becoming* siblings of Christ, adopted into the triune life of God not as slaves but as God's children and God's heirs (Gal. 4:4–7). Our being is both contextual and situated and a constant, transformative "becoming." In other words, in Christ we "are"—not only in the sense of the Spanish verb *ser* but also in the sense of *estar*, a difference that is significant yet almost untranslatable into English. *Estar* derives from the same root (the Latin *stare*) as "to stand"; it means "being" in a particular place and a particular state. Being as *estar* localizes, concretizes, and contextualizes being as *ser*. We know and we do by "being" (in the sense of *estar*) in a particular time and place. This is what standpoint epistemology tries to convey: being in a particular time and place allows us to "see" and to "do" particular things; yet, all that we will be and know and do is not yet manifest (1 John 4:2). God often calls us to be (*estar*) in a new place—that is, to shift where we have been standing.

---

[28] Amardo Rodriguez, "The Performative Nature of Knowledge," in *Liminal Traces: Storying, Performing, and Embodying Postcoloniality*, ed. Devika Chawla and Amardo Rodriguez (Boston: Sense Publishers, 2011), 65–73.

It is, in short, possible to "know" and to "do" Christology in a way that contests the cooptation of Jesus by normative whiteness and by violent forms of masculinity by shifting where we take a stance ("being" in the sense of *estar*). Depending on where we find ourselves to begin with, those shifts may be subtle or quite drastic, but regardless they will decenter us with respect to the way this society imagines what is beautiful, good, and true. The Johannine Jesus says to his disciples: "I still have many things to say to you, but you cannot bear them now" (John 16:12). Our Christological work is to get ourselves to a place where the promised Spirit of Truth (John 16:13) can help us understand what it is that Jesus has to say to us today.

Implications for Anabaptist Identity and Beyond

A review of the Christology of early Anabaptists (and beyond) is not very reassuring with regard to the matter of a robust Christology that avoids docetism and other distortions that seem to continue to plague contemporary perceptions of Jesus.[29] Admittedly, since Anabaptists did not tend to work out systematic theologies, a helpful principle can be—as Thomas Finger points out—to pay attention to what their convictions about the *work* of Jesus implied about the *person* of Jesus.[30] On this basis, he distills three basic Christological convictions visible in various ways across the early Anabaptist movement(s): (1) a sense that Jesus opposed and overcame the "world" and its powers; (2) an emphasis on the self-emptying (kenosis) of Jesus; and (3) the centrality of an active community of faith.[31] He adds, "Genuine trust in such a God and confession of such a Jesus as Lord engenders a life of discipleship in community guided by nonviolent shalom in every respect."[32]

---

[29] Thomas N. Finger, *A Contemporary Anabaptist Theology: Biblical, Historical, Constructive* (Downers Grove, IL: Intervarsity, 2004), 329–464.
[30] Finger, *Contemporary Anabaptist Theology*, 365.
[31] Finger, *Contemporary Anabaptist Theology*, 365.
[32] Finger, *Contemporary Anabaptist Theology*, 365.

I find Finger's framework helpful. However, in light of what I have argued in this chapter about the need for Christology to decenter whiteness, disarticulate violent masculinities, and avoid disembodied ways of understanding our lives in the world, the three basic Anabaptist Christological convictions he sketches out need to be sharpened, lest the figure of Jesus continue to be coopted by our culture of racism, violence, and dehumanization. Continuing the struggle of Jesus against the dominant system and its powers therefore entails a conscious path of anti-racist commitment, something quite urgent given the normative "whiteness" of many Anabaptist spaces in North America. The servant-like kenosis of Jesus cannot be an excuse to misuse the bodies of women or to exalt women's supposedly servile qualities; a necessary practice in our churches is making the space and time to listen to the voices and stories of women, learning to be vigilant about their welfare in our communities. A life of discipleship in community can be neither mutually interactive nor nonviolent if all the members of the community—regardless of age, ability, sexual orientation, gender, class, race, or ethnicity—are not fully able to live into their dignity bodily and fully as persons created equally in the image of God.

For Anabaptists, the practice of following Jesus (and thus living out the logic of the "politics of Jesus") continues to be at the center of our spirituality and faith. But we need to discern constantly whether our expressed or implicit Christologies are helping or hindering us in living concretely and materially in ways truly consonant with the life and teachings of Jesus of Nazareth. Our primary help in finding ways to do so is listening carefully for the prodding of the Spirit, developing our potential to live as part of communities who believe that the Spirit can manifest the way of Jesus in ever-renewed ways.

2

Jesus and the Stories of Our Lives

Carol Penner

Let me tell you a story about Anabaptist women. From the beginning of the movement in the 1500s, they were eager to share their faith in Jesus with others. Unlike men in the Anabaptist movement, women rarely had the opportunity to write down their theology so it could be shared across time and space. Yet from the sixteenth century on, exceptional Anabaptist women can be found who defied the odds and shared their theology in writing so we can read it today. By the twentieth century, many things had changed for women in North America: several waves of feminism gave them access to higher education, they could pursue vocations outside the home, and birth control offered freedom from continual childbearing. Anabaptist women had more time and opportunities to write theology. They began to share their ideas in Mennonite periodicals, if the male editors of the periodicals liked what they were writing. One of the first places where Anabaptist women controlled the agenda and format of theological writing was in the *MCC Women's Concerns Report*, published from 1973 to 2004. The way women did theology in this groundbreaking periodical offers direction for the future of Anabaptist women's theology.

Let me tell you a story about why the *Report* is so important to me. I grew up worshiping in a Mennonite congregation; I wanted to deepen my faith, so I studied theology and peace studies at a Mennonite Bible college. After graduation I worked as a homemaker, babysitting two small children for a single mother. I arrived at her house one morning to find the front door pulled off its hinges. Hearing a man's voice yelling, I ran in to find the woman I worked for cowering in a corner while her ex-husband threatened her with a raised fist. The children were crying in the doorway. He eventually twisted her arm behind her back and forced her into his car. I called the police, who worried he was going to kill her because he had threatened to do so before. Thankfully, she survived.

This was a traumatic experience for that family—and for me. I felt powerless to intervene and felt stuck when I tried to make sense of what had taken place. In my years of studying Anabaptist peace theology, all of it written and taught by men, I had learned about conscientious objection to military service and the importance of peace, but no one had prepared me in any way to deal with violence in the living room. I didn't know where Jesus was in this picture or what it meant to be a peacemaker there.

Through conversations with friends in the following months and years, I began to realize the extent of the violence around me: harassment, rape, child sexual abuse, and wife battering were all part of my friends' lives. After a long while, I was even able to name the violence in the home where I grew up. Graduate studies exposed me to feminist theology, which helped me understand the religious history of patriarchy and violence against women. Around that same time, a friend introduced me to the *MCC Women's Concerns Report*. In its pages, theology started with the real stories of Anabaptist women, including stories about violence and abuse. Writers asked vital questions and wrestled with God. They had suggestions about how followers of Jesus could work for change in church and society. The *Report* came into my life like water and a compass during a dry and dusty journey in the wilderness.

In the first section of this chapter, I provide a thumbnail history of the *Report* and its significance. Following that, I describe the theological methodology of the *Report* and then show how revolutionary this methodology is by describing the Jesus found in its pages. In the final section, I outline how this methodology can reshape Anabaptist peace theology as we move toward the next century.

A Place for Women: The *MCC Women's Concerns Report*

In spring of 1973, women board members of the Mennonite Central Committee (MCC) Peace Section presented their concerns to the rest of the board,[1] asking that "women's interests in justice and peace" be included as part of its agenda.[2] A task force was approved at this meeting, and in August 1973 the first newsletter

---

[1] This was two years after women were first included as members of the Peace Section board. Mennonite Central Committee is an Anabaptist service organization that also creates spaces for theological reflection; the Peace Section was one of those spaces. Linda Gehman Peachey, "Naming the Pain, Seeking the Light: The Mennonite Church's Response to Sexual Abuse," *Mennonite Quarterly Review* 89, no. 1 (January 2015): 113.

[2] Luann Habegger, "Note to Readers," *Report from the Peace Section Task Force on Women in Church and Society* 1 (August 1973): 1.

was issued, called *Report from the Peace Section Task Force on Women in Church and Society*. The name was changed in 1982 to *MCC Women's Concerns Committee Report*. Published every two months, it was available by subscription.³ Altogether 171 reports were published, the last dated January–February 2004.

The *Report* was always edited by women, making it one of the first theological publications to be controlled by Anabaptist women.⁴ Each issue consisted of half a dozen or more articles written by women from different denominations of the Anabaptist church: Mennonite, Mennonite Brethren, and Brethren in Christ. Each *Report* centered on a theme of interest to women, covering such diverse topics as childbearing, power, mentoring, sexuality, friendship, aging, poverty, divorce, materialism, addictions, and health. Violence was frequently addressed within those topics, but there were also specific issues of the *Report* on rape, pornography, wife battering, incest, sex tourism, pastoral misconduct, and militarism. Some *Reports* were devoted to hearing marginalized voices, through issues focused on third world women, Black women and feminism, Asian women doing theology, Latin American women's groups, and women with disabilities in the church, to name a few. While faith perspectives were present in all of the issues, some were more explicitly focused on theological topics, with numerous issues on women in ministry, women as theologians, theology and gender, worship, ritual, and biblical interpretation.

It may be hard for younger women today, who have grown up with feminist voices in their church press and who can readily access any perspective they want by searching on the internet, to realize how isolated feminist women in Anabaptist churches felt

---

³At its peak circulation, 2,000 copies were distributed: "Over two thousand copies of the *Report* are mailed from MCC headquarters in Akron, Pa. to subscribers in the U.S. (1,625 individuals), Canada (434) and abroad (125)." Margaret Loewen Reimer, "The Task Force Report," *MCC Women's Concerns Committee Report* 50 (July–August 1983): 9.

⁴The editor chose topics in consultation with a larger committee; the committee then found a compiler for each issue who was knowledgeable about a particular topic. There was some oversight by MCC, which intervened occasionally, at one point vetoing the publication of a specific illustration of a nude woman (from a work by Rembrandt). Occasionally a man was invited to write an article in the *Report*, but men were never part of the planning committees.

in the 1970s and 1980s. Books and periodicals were the primary means for sharing written theology, and Anabaptist publishing was almost entirely controlled by men. Women's voices were absent, marginalized, or edited to the way men wanted them to sound.[5] Few places existed within the church where women could read feminist perspectives.[6] Many congregations resisted the feminist movement and were suspicious of women who wanted to change the roles in which they had been confined. As *Report* editor Emily Will wrote: "Sometimes outright hostility to our vision of equality for women with men silences us or forces us to go underground"; the *Report* helped women see "we aren't alone and we can trust our inner voices, voices that dare to utter 'God.'"[7] Having a space where women could write about faith was very significant in a context where women's voices were routinely banned or devalued.[8]

Ways of Doing Theology in the *Report*

Hundreds of women wrote for the *Report*, sharing many perspectives and ideas, but the journal's method for doing theology was constant: it was Anabaptist, story-based, and feminist.

---

[5] For example, Katie Funk Wiebe is widely remembered as a strong feminist; however, when she wrote for the *Mennonite Brethren Herald* in the 1970s her feminist perspectives were toned down or muted. See Carol Penner, "Women Moving into Ministry: A Canadian Mennonite Press Survey," *Journal of Mennonite Studies* 37 (2019): 176.

[6] As one woman writing in the letters section observed, "There are not many other places to get info/reflections etc. from an Anabaptist female point of view." "Thanks to All the Subscribers," *Report* 154 (March–April 2001): 15.

[7] Emily Will, "Remembering," *Report* 109 (July–August 1993): 5. A letter writer wrote, "At first I could not believe my eyes that such deep-feeling feminism was being printed through a Mennonite publication. The reading has not just turned my thoughts around, it has brought tears of joy to my eyes that my feminist 'controversies' are being upheld, supported, and talked about by a Mennonite publication. You have shed light into my darkness, rekindled my trust in Mennonite culture. What strength I have found!" Kate Neudorf, "Letters," *Report* 65 (March–April 1986): 13.

[8] For example, "I have felt so encouraged and uplifted by the knowledge that there are other women who feel as I do—that I DO count in God's kingdom and that I am NOT inferior in God's sight, although it seems my church and its constitution teach the opposite." A Canadian reader (name withheld), "Letters," *Report* 64 (January–February 1986): 12.

Anabaptist

In a 1982 article, Ruth Krall emphasized that revelation from God happens in community through "discerning dialogues."[9] The early Anabaptists rejected a hierarchical view of divine revelation, where leaders are believed to hear God's voice more clearly than other believers can. Di Brandt observed that the Anabaptist faith heritage had warped over time: "This belief that God could speak through all members of the community was not followed in practice, as women were required to be submissive and silent in the gendered hierarchical leadership historically found in most Mennonite churches."[10] The *Report* was a venue where women could claim their place in the Anabaptist community as followers of Jesus. Carol Dyck compared the distortion of human society to a one-winged bird in flight, because "women's perspective has been consistently downplayed and devalued."[11] Gayle Gerber Koontz explained how gender bias in the church had distorted the Anabaptist belief in the priesthood of all believers.[12]

The editors strove for inclusivity by publishing the voices of women from various walks of life. Writers included pastors and theologians, as well as homemakers, social workers, librarians, and shopkeepers. Instead of featuring an expert presenting an extended essay on the chosen theme, each issue featured women from different churches and different parts of the United States and Canada. The editors made a consciously Anabaptist choice to listen to a variety of voices in order to foster dialogue in the Christian community. Encouraging love and understanding within the church was a value expressed through the *Report*, primarily through the method of storytelling.[13]

---

[9] Ruth Krall, "Development of Sexual Ethics," *Report* 44 (July–August 1982): 2.
[10] Di Brandt, "Pornography Silences Women," *Report* 64 (January–February 1986): 6.
[11] Carol Dyck, "Capturing God's Mystery in Song," *Report* 76 (January–February 1988): 13.
[12] Gayle Gerber Koontz, "Focus on Women in Ministry," *Report* 19 (April–May 1978): 1.
[13] For example, "Our hope is that these stories will evoke in you a non-judgmental response of compassion and understanding." Gwen Groff and Emily Will, "Sharing Our Stories," *Report* 70 (January–February 1987): 1.

Story-Based

Over the *Report*'s thirty-year history, the Women's Concerns Committee consistently encouraged women to tell their own stories, uniting life experiences with faith reflection. This method, favored by liberation theology movements, allows people from different socioeconomic classes to participate regardless of whether they can afford theological education.[14] This narrative approach connecting faith and life was reinforced through the artwork of women, found in each issue of the *Report*.[15] Illustrations also helped make the *Report* more accessible for people who might have felt intimidated by reading large blocks of text.

The letters section of the *Report* frequently reflected the significance of stories. One woman wrote, "Personal experiences shared mean the most to me. We hear enough advice both from the pulpit and other Christians of the correct theological response, but not enough on how I've put my theology into practice and, yes, even failed."[16] Stories helped women root their theology in their lives: "To have survivors share their stories is a way for the Latino community to recognize that this problem exists even in their religious homes."[17]

Anniversary issues provided an opportunity to look back at the periodical as a whole. In the thirtieth-anniversary edition, editor Muriel Thiessen Stackley wrote that the *Report* had been a catalyst in Mennonite and Brethren in Christ circles: "It has broadened our awareness, helped define our theology, educated us, offered practical information, described relationships, evoked tears of empathy, enlivened our language, defined our careers, and affirmed the leadership of women—all this by telling women's stories, by providing space for them to tell their own stories."[18] In the final

---

[14]See, for example, the way story is woven into biblical interpretation in Ernesto Cardenal, *The Gospel in Solentiname* (Maryknoll: Orbis, 1992).

[15]The artwork of Teresa Pankratz featured in this book is taken from the illustrations she did for the *Report*.

[16]"Reader Feedback," *Report* 73 (July–August 1987): 14.

[17]Elizabeth Soto Albrecht, "Compilers' Comments," *Report* 157 (September–October 2001): 3.

[18]Muriel Thiessen Stackley, "The *Report*: Helping us 'Rethink,'" *Report* 109 (July–August 1993): 10.

edition of the *Report*, editor Gwen Groff observed: "*Report* provides a vehicle for women to tell their own stories in their own voices. That fits one of the most basic tenets of feminist theology; our own stories are valid places to look for God at work in human history."[19]

Sharing stories was only the first step. Writing in the *Report* issue on violence against women, I observed, "Simply sharing stories was not enough to end the cycle of violence. People who risked their stories in the 1990s are more careful now. What's the point of sharing our pain in the church? How does it contribute to change?"[20] Storytelling needed to be augmented with power analyses and strategies for change.

Feminist, Womanist, and *Mujerista*

Feminist theology centers itself on women's stories. Women need to "begin naming their own separate knowledge of themselves in their own women's style."[21] Feminism also pays careful attention to power and the way it is distributed in systems and structures. It holds gender equality as a high value: the term "equality" was present in the masthead of the *Report* as a guiding principle.[22] Feminism seeks to listen to the voices on the underside of power relations. When women in the *Report* started listening to each other's stories, they saw patterns of power imbalances. Rhoda Glick described this dynamic: "What we thought were personal problems turn out to be the effects of systems geared against us."[23] The *Report* named women's realities in the public sphere, giving space for theological reflections on power and how it is distributed.

As I mentioned earlier, the *Report* resonated with me because I could identify with many of the stories and perspectives I found

---

[19] Gwen Groff, "Looking Back: Women's Concerns Directors Reflect," *Report* 165 (January–February 2003): 2.
[20] Carol Penner, "An Anabaptist Theology Opposing Violence against Women," *Report* 164 (November–December 2002): 2.
[21] Brandt, "Pornography Silences Women," 7.
[22] The word "equality" was present in the *Report*'s masthead from issues 45 to 164.
[23] Rhoda S. Glick, "Inspiration for the Church," *Report* 171 (January–February 2004): 10.

there. It was only much later, and with the help of diverse writers featured in the *Report*, that I began to see why I felt so comfortable with much of the publication's writing. I am North American, a cradle Mennonite,[24] white, and middle class; many of the writers in the *Report* were just like me. I resonated with what they wrote because they reflected my own context.

Women of color writing in the *Report* described the disparities between the context of white women and that of African American and Latina women, pointing out white biases in the *Report*. Over time, writings by women of color appeared more frequently in the *Report*. The January–February 1985 *Report* focused on "Black Women and Feminism." Joy Lovett described the historical discrimination Black women have faced from both white men and white women. Speaking from the perspective of Black women, Lovett declared, "Lately, she's grown weary of the feminist movement's effort to recruit her energies, while failing to deal with its racism and to address many of the issues vital to her."[25] Wilma Bailey spoke plainly about the racism of white Mennonite women and the intersection with economic disparity:

> Typically, white Mennonites are pretty well off. They are soundly in the middle class and their minds are adjusted to a whole different place. They've got all that prejudice that they won't deal with. . . . They don't seem to be willing to come over to the Black side of things. In the past what has happened when they want to form coalitions is that the Blacks come over to them and support them and what they want to accomplish.[26]

The disconnect between feminism championed by white women and the realities of Black women's lives meant that Black women were reluctant to use the word "feminist" to describe their own theology. Instead, they used the word "womanist" to describe a theology originating in the lives of Black women.

---

[24] By this, I mean I grew up in a Mennonite church, with parents who were Mennonite.
[25] Joy Lovett, "Black Women: A State of the Union," *Report* 59 (January–February 1985): 8.
[26] Wilma Bailey, quoted in Joy Lovett, "Where There Ain't No Light," *Report* 59 (January–February 1985): 10.

Latina women also noted the absence of their realities and stories in the *Report*. In a 2001 issue, "Domestic Violence: A Concern for All," editor Elizabeth Soto Albrecht wrote, "The uniqueness of this issue of *Report* is the voices of Anabaptist Latina women that we are hearing for the first time."[27] Writers who center their theology on Latin American women are called *mujerista* theologians. Printing several bilingual issues of the *Report*, where stories written in Spanish were translated into English, was a way of including diverse voices. From a Canadian context, April Yamasaki also commented about racism in the church: "To the extent that this community excludes those who are on the margins of society and church life, to the extent that it excludes the poor, to the extent that it excludes those of other races and cultures, to the extent that it excludes those who are different from ourselves, this community is incomplete."[28] By the end of its publication, the *Report* was attempting to decenter white writers and center women of color.

The fact that the voices of women of color came through eventually in the *Report* can be attributed, at least in part, to the way power was distributed in the editorial process. The women who controlled the *Report* were committed to the feminist value of sharing power. It was decided early on that the leadership should rotate every three years in order to disperse opportunity and not concentrate power in the hands of one person.[29] Each editor invited a different compiler to work with them for each issue. This distribution of power differed from most Mennonite periodicals, where editors controlled every issue and served for decades in their positions.

Feminist/womanist/*mujerista* theologians not only had the goal of describing what was happening; they also had the goal of changing the world. In an issue on sex tourism, Ethel Yake Metzler wrote of women doing just that:

> Thus, I found that Christian women in Asia are not only doing theology in the seminaries and libraries, but also on the streets

---

[27] Soto Albrecht, "Compilers' Comments," 3.
[28] April Yamasaki, "In Search of Wholeness," *Report* 105 (November–December 1992): 4.
[29] "A significant strength of the WTF [Women's Task Force] is its inter-Mennonite duo-nation representation. In order to truly disperse opportunity, we soon decided that members would function for only three years, and that chairing duties would rotate." Dorothy Yoder Nyce, "Ten Years Later," *Report* 50 (July–August 1983): 3.

and in factories. They are ministering to women trapped in oppressive traditions and lacking legal rights [prostitutes] . . . Ordinary churchwomen like you and I, they are taking bold and risky actions in often repressive political climates.[30]

The feminist/womanist/*mujerista* perspectives encouraged in the *Report* enabled Anabaptist women not only to tell stories of power abuse but also to envision and strategize about how women could exercise power. Writers reimagined power relationships in the new reign of God that Jesus came to introduce. They imagined new ways of structuring Anabaptist communities.

Meeting Jesus in the Pages of the *Report*

The *Report* was one of the first women-controlled theological publications: using their Anabaptist, story-based, feminist/womanist/*mujerista* methods, hundreds of women reflected on their faith and on Jesus. Studying all 171 issues of the *Report*, I tracked the scriptural references to Jesus and the adjectives and concepts used to describe him. A particular image of Jesus emerges in these pages.

Jesus is central to the *Report*. For many years his name was in the periodical's masthead: "Women's Concerns Report is published bimonthly by the MCC Committee on Women's Concerns. We believe that Jesus Christ teaches equality of all persons."[31] The most frequent description of Jesus was that he taught equality.[32] The second most common descriptor of Jesus was that he was radical: "If we choose to be radical like Jesus, we will begin by rejecting all relationships of dependence and domination."[33] Contributors

---

[30]Ethel Yake Metzler, "Asian Women Doing Theology," *Report* 72 (May–June 1987): 1.
[31]Masthead. *Report* 155 (May–June 2001): 19. As mentioned above, the word "equality" was used in that description from *Report* 45 to *Report* 164.
[32]In addition to the masthead reference, there were ten other references to Jesus teaching equality. "References" here refers not to the number of times the word was used but rather to the number of articles that used that concept.
[33]Dorothy Yoder Nyce, "Genesis 1–3: A Place to Begin," *Report* 49 (May–June 1983): 3. The adjective "radical" was used by seven different *Report* writers to describe Jesus.

described him as a liberator[34] who rejected male stereotypes[35] and broke norms of acceptable behavior in order to follow God.[36] Jesus broke with the patriarchal culture of his day; he was a biblical interpreter[37] who treated women in a way that was revolutionary for his time.[38] Jesus challenged the primacy of the patriarchal family by calling the disciples away from their families and their work, inviting them to a new community not based on biological kinship.[39] Jesus called followers to the common human task of birthing children of God rather than primarily offspring.[40]

Writers in the *Report* characterized Jesus as someone on the margins, a person to whom the oppressed could relate. Jesus was a poor peasant, an outcast who was eventually painfully executed like a criminal. Janet Umble wrote, "Such a Christ surely understands the pain and loneliness of a woman whose body and spirit are damaged by those more powerful than she. . . . Jesus identifies with powerlessness and suffering."[41] Michelle Armster observed that "Jesus was not a white man. He was a man whose features, hair and skin color were more like mine."[42] Diane Driedger described a Jesus who related to people who were sick or had disabilities: "He affirmed the worth of everyone, whether they were blind, had leprosy or were hemorrhaging. Through his example, we

---

[34] For example, "Jesus came preaching the good news of salvation . . . the message is again and again one of liberation from oppression." Mary Kauffmann-Kennel, "The Church: A Roadblock for Battered Women," *Report* 74 (September–October 1987): 5.

[35] For example, "I think Jesus was the original liberated man. He did not fit many of the characteristics of the male role as our culture defines it." Elizabeth Yoder, "The Christian and the Cult of Masculinity," *Report* 13 (February 1977): 2.

[36] For example, "Jesus went against the accepted code of behavior when he talked to the Samaritan woman at the well." Marilyn Troyer Yoder, "Toward a Curriculum for Free People," *Report* 5 (April 1974): 3.

[37] Patricia Haverstick, "Looking Forward: Compiler's Comments," *Report* 170 (November–December 2003): 2.

[38] Mary Massey, "*Imago Dei:* The Importance of the Revised Standard Version," *Report* 152 (September–October 2000): 4.

[39] Reta Halteman Finger, "Community and Individual in the New Testament," *Report* 121 (July–August 1995): 7.

[40] Dorothy Yoder Nyce, "Childbearing and the Bible: A Dictionary Approach," *Report* 55 (May–June 1984): 3.

[41] Janet Umble Reedy, "Reflections," *Report* 74 (September–October 1987): 9.

[42] Michelle E. Armster, "Who Is It?" *Report* 156 (July–August 2001): 8.

as followers are called to be advocates with disabled persons."[43] Through a feminist lens, the writers of the *Report* saw a Jesus who cared for the marginalized and powerless.

Anabaptists have often been characterized as people who have a canon within the biblical canon, with a strong emphasis on Jesus's teaching on the Sermon on the Mount.[44] This is not seen in the *Report*; in fact, there were almost no references to any texts within the Sermon on the Mount. Instead, the gospel stories most referenced are the interactions Jesus had with women and with other poor and marginalized people. The three stories quoted most often were those of Mary and Martha, the woman at the well, and the women at the empty tomb who were sent to proclaim the resurrection.[45]

As women shared their own stories in the *Report*, they described a Jesus who met them in those stories. Judith Snowden wrote,

> I saw Jesus as a compassionate man who was in solidarity with those who were wounded, with women, children and even Gentiles. Yet he too was abused by the religious community of his time, even to the point of death. . . . I was not alone.[46]

Elizabeth Soto found herself in the biblical text:

> She [the Syrophoenician woman] was an outsider . . . with a sick daughter. She is carrying the burden of her daughter's illness. Similar to Latin American women, she does whatever is possible for her child's health. She leaves her family/home, breaks societal male-female relation patterns, trespasses on religious barriers, and falls at the feet of Jesus. . . . Many Syrophoenician women in our churches bring their wounds to us for healing and liberation.

---

[43] Diane Driedger, "Disabled Women and the Church," *Report* 80 (September–October 1988): 13.
[44] Leo Driedger and Donald B. Kraybill, *Mennonite Peacemaking: From Quietism to Activism* (Scottdale: Herald, 1994), 30.
[45] The Mary and Martha story was used eleven times in different articles, the women witnessing to the resurrection was used seven times, the Samaritan woman at the well was used six times, and the woman caught in adultery was used four times.
[46] Judith Snowden, "Who Will Listen? Who Will Hear?" *Report* 150 (May–June 2000): 5.

As long as we continue to see it as their problem and not ours, we will deliver a handicapped Gospel.⁴⁷

Dorothy Yoder Nyce identified with the woman who touched Jesus's clothes: "Women still bleed. Perhaps some hemorrhage, their faith tugging at the robes of the church whose institutions prove insensitive to the touch."⁴⁸ Telling the message that Jesus came to bring change to the world today was one of the *Report*'s reasons for being.⁴⁹

Emma Richards pointed out that by emphasizing a Jesus who believed in equality, feminists were challenging the Anabaptist tradition, which has sanctioned the submission of women to men.⁵⁰ The Jesus that Anabaptist women portrayed in the *Report* was remarkably different from the Jesus presented by male Anabaptist writers, who often emphasized a servant Jesus who called others to suffer.⁵¹ This servant emphasis has not been good news for women: "Taking up the role of servant has led many women not to salvation, wholeness, and liberation, but to abuse, sickness, and self-abnegation," wrote Christina Bucher.⁵² Beth Graybill emphasized resisting suffering rather than passively accepting it: "Our tradition of nonresistance has helped contribute to violence against women by implicitly encouraging women to accept abuse as Christ-like suffering, rather than to resist. But Jesus taught us to pray, 'Deliver

---

⁴⁷Elizabeth Soto, "The Syrophoenician Woman," *Report* 164 (November–December 2002): 10.
⁴⁸Quoting Dorothy Yoder Nyce, "MCC Acts on Task Force Recommendation," *Report* 8 (May 1975): 1.
⁴⁹Stackley, "The *Report*: Helping Us 'Rethink,'" 10; Ruth Brunk Stoltzfus, "Women in the Bible," *Report* 153 (January–February 2001): 6.
⁵⁰Emma Richards, "What Do Participants Say: Emma Richards," *Report* 63 (September–October 1985): 13.
⁵¹"Christians in the Anabaptist tradition have long equated discipleship and servanthood." Christina Bucher, "Servanthood in Isaiah," *Report* 89 (March–April 1990): 5.
⁵²Bucher, "Servanthood in Isaiah," 5. Cf., "At times the dissonance between my developing personhood and the patriarchal interpretations of servant theology was painfully evident." Vange Thiessen, "Serving with a Feminist Perspective," *Report* 89 (March–April 1990): 3.

us from evil.'"⁵³ Writers in the *Report* emphasized that Jesus's call to servanthood was not about accepting suffering but rather about throwing off that which limited and confined people. Jesus's call was empowering and "frees us to act," wrote Bucher. "It calls us to wholeness, to the fullness of life."⁵⁴

Women interpreting the biblical text in the *Report* presented a new articulation of the gospel for Anabaptist Christians, a gospel that is good news for women and other groups on the margins of power. The methodology of the *Report* produced a vision of Jesus strikingly different from what has traditionally been seen as Anabaptist theology; what is commonly called "Anabaptist theology" is revealed as "male Anabaptist theology."

A Way Forward

Having examined the methodology of the *MCC Women's Concerns Report* and offered examples of the theology it produced, I now use this methodology to suggest three important areas for Anabaptist theology as we move further into the twenty-first century.

Advocating for Women Doing Theology

As Anabaptists, we need to take the concept of hermeneutical community seriously. We need to hear from parts of the church that are still marginalized. The majority of Anabaptist women in North America worship in churches that do not allow women in the pulpit. The Amish and Conservative Mennonites are the largest Anabaptist groups, and they are entirely patriarchally structured, so that women have limited venues for sharing their theology. The Mennonite Brethren still have few women in leadership.⁵⁵ The majority of women in the Anabaptist tradition are prevented from sharing their theology in public forums through speaking or writing.

---

⁵³Beth Graybill, "Toward a New Theology: Pacifism and Women's Resistance," *Report* 164 (November–December 2002): 3.
⁵⁴Bucher, "Servanthood in Isaiah," 5.
⁵⁵I was a lead pastor in the Mennonite Brethren denomination from 2014 to 2016; I was one of only three women lead pastors in all of Canada.

The *Report* itself did not do a good job bridging the divide between liberal and conservative groups of women. Even though conservative groups were members of MCC, voices of women from this part of the church were rarely heard in the *Report*. As Anabaptist feminist/womanist/*mujerista* women doing theology, we must analyze how power has been and is being used. The *Report* began as a way to combat inequality in the church. It aimed to be a forum for women to share their theological perspectives. Conservative elements within the church wanted to remove advocacy for women from the agenda of MCC.[56] The end of the *Report*'s publication was premature, in that most Anabaptist women had hardly even started to find their theological voice. The MCC is one of the few organizations where Anabaptists of many kinds cooperate: Could the empowerment of women to share the good news of Jesus Christ be a renewed ideal for MCC? Is Mennonite World Conference a forum where this agenda could be raised? Where will women hear each other's voices?

Another marginalized group within the Anabaptist church consists of LGBTQ+ people. The MCC limited the inclusion of their voices in the *Report*.[57] The Anabaptist church has silenced and punished queer voices in the church, and our theology needs to listen to their pain and their perspectives on Jesus. Including both conservative voices and LGBTQ+ voices as part of the hermeneutical community is a challenge that could take us into the next century.

I am writing from Canada, but the majority of Anabaptists live in the Global South. If we want to facilitate dialogue between groups of women in the Anabaptist church, the economic power of the United States and Canada needs to be factored in. How can that

---

[56] For example, some conservative pastors deemed a conference on women in ministry in British Columbia sponsored by MCC Women's Concerns "too radical." They threatened to withdraw their church's financial support from MCC, and the MCC BC board did withdraw its endorsement. Esther Epp-Tiessen, *Mennonite Central Committee in Canada: A History* (Winnipeg: CMU Press, 2013): 207.

[57] Editor Debra Gingerich writes, "In fact, since there has been so much recent debate over whether or not homosexuals should be a part of the church, we did plan to include an article by a lesbian. We were not given permission to do so. Apparently, even when listening to women who are challenging how we define who is in and out of the church, the issue of homosexuality is too controversial to discuss." Debra Gingerich, "Compiler's Comments," *Report* 163 (September–October 2002): 3.

power be harnessed to foster dialogue? How can Anabaptist women work together to build bridges, hear each other's stories, and learn how Jesus is working in our lives? Is there a desire to do this? Do we care enough about each other to respect the other's points of view, even when it is difficult? Are we in the United States and Canada willing to hear how lifestyles of people like me contribute to the suffering of our sisters in the Global South?

Anabaptist women should be fearless and bold in setting the theological agenda for their own writing. In my research of the *Report*, I discovered that women found other women's writings the most helpful in developing their own theology. Women were cited three times more often than men.[58] The women theologians quoted most were Mary Daly (six times), Katie Funk Wiebe (six times), Rosemary Radford Ruether (five times), Virginia Ramey Mollenkott (five times), Madeleine L'Engle (five times), and Ruth Krall (two times).[59] When male theologians were quoted, none were mentioned more than twice.[60] Interestingly, of all the women quoted, 8 percent were Anabaptist, while of the men quoted, 30 percent were Anabaptist.[61] Clearly women wanted to draw on Anabaptist sources, but at the time they were writing, women Anabaptist writers were not well known. How would Anabaptist

---

[58] This statistic refers to the times a writer is directly quoted or a specific idea of theirs is explained, not how many times their name was mentioned.

[59] The following theologians were quoted once: Kelly Brown Douglas, Barbara Brown Zikmund, Elizabeth Cady Stanton, Lydia Harder, Nancy Hardesty, Georgia Harkness, Carter Heyward, Elizabeth Johnson, Julian of Norwich, Emma LaRocque, Sallie McFague, Nelle Morton, Kathleen Norris, Judith Plaskow, Marjorie Proctor-Smith, Letha Scanzoni, Mary Shertz, Starhawk, Mary Ann Tolbert, Phyllis Trible, and Dorothy Yoder Nyce. Feminist writers quoted were Alice Walker (thrice), Gloria Steinem (thrice), Betty Frieden (twice), and quoted once were Maya Angelou, Anita Diamant, Carol Gilligan, bell hooks, Dorothy Sayers.

[60] Male theologians mentioned twice were Gordon Kaufman, Thomas Merton, Walter Wink, and John Howard Yoder. Mentioned once were David Augsburger, Leonardo Boff, Frederick Buechner, Donald Capps, John Driver, Richard Foster, Matthew Fox, Frederick Keene, Martin Luther King Jr., C. Norman Kraus, Donald Kraybill, James Nelson, Parker Palmer, James Newton Poling, Dennis Quinn, Paul Ricoeur, Oscar Romero, A. W. Tozer, Thomas Troeger, and Desmond Tutu.

[61] Male Anabaptist theologians were quoted eight times, and female Anabaptist theologians were quoted five times.

theology be different if the theology taught in churches and schools included women's and men's voices equally?

The *Report* provides an alternative Anabaptist tradition that can be mined and explored. More work needs to be done unearthing the voices of Mennonite women from different time periods. These texts by women can become normative for students who are studying theology rather than just being featured in a single class devoted to "women's voices." As Anabaptist women and their allies find positions in theological schools, and as we listen to marginalized women's voices in the hermeneutical community, our theology will grow and develop. As Anabaptist women find their voices and share their writing, we will hear new perspectives about the gospel of Jesus Christ.

Telling Our Stories against All Odds

The inclusion of personal stories in our theological writing will be central. Stories make theology accessible: you don't need a degree in theology to read a story. Personal stories allow the reader to know who you are, why you are writing, and who could benefit from your writing. If I identify myself as a white, North American, middle-class woman who is writing about abuse because I have witnessed abuse and want abuse to stop, people know my commitments. Too much of Anabaptist theology, sometimes even authored by women, is written as if disembodied brains are looking down on the world from on high. This is patently false; we write from social locations, and our theology has political implications. I believe it is important to name our social contexts, and telling our stories is a way to do this.

There are forces aligned against contextualizing theology and telling stories in academic settings. In the past several years I was invited to participate in two different Anabaptist academic conferences. I submitted both my papers for consideration in the volumes that were going to be published from these events. Both times the peer review comments asked me to take the "story elements" out of my papers, where I explained who I was, why the research was important to me, and how I got involved with it. I faced a dilemma: I was not tenured faculty, and showing my publication record was important for continued employment. I did not feel that I could argue with people much senior to me in academia and still get published. I bowed to the pressure and removed the story sections of my papers that made them interesting, accessible, and I think ethically responsible. There are still gatekeepers in our Anabaptist institutions that smother a narrative method of doing theology. Women need to be bold, but change will take longer than we think.

As we move forward as Anabaptist women doing theology, we must stay keenly tuned to the way power shapes the stories we share. Sometimes we have power, and sometimes we do not. How do those of us with power use it to empower others? This is something I struggle with as a white woman. We need to be honest about when we have done well and when we have failed. Who is being heard? Who benefits?

Listening to the Stories of the Earth

As women listening to each other's stories, we must listen to stories of the marginalized. In that vein, I think the most marginalized voices in our world today are nonhuman voices. Our hermeneutical community needs to listen to the stories the earth is telling us.

Last year I found the body of a huge fish washed up on the shore of Lake Ontario near where I live. I had never seen anything like it. It turned out to be a fish on the endangered species list called the lake sturgeon. It used to be one of the most plentiful fishes in the Great Lakes. The lake sturgeon is communicating in the only way it can; will we listen? What does theology look like if we confess that creation is groaning, and it is groaning because of what we have done to it? I am now asking, If Jesus is Living Water, how is that related to Lake Ontario?

There are other voices we need to listen to if we want to do theology with the earth in mind. I am writing this on the traditional territories of Anishinaabe, Ojibway/Chippewa, and Haudenosaunee peoples. They were stewards of the land for thousands of years before white settlers came. Their long connection with the land and water offers wisdom that certainly cannot be historically found in Anabaptist theology or in any white Christian theology. We need to hear the stories that First Nations peoples are willing to share with us. The specter of climate change looms over all life on earth:

this will be our number one issue as a peace church. The biggest challenge for theologians in the coming century will be to navigate political and economic power differentials and live into the moral responsibility that economically rich countries have to care for the earth and for all affected by climate change. Anabaptist, feminist/womanist/*mujerista*, and story-based theologies can help foster compassion in these challenging times.

Conclusion

Anabaptist women have been empowered by Jesus to share good news. As Dorothy Yoder Nyce writes, this has always been the case: "An astonishing thing about Anabaptism is not so much the activity of the ordained leaders, who usually were chosen out of the laity . . . but the missionary commitment of the ordinary members."[62] The *MCC Women's Concerns Report* was one way that ordinary women shared the good news with each other. Through storytelling and feminist/womanist/*mujerista* analysis, this publication provided a new theological vision for the Anabaptist church in the form of a Jesus who empowered the marginalized and oppressed.

I am not a young woman, and I will be long gone by the end of this century. But I can imagine the ways that Jesus will be empowering Anabaptist women to creative and life-giving work in our church and in our world, where peace will be so badly needed. They will tell the stories of Jesus as they live the stories of their lives. I am praying for them.

---

[62]Dorothy Yoder Nyce, "Leadership and Ordination Intertwined," *Report* 43 (May–June 1982): 3.

3

The Politics of Suffering and JustPraxis

Elizabeth Soto Albrecht

Most Christian teaching about suffering has been an obstacle for women healing from gender-based violence. It suggests that everything happens under the perfect will of God and that we should voluntarily "take our cross" and suffer for Christ's sake. I want to chart a new path: the process of justice-liberation, which I call JustPraxis.[1] I argue that in order to stop suffering produced by human actions (whether intentional or unintentional), we need to disrupt the cycle of violence. This process of proclaiming liberation is based on truth-telling and breaking silence, giving meaning to our pain. JustPraxis includes compassion and communal healing for those suffering from hurt and violence caused by human wrongdoing. It is deeply connected to the liberative work of Jesus Christ and the wisdom of Sophia. I aim to deconstruct suffering as it is found in many socioeconomic realities. In writing this chapter I recount my journey as a Latina practical theologian liberating the politics of Jesus from the predominant Christian teaching of voluntary suffering and uncovering the politics of suffering acted out in Jesus's doing and being. In my view, the politics of suffering is embedded in the politics of Jesus.

I begin by naming my own commitments and roots as I draw on feminist, Latina, and liberation theologians to discuss praxis. I then describe the traditional, inherited, patriarchal concept of suffering, as articulated by John Howard Yoder. I move away from a *theology* of suffering to a *politics* of suffering, away from an abstract view of suffering to one that deals with concrete realities. Then I apply this to Christology, showing how Jesus is a model in charting this new path of JustPraxis.

This constructive theological exercise is an invitation to perceive how we can create new paths from woundedness, pain, and suffering. I address a politics of suffering that has liberation from suffering as its

---

[1] I created the word JustPraxis, inspired by two authors. Obery M. Hendricks Jr. concludes, "For the polities of Jesus seeks not possession of worldly power, but to serve the justice of God." Obery M. Hendricks Jr., *The Politics of Jesus: Rediscovering the True Revolutionary Nature of the Teachings of Jesus and How They Have Been Corrupted* (New York: Doubleday, 2006), 331. Similarly, Miguel De La Torre, from his Hispanic perspective, makes "a preferential option for a Jesús who provides my particular Latino/a community (as well as other marginalized communities) with realistic spiritually based political praxis that could lead us toward a more just social order." Miguel A. De La Torre, *The Politics of Jesús: A Hispanic Political Theology* (Lanham, MD: Rowman & Littlefield, 2015), 14.

divinely given goal, based on God's salvific plan for humanity. Salvation addresses the living reality of all peoples, not only the individual soul. JustPraxis focuses not on cognitively complex answers but on life-giving alternatives found in the messiness of our pain.

Praxis Rooted in the Soil of My Latina Identities

When I was a child attending the Catholic Church with my family in Chicago and Puerto Rico, voluntary suffering was prescribed by the nuns and priests as good for our souls. In order to demonstrate our faithfulness, we were forced to face the crucifix as catechumens: the cruel face of the suffering Christ on the crucifix was front and center, producing more fear/*temor* than obedience. Jesus was presented in my childhood as the one who suffers; therefore, it was acceptable for all to suffer. I found solace in the Christmas baby Jesus and Mother Mary.

During my conversion in a Pentecostal church as a young adult, I experienced the message of the fire of hell, and our problems were demonized. Financial hardship, unemployment, interfamily violence, church conflicts, and all kind of physical and mental illness were interpreted as an attack from the devil on our Christian faith. Poverty, racism, and sexism were interpreted as the way God tested our faith to become better believers. Spiritualization of suffering was a way of coping, instead of recognizing that humans commit violent acts and need to be held accountable.

The message always present was, *It's OK to suffer*. Because God is willing it in the spiritual realm, we must just passively accept it as voluntary suffering, seeing it as good since we cannot stop it. We were taught to spiritualize even the suffering of natural disasters. Latin America so often experiences the suffering caused by natural disaster; the poor are totally devastated from hurricanes, tornadoes, and earthquakes. The marginalized do not have homeowner's insurance. Their poorly constructed houses cannot be rebuilt; they lose even the little they once had.

Human-made disasters, such as patriarchy, were also something to be accepted. The dominant religious narrative in women's lives in Puerto Rico and Colombia was, *As a wife, it's reasonable to tolerate abuse; you should put up with it as your voluntary suffering.* It was culturally normal that wives were socially blamed for their suffering. In general society, the Latino patriarchal realities were bad; but in church it was worse, using Scripture and prayer as instruments of appeasement and acceptance.

Later, in my adult faith journey after I had migrated to the United States, simple Mennonite folks encouraged me to live a life of self-sacrifice, a lifestyle to which I submitted for the good of the community. To be a servant—to sacrifice one's life—was to suffer and that was deemed good and acceptable. In this Anabaptist community, martyrdom was almost prescriptive: the right way to be a disciple of Jesus, who suffered for our sake, was to take on suffering. This faith community was not unique. Violence toward women in some Christian communities is tolerated. Literal biblical interpretations about female subordination further traumatize and make women's wounds difficult to heal. As women, we are taught to accept suffering and not to question the human-made systems and structures that keep us enmeshed.

In my life, liberation came when I questioned these theological assumptions, allowing justice to shine light on the truth of suffering. As a young adult seminarian, I heard and read about a different Jesus preached in Mennonite Puerto Rican churches, founded on the liberative work of the life and teachings of Jesus. I asked myself, *I refuse to suffer—does that mean I am less of a Christian? Can I keep faith in Jesus and find truth in other life-giving narratives?* I found that using only theological language constrained me. To disentangle my inherited theology, I had to explore the term "politics of suffering"—a concept that has been used in theories of politics and social science, most recently in writing about Palestinian refugees in Syria and in writing about Aboriginal living conditions in Australia.[2] African scholar Patrick Chabal defines the politics of suffering as the "journey into the politics of everyday life."[3]

As a Puerto Rican, second-generation migrant, Latina, and Mennonite, I see reality differently than my white male and female

---

[2] Nell Gabiam, *The Politics of Suffering: Syria's Palestinian Refugee Camps* (Bloomington, IN: Indiana University Press, 2016); Patrick Chabal, *Africa: The Politics of Suffering and Smiling* (London: Zed, 2009).
[3] Chabal, *Africa*, 172.

colleagues. As a Latina theologian, I recognize that I have been given not only a patriarchal biblical interpretation but also another layer: that of a colonized/occupied people. W. E. B. Du Bois described the African American reality as double-consciousness. Later, womanist theologian Jacquelyn Grant identified "the triple nature of Black women's consciousness."[4] I dare to say that Latina women in the United States carry three or four consciousnesses, "this sense of always looking at one's self through the eyes of others."[5] Our otherness[6] arises from our country of origin, our migration/immigration status, our woman-self, and our religious identity. Postcolonial African feminist Musa W. Dube adds the term "double colonization": oppression "by two structure systems: imperialism and patriarchy."[7] Since I experience oppression differently from our Black communities, we meet in the margins. In order for us not just to exist separately, we must collaborate in our mutual struggles to be as equals. I need constantly to decolonize my belief, arriving at my own understandings of Jesus and Wisdom Sofia, who informs my struggles and sufferings in the United States, the matrix of my praxis. It is in praxis that I find my voice, naming my Latin identities in this politics of suffering and not allowing white systems to place me in a limited box on their terms.

Suffering as a Political Problem

Ministry is the arena where action-reflection is done in the ever-transforming movements of being aware, guided by praxis at its

---

[4]Jacquelyn Grant, "The Sin of Servanthood," in *A Troubling in My Soul: Womanist Perspectives on Evil and Suffering*, ed. Emilie M. Townes (Marynoll, NY: Orbis, 1993), 212.
[5]W. E. B. Du Bois, *The Souls of Black Folk*, ed. Brent Hayes Edwards (New York: Oxford University Press, 2007), 8.
[6]Fernando Segovia redefines "otherness" in a more liberating and redeemable way. Fernando F. Segovia, "Toward a Hermeneutics of the Diaspora: A Hermeneutics of Otherness and Engagement," in *Reading from This Place, vol. 1, Social Location and Biblical Interpretation in the United States*, ed. Fernando F. Segovia and Mary Ann Tolbert (Minneapolis: Fortress, 1995), 57–74.
[7]Musa W. Dube, *Postcolonial Feminist Interpretation of the Bible* (St. Louis: Chalice, 2000), 113.

core. Feminist theologians define the term "praxis" as "the social activity of emancipation in Christian feminism."[8] Rebecca Chopp defines Christian praxis more specifically as "the work of God and Christians in alleviating oppression, in forming communities of survival and hope, and in providing new ways of flourishing."[9] Ada María Isasi-Díaz reinforces this through *mujerista* theology, "a liberative praxis: reflective action that has as its goal liberation."[10] Praxis, according to Isasi-Díaz, "enable[s] Latinas to understand the many oppressive structures that almost completely determine our daily lives."[11] The inter-connectiveness of theory-practice is a dance in which one informs the other in a nonlinear and nonhierarchical way. It is a continual dialogue of reformulating based on reality, providing practical implementations toward change. When we speak of praxis, it informs both the means and the end we seek to change, working to free self and others.

Praxis cannot confine any practical issue to a religious realm. In her book *Political Theology*, German theologian Dorothee Sölle sought to bring faith and action together, asserting that our theological statements do carry political meaning.[12] Feminists have argued for decades that "the personal is political." Accordingly, we have searched to define the political nature of our sexuality, race, class, and gender, which are all social constructs. Praxis does not explore theory, yet it makes implicit the need to question theories that are nonfunctional for our reality today. To question the assumptions about God taught by my upbringing, I needed to disarm the patriarchal apparatus, necessitating the work of justice, offering light into the intersectionality of the real issues of ethnicity, race, gender, and class. Praxis describes our political existence, where we read the text of our bodies and the pain we experience. Pain is agency. Pain is power that speaks to and demonstrates the injustices. The pain in our bodies is the text.

---

[8] Rebecca S. Chopp, "Praxis," in *Dictionary of Feminist Theologies*, ed. Letty M. Russell and J. Shannon Clarkson (Louisville: Westminster John Knox, 1996), 221.
[9] Chopp, "Praxis," 222.
[10] Ada María Isasi-Díaz, *Mujerista Theology: A Theology for the Twenty-First Century* (Maryknoll, NY: Orbis, 1996), 62.
[11] Isasi-Díaz, *Mujerista Theology*, 62.
[12] Dorothee Sölle, *Political Theology*, trans. John Shelley (Philadelphia: Fortress, 1974), 3.

When we define suffering as a political problem, we must see it as a direct result of systems of oppression that allow abusive actions, causing harm and pain. This is everyday life for the oppressed. Womanist theologian M. Shawn Copeland defines suffering as "the disturbance of our inner tranquility caused by physical, mental, emotional, and spiritual forces that we grasp as jeopardizing our lives, our very existence."[13] The politics of suffering requires us to dismantle the systems of oppression that sustain sexism, classism, and racism since they share the same root causes. Human suffering, as explained by Cynthia Halpern, has been the most urgent and least understood question of contemporary politics. Suffering must be understood "as a *political* question . . . that opens up a public moral space . . . and that demands a public response through the exercise of power."[14] Sölle names three phases of response, from submissiveness to conquest: "The conquest of powerlessness—and this may at first consist only in coming to know that the suffering that society produces can be battled—leads to changing even the structures."[15] The politics of suffering aims to address the problem of accepting suffering.

John Howard Yoder wrote extensively on the meaning of Jesus's suffering and developed the concept of "voluntary subordination": since Jesus took on suffering of his own free will, Christians should also submit when suffering comes their way. However, it is one thing for a male in a position of power to submit voluntarily; it is a much different thing for a poor woman of color to submit voluntarily.[16] Yoder's thesis seems absurd to the oppressed and not valid for women's reality. His position comes from his reliance on an antiquated nonresistant pacifism common in Anabaptist writers before him that he at times also advocated.[17] The points of

---

[13]M. Shawn Copeland, "Wading through Many Sorrows: Toward a Theology of Suffering in Womanist Perspective," in *A Troubling in My Soul: Womanist Perspectives on Evil and Suffering*, ed. Emilie M. Townes (Maryknoll, NY: Orbis, 1993), 109.
[14]Cynthia Halpern, *Suffering, Politics, Power: A Genealogy in Modern Political Theory* (Albany, NY: SUNY Press, 2002), 2.
[15]Dorothee Sölle, *Suffering*, trans. Everett R. Kalin (Philadelphia: Fortress, 1975), 73.
[16]I am in full agreement with Teresa M. De Farrari, "The Politics of Jesus: Vicit Agnus Noster," *Catholic Biblical Quarterly* 36, no. 1 (1974): 149–50.
[17]For example, Harold S. Bender, "The Anabaptist Vision," *Church History* 13 (March 1944): 3–24; Guy Franklin Hershberger, *War, Peace, and Nonresistance* (Scottdale, PA: Herald, 1944).

reference are not equal in currencies of power; hence, to prescribe voluntary subordination is abusive. Yoder's proposition promotes an unjust status quo.[18] Yoder's peace stance did not allow him to view suffering as a political problem; furthermore, his white male privilege blinded him to the true political nature of suffering reinforced in his innovative (yet hurtful) teachings on voluntary subordination.

Yoder succeeded in taking Jesus out of the shadows of apolitical existence, convincing readers that Jesus proclaimed and worked toward radical change. In that, I agree: the heart of the gospel proclamation of salvation is liberation. The oppressed people of Jesus's time did not even fully understand the implications of his teaching and actions; they received it as a fertile seed that would grow inside of them. It was reinforced by the disciples and the emerging community of believers. Still, Yoder did not go far enough. As a Euro-American, privileged white man, he did not know what being oppressed and suffering under unjust systems felt like. Furthermore, he never totally recognized his own abuse of power and the profound damage he caused by sexually abusing so many sisters in the Mennonite church. He failed to see his own culpability and complicity in systems of oppression.

Ultimately, subordination has led many women into suffering. The idea of voluntary suffering is oppressive and masochistic in nature, infringing on our freedom in Christ and, worse, perpetuating more abuse. It has kept us women from healing. Furthermore, for the oppressed there is no such thing as voluntary suffering: the status quo of these teachings has saturated our souls with chains of oppression. Feminist theology moves away from asserting that suffering is God's will toward recognizing the systems and ideologies that promote suffering, acknowledging that "God who is the lover of life does not desire the suffering of people."[19] I join with many womanist writers in saying that, as women of color, we

---

[18] For more in-depth reading, see Rachel Waltner Goossen, "Historical Justice in an Era of #MeToo: Legacies of John Howard Yoder," *The Martin Marty Center for the Public Understanding of Religion*, December 7, 2017, https://divinity.uchicago.edu/sightings/historical-justice-era-metoo-legacies-john-howard-yoder.

[19] Sölle, *Suffering*, 108.

"reject suffering as God's will," and we reject suffering coming from both sociopolitical and religious arenas.[20]

The Cross as Transitional Bridge

The cross as a symbol of self-suffering should not be part of our Christian understanding and should not be at the center of Christianity. For many Latinas/Latinos, the cross became the sword of elimination wielded against the natives of our lands, genocide done by massacring (like the Spanish Conquistadores who killed the *Tainos* of my country Puerto Rico), all in the name of Christ. Some feminist writers eliminate the cross altogether from their interpretation of Christianity; some womanists re-interpret its value; others, like me, try to decentralize it.[21] For many, the cross is on the side of death, which is why placing it as a transitional bridge is a much more helpful image.

I prefer to interpret the cross as a transitional bridge, a traumatic event ending with the power of God manifested in the resurrection. The cross was not divinely imposed but was a result of human intentions. Jesus lived in an occupied and oppressed political world. The cross was a clear political statement of destruction and death. The Roman Empire made it a visible way of terrorizing the inhabitants of their occupied lands, and the temple leaders knew how to use it to eliminate their enemies, too. Jesus was killed, eliminated by the evilness of both religious leaders and Roman political powers. I agree with David T. Ngong, who argues that "the cross does not validate suffering but rather demonstrates that suffering is an aberration."[22] Delores Williams reminds us, "Jesus came for life

---

[20]Emilie M. Townes, "Living in the New Jerusalem: The Rhetoric and Movement of Liberation in the House of Evil," in *A Troubling in My Soul: Womanist Perspectives on Evil and Suffering*, ed. Emilie M. Townes (Maryknoll, NY: Orbis, 1993), 83.
[21]Rita Nakashima Brock and Rebecca Ann Parker wrote an extensive survey of history of the Christian church taking us back to more life affirming symbols present in the early church, moving away from the focus of the cross. Rita Nakashima Brock and Rebecca Ann Parker, *Saving Paradise: How Christianity Traded Love of This World for Crucifixion and Empire* (Boston: Beacon, 2008).
[22]David T. Ngong, "Protesting the Cross: African Pentecostal Soteriology and Pastoral Care," *Journal of Theology for Southern Africa* 150 (November 2014): 5.

and to show us something about life and living together and what life was all about."[23] Jesus is a reminder of "the world's crucifying violence" and how as victims we can overcome the "absolute indignity" of our crucified oppression, particularly as Black/Brown bodies.[24] However, because many Christian churches preach the cross from a patriarchal viewpoint, it is hard to find a safe place for those seeking healing from the crucifixion experiences of religious violence. Thus, we are called to create safe places, transitioning us out of death into life, experiencing our resurrection-liberation.

JustPraxis as Power to Change

Christ knows what pain and suffering are all about. This is the Jesus I love who moves me into action, empowered by the Holy Spirit, the Sofia that guides me to proclaim, *This should not be*. We will not address the suffering of our people (sexual abuse, mass incarceration, homelessness, racial discrimination) through humiliating subordination. Suffering requires a response with actions of pastoral compassion and lamentation. Crucifixion *no tiene la última palabra, ni la muerte* (does not have the last word, and neither does death). We find hope in resurrected healing. Emilie M. Townes describes resurrection as "God's breaking into history to transform suffering into wholeness—to move the person from victim to change agent."[25] Susanne Guenther Loewen gives meaning to the cross as a place to name our pain, to "witness to God's call for nonviolent resistance and conscientious objection to all the ways we are living in death. With compassionate desire, we might then step into liberation, healing, and life."[26] My perspective as a

---

[23]Delores Williams quoted by Kelly Brown Douglas, *What's Faith Got to Do with It? Black Bodies / Christian Souls* (Maryknoll, NY: Orbis, 2005), 90.
[24]Kelly Brown Douglas, *Stand Your Ground: Black Bodies and the Justice of God* (Maryknoll, NY: Orbis, 2015), 192.
[25]Townes, "Living in the New Jerusalem," 84.
[26]Susanne Guenther Loewen, "Can the Cross Be 'Good News' for Women? Mennonite Peace Theology and the Suffering of Women," *Anabaptist Witness* 3, no. 2 (December 2016): 109–21, http://www.anabaptistwitness.org/wp-content/uploads/2016/12/Loewen-Can-the-Cross-Be-Good-News-for-Women.pdf.

*mujer-lista*²⁷ feminist leads me away from prescribing the cross and instead leads me toward JustPraxis.

JustPraxis is Jesus's way of bringing peace and healing. Implicit in JustPraxis is the justice of God and the very motif of "making things right." It is not mainly about restitution or reconciliation, although that could be part of the action; it is about living out the true meaning of justice as *mishpat*, which is more than punishment of wrongdoing. *Mishpat* also means giving people their rights and taking up the care for the widows, orphans, and the poor.[28] Another word related to justice in Hebrew is *tzadeqah*, a life of right relationships, not only with God but also socially. Jesus's politics was good news for the rich and powerful, if they let go of positions of power and privilege. It is JustPraxis, our human response, that offers the tools to restore right relationships.

In liberating the politics of Jesus, we find a true historical and political person in Jesus. Following the politics of Jesus is not about blindly imitating Jesus but rather creating a path forward out of oppression. In his classic text, *The Spiral of Violence*, directed to the youth in Brazil, Helder Camará teaches "justice as condition of peace."[29] When we take seriously our own context and the text of our walk with Jesus, we can better understand the impact of the politics of Jesus in his social location and in our world today. Within the teachings of the Sermon of the Mount is an invitation to "seek first his kingdom and his righteousness" (Matt. 6:33a NIV), to pursue right actions. Today, beyond political ideology or partisanship, our alignment should be with God's justice. JustPraxis is one way to incarnate God's justice, moving us away from suffering as we address together that which produces pain.

JustPraxis is about redistributing power to make changes in institutions and systems, reviewing and transforming policies to be fair and equal to all. In its most healthy sense, power is about producing change, dynamic energy to move and make things happen.

---

[27] I coin the word *mujer-lista* as an Anabaptist woman ready/*lista* to do the active work of justice from a *mujerista* perspective.
[28] Timothy Keller, *Generous Justice: How God's Grace Makes Us Just* (New York: Riverhead, 2012), 3–4.
[29] Helder Camará, *Spiral of Violence* (London: Sheed and Ward, 1971), 56, http://www.alastairmcintosh.com/general/spiral-of-violence-camara.pdf.

During the colonization period, power was associated with control and dominion. Today, in a post-colonization world, we opt to conceive of power as a shared commodity of mutual respect. Musa Dube names her task this way: "to cultivate postcolonial strategies . . . that resist and decolonize both patriarchy and imperial oppression and seek to articulate . . . liberation."[30] Womanists call it "power as cooperation," moving away from power-over toward power-with, calling us "to develop our . . . capacities for . . . interconnectedness."[31] The powerful need to learn to release power, whereas the powerless need to unleash theirs. We can move from using the imperialistic concept of power-as-domination to power-as-agency, as capacity for change. JustPraxis is the call to do this change, to redistribute power toward the vulnerable. To paraphrase Mary's Magnificat, it is to scatter the proud, to bring down the powerful and lift up the lowly, and to fill the hungry and send the rich away empty (cf. Luke 1:46-55).

JustPraxis in Action

As Anabaptists, we claim our faith to be Christ-centered.[32] Yet, it is not a simple matter to live into JustPraxis. JustPraxis moves us to create bridges not walls, inclusion not exclusion, and openness to innovative approaches. Liberation begins in the search for the root causes of suffering, allowing God's love to be present and working for justice. Yet this does not happen alone but among communities of wounded healers that find each other in the journey toward wholeness. JustPraxis declares the need for change.

I have learned to lean into the pain, as a spiritual practice, even as my wounded self wants to leave it and reject it. As I have journeyed with children, men, and women in their pain, I have attended to my own afflictions. This can only be done because we have support systems ready to listen and impart their healing on us. I find truth by walking with marginalized communities in *lo*

---

[30] Dube, *Postcolonial Feminist Interpretation*, 43.
[31] Townes, "Living in the New Jerusalem," 87.
[32] Palmer Becker, *Anabaptist Essentials* (Harrisonburg, VA: Herald, 2017), 34.

*cotidiano*³³ (everyday life)—not from a desk but from my wounds and sufferings with the people. As an active pacifist Christian, I recognize Jesus as the center of my faith. What is compelling has been his life—his realistic teachings and deeds here on earth— not his death. JustPraxis challenges our misconceptions of God, demands that we re-know God, and invites us to use new names and images more inclusive of the divine being. In my spiritual journey, I created the name CristoSofia, claiming the wisdom (*Sofia*) of God present as a female image of the divinity in Jesus the Christ. I have highlighted the feminine sign of God within Christology as part of my healing journey. Grounded in CristoSofia, I find my voice and my authority to construct and deconstruct. JustPraxis is a calling to be part of the body of Christ, the *ekklesia* of love and justice that holds hope in the midst of pain.

During my early years of walking with sexual abuse victims in the church, I accompanied Anita, a young Latina teenager studying in one of our schools in the mid-1980s. Anita ended up in a mental health hospital, struggling as a victim of sexual abuse from her Latino pastor back home. I went to pick her up at the hospital and traveled that evening to her home city, back to her mother's house. She told me of her pain with anger and tears. It was not right for a pastor of one of our city churches to sexually violate this young girl. Later in their living room, her sister too shared her story of abuse by the same pastor. I was upset and promised I would take this case to the white bishop, no longer trusting the Latino bishop who oversaw the Latino pastors of that same conference. I hoped that justice could be done by exposing the story to the highest power I could reach. Thirty years ago, justice was to get him removed from that church, even if the Latino congregation had forgiven him the Sunday before. Justice for Anita was to at least feel safe in her mother's house.³⁴ This child of God would need to be accompanied professionally to start her journey toward healing. Praying and

---

³³See Isasi-Díaz, *Mujerista Theology*, 66–73; Loida I. Martell-Otero, Zaida Maldonado Pérez, and Elizabeth Conde-Frazier, *Latina Evangélicas: A Theological Survey from the Margins* (Eugene, OR, Cascade, 2013), 41 and 79.
³⁴For a discussion of the elements of justice-making, see Marie M. Fortune, *Is Nothing Sacred? When Sex Invades the Pastoral Relationship* (San Francisco: Harper and Row, 1989), 114–18.

listening was not enough. JustPraxis was emerging through my actions.

The core of JustPraxis is manifested in liberation from suffering. In the need to heal, JustPraxis is not about working for peace but rather about building the essentials for justice to be actively present. Mercy as the expression of love and truth translated by faithfulness are essentials, but peace needs to encounter justice. It will go before God preparing the way, as the psalmist so well depicts: "Mercy and truth have met together. Grim justice and peace have kissed!" (Ps. 85:10 TLB). The invitation is in the question, *What do you need?* articulated to a victim of sexual violence within the church, prompting us to search for the root cause of the suffering and moving us toward liberation. Countless times I have had to articulate my mantra, *Dios no desea sufrimiento para tu vida* (God does not desire suffering for your life), to victims I have journeyed with through tears and anger.

In my embrace of JustPraxis, I realized that if I continued to nurture hate and ill feelings toward my enemy, I would further injure my body, mind, and soul. I am now able to love even my enemies because of the spiritual practice coming from the power of reclaiming healing for myself and others. After all, the enemy and I share the brokenness of humanity. There is plenty of grace for all even as it is necessary with righteous indignation to hold the abuser responsible and seek restitution for the wrong committed.[35] Today it is not enough just to stop the violence; there is a higher call to create policies and procedures for earlier intervention and preventive approaches. JustPraxis seeks justice for not only individuals but also entire communities. Here the power of togetherness allows the bodies to speak, cry, and move, resisting the normalization of historical violence. The political implications of JustPraxis are made tangible; its manifestation is in the body of those claiming justice, always searching for liberation.

The politics of Jesus was expressed here on earth, so we can continue to pray-act together: may "your will be done, on earth as it is in heaven" (Matt. 6:10). I aim for JustPraxis because there is much justice to be done before heaven will happen here on earth, where it matters.

---

[35] Fortune, *Is Nothing Sacred?* 116–17.

PART TWO

Living the Politics of Jesus in Context

4

Hospitality as Revolutionary In-Subordination in South Africa

Karen Suderman

An excellent case study of power structures, superordinate and subordinate, lies within the South African context. The iron-fisted structure of the apartheid regime created an extremely detailed caste system. The white minority sat at the apex of this structure while the black majority suffered and struggled as subordinates. The success of the struggle against apartheid was the culmination of millions of revolutionary acts both insubordinate and in subordination through powerful grassroots and underground movements. Political movements such as the African National Congress, the United Democratic Front, and the Communist Party (only to name a few) all worked together and in their own ways to mobilize the masses and create a platform for voices to be heard. Strikes, boycotts, and demonstrations were commonplace. South Africa echoed with the call and response freedom cry: *Amandla, awethu* (the power is ours). These were the overt revolutionary acts of insubordination used by those struggling against apartheid in the explicit power struggle that took place on a daily basis.

Other revolutionary acts were quiet but equally powerful. While the apartheid regime itself was in power for forty-six years, the colonial history and imagination of segregation existed for three centuries before that. Those who were oppressed and those in subordinate positions had immense time to hone the skill of acting as a revolutionary. These acts became a habitual part of daily life. The effects of these carefully honed skills were incredible. While the aforementioned parties and movements are the legend of the struggle against apartheid and have earned mention in the annals of South African history, what I point to as small, daily acts of revolution are the lore of the struggle against apartheid. These stories exist under the surface and are not often mentioned in history books. These acts began with a large pot, a wooden spoon, and an open door.

I had the privilege of calling South Africa home from 2009 to 2016. I witnessed firsthand the reverberating pain and mistrust that is the legacy of colonialism and apartheid. I also witnessed the dogged determination of many in the nation to move beyond the apartheid imagination and to witness a new reality. As workers with Mennonite Church Canada Witness, my husband and I were invited to South Africa to help organize and coordinate the Anabaptist Network in South Africa (ANiSA). Among many things, a key role I played within the network and our larger ministry was one of hospitality. Remembering and practicing hospitality across racial boundaries in the context of apartheid South Africa was not only frowned on; it was illegal. Yet many dared to open their homes and lives to one another, creating alternate spaces of justice and equality—revolutionary acts of insubordination even while occupying subordinate roles to those favored by an oppressive regime. Hospitality was neither an augmentation to a revolutionary act nor a meager submission to the system of power. Hospitality *waged* revolution in an inhospitable system. Even in postapartheid South Africa, hospitality has a key role to play in freeing the imagination of what it means to engage the other and how to walk together.

In this chapter, I critically engage the idea of "revolutionary subordination" by John Howard Yoder and reframe it in light of examples and experiences from South Africa. While elements of Yoder's interpretation of revolutionary subordination are worth our attention, several issues arise that undermine Yoder's understanding of the term. I offer a reinterpretation of the phrase "revolutionary subordination" and use South Africa as a case study to highlight daily acts of revolution from ordinary radicals.

Reframing "Revolutionary Subordination"

"Revolutionary Subordination" remains arguably the most contentious of Yoder's chapters within *The Politics of Jesus*. Often seen as a theological and exegetical treatise that has perpetuated the subjugation of women, this chapter has been the source of strong rebuttals from many North American feminist theologians. At risk of upsetting my sisters and brothers reading these words, I argue that elements of revolutionary subordination can be emancipatory. Noting that Jesus left a lack of ethical compass for the early church, Yoder seeks to trace the ethical models used by the early church.[1] Using Paul's writing as a rubric, Yoder outlines the *haustafeln* (literally "house table," the name given to the ethical model used by the early church) in contrast with stoic ethics.[2] While the *haustafeln*

---

[1] John Howard Yoder, *The Politics of Jesus: Vicit Agnus Noster*, 2nd edn (Grand Rapids: Eerdmans, 1994), 168.
[2] Yoder, *Politics of Jesus*, 169.

reflected the social order of the time, it also carried elements that demonstrated an alternative way of being in light of the ethics Jesus demonstrated throughout his ministry.

Yoder's exegesis points to a few liberative elements worth noting. One of the most salient features of the *haustafeln* is the notion that those in subordinate positions are the primary subjects of Paul's address.[3] By contrast, those in power (namely, men) are addressed in stoic social ethics. Thus, according to Yoder, those in subordinate positions are the moral agents within the *haustafeln*.[4] Additionally, while single roles are addressed in stoic ethics (e.g., father, friend, sibling), roles are addressed in pairs within the *haustafeln*, with the subordinate role coming first (e.g., slave/master, child/parent, wife/husband).[5] Moreover, while addressing pairs and relationships, the *haustafeln* calls for mutual submission.[6] Slaves submit to masters, and masters must be aware that they, too, have a master in heaven; wives submit to husbands, and husbands must love their wives as Christ loves the church.[7] The argument points not to caving into and accepting the social order as it stands but rather to constantly evolving relationships that move toward the way things ought to be in the order of the Kingdom of God. Yoder is also careful to point out that, in his view, he is simply talking about social order. The word "subordinate," in Yoder's use, must not be mistaken for the word "subjugate." The key for Yoder is the root word "ordinate"; he sees himself as examining a social order as it existed. The prefixes "super" or "sub" simply apply to where people are located within the social order, he argues; it was not intended as a denigrating model of subjugation.[8] In other words, Yoder sees himself as *describing* the way a community's moral ethical code operated within a specific context rather than *prescribing* how he thinks all moral ethical codes ought to operate.[9]

All of this said, Yoder's interpretation of Jesus's motto of revolutionary subordination as "willing servanthood in the place

---

[3] Yoder, *Politics of Jesus*, 171.
[4] Yoder, *Politics of Jesus*, 171.
[5] Yoder, *Politics of Jesus*, 169, 171.
[6] Yoder, *Politics of Jesus*, 177.
[7] Yoder, *Politics of Jesus*, 177–8.
[8] Yoder, *Politics of Jesus*, 172.
[9] Yoder, *Politics of Jesus*, 187.

of domination" is deeply problematic.¹⁰ First, this definition for "revolutionary subordination" only crops up toward the end of Yoder's argument, a significant structural weakness to the chapter. Without a lens through which to read the chapter, the reader is left with little to guide their understanding of Yoder's words. Placing the definition toward the beginning of the chapter would have informed the reader of the interpretive lens through which the *haustafeln* was being viewed and may have mitigated some of the chapter's tendency to be understood in a different light. Second, Jesus, a man, was in fact a superordinate within the societal structure of the time. As a male, he had the ability to choose between servanthood and domination. For those in subordinate positions, the choice between servanthood and domination was far more limited, if it existed at all. Those who are subordinate have only the choice of servanthood because they are dominated. Thus, the interpretation and reception of Yoder's chapter depends on one's position within societal orders. Reading Yoder's chapter, those with the option—the superordinate—are urged to exercise voluntary servanthood. However, those without the option—the subordinate—are only reminded that their choice is not willfully but circumstantially made. Thus, Yoder's female readership—myself included—understandably perceives that the chapter is a focused and exegetical reminder that theirs will always be the place of servanthood, not because they chose it but because their role in society determines it for them. Thus, the moral agency of those in subordinate roles is problematic, undercutting the emancipatory and revolutionary ethics of the *haustafeln*, which sits at the foundation of Yoder's argument.

A new framework is needed. Another word or phrase is required to help us rethink what emancipatory power lies within the notion of revolutionary subordination. I suggest the word "in." The phrase "revolutionary subordination" is a direct adjective plus a noun. The adjective "revolutionary" describes the nature of the noun "subordination." Revolutionary tells us what the subordination ought to look like. Thus, the focal word and key concept in the phrase is "subordination." Adding the preposition "in" to the phrase—namely, "revolutionary in-subordination"—changes the nature of the phrase dramatically. A preposition describes the

---

¹⁰Yoder, *Politics of Jesus*, 186.

relationship of the words in a phrase, in this case revolutionary and subordination. To be revolutionary *in*-subordination inverts the emphasis of the phrase—that is, we are to be revolutionary in our subordination. This, to my mind, is a far more compelling expression. While acknowledging that there are power structures and orders in any given society, how can we use our position within that structure to act in a revolutionary manner, for we are all subject to one power or another? To go a step further, in this case "in" can also be used as a prefix. The phrase would therefore become revolutionary *insubordination*—that is, to act outside of or push the parameters of one's "ordinate" or role in society. What is any revolutionary act than an act of insubordination? While it is seemingly contradictory to be simultaneously insubordinate and in-subordination, both modes are legitimate and complementary to a revolutionary life.

Hospitality as Revolutionary in-Subordination in South Africa

The apartheid system in South Africa was extremely effective at creating mistrust and enmity. Dividing people from each other—not only white from black but also white from black, from Indian, from colored[11]—created perceptions and stereotypes of the "other" based on fear and thinly veiled hate. The apartheid regime took great care to ensure that South Africans were blinded to common humanity. Rather than choosing to seek and see what might bring South Africans together, South Africans were conditioned to see and fear differences. Moreover, these differences were used to create a value system, which favored some with immense privilege and left the majority of the country's inhabitants with little. This was created at all levels in South African culture and society through city planning and infrastructure, laws, formal education, and public communication and propaganda. Conditions were created in which people's knee-jerk reaction to one another would be to slam the door and lock it rather than to hold it open.

---

[11]The term "colored" in South Africa refers to people who are of mixed-race descent.

Involvement with the struggle against apartheid was risky no matter who you were. If you were Black, Indian, or colored, you were subject to the brutality of police response. Violent responses to protest were common. Rubber bullets, stun grenades, tear gas, and live ammunition were commonly used tools. Prison, or worse, was the repercussion. Those in positions of privilege within the apartheid system—namely, those who were deemed white—risked being ostracized from their communities, congregations, and families if they demonstrated sympathy to the struggle.

Many across the racial spectrum accepted the risk. Many chose to hold the door open in defiance to the contorted imagination the apartheid regime fostered. A dear friend shared some stories of such defiance. She was growing up in Soweto when the student uprising erupted in June 1976. She told stories of how several Mamas took to the streets with their braais (South African charcoal barbecues) and *poitjke* pots (three-legged cast-iron stewing pots) to feed the protestors as tensions increased and the demonstration stretched into days.

On other occasions Mamas cooked large meals in front of their homes while clandestine gatherings took place within. The African National Congress (ANC), among many other liberation movements, was banned during apartheid, and members were forced underground. Meetings, therefore, needed to happen in secret, and they were often raided and broken by the police. Cooking outside gave the ruse of a social gathering to diffuse suspicion. If police arrived, the Mamas always offered to share the food they cooked with the police, though it was often refused.

Within the social construct of apartheid, Black women were on the bottom rung of the social order while white men were at the apex. The Mamas cooking outside of their homes were doing none other than operating within the parameters of their subordinate position in society. However, in a couple of ways they were being far from complicit to their subordinate position, acting in revolutionary ways even in their subordination. The most obvious act of revolution in-subordination was welcoming ANC members into their homes, playing the role of host to those in need of welcome. The role of host and cook fell well within the parameters of the Mamas' subordinate role; in its strictest sense, there was no act of subversion in their act of welcome. Allowing members of the banned ANC to meet, however, enabled the struggle against apartheid to continue. Thus, the Mamas were being revolutionary in their subordinate role. Allowing ANC members to gather in one's home posed a great risk to both guest and host. They made themselves vulnerable to the brutality of police response, bans, beatings, and incarceration.

The Mamas' second act of revolution in-subordination is both more direct and more subversive. The Mamas—functioning within their ordinate role as cooks—dared to look the police at apex of power in the eye and invite them into a shared experience. Despite the extreme power differential between themselves and the police, the Mamas asserted their humanity with an invitation to share food—a deeply revolutionary act. This assertion recognized the humanity in the police. Offering food carried the potential to strip the police of their dogs, guns, uniforms, and weapons and have them stand before the Mamas as human beings and to have the police recognize the Mamas in the same light. Sharing food together marks an entrance into relationship. It is difficult to eat with a person and not learn about them and find commonality. Common humanity was the ultimate ideological antidote to apartheid.

Hospitality as Revolutionary Insubordination

David and Annemie Bosch perpetrated radical hospitality to both friend and foe and acted in profoundly insubordinate ways. When mixed-race gatherings in private homes were illegal, they hosted meals and Bible studies for *all* who wanted to participate, and many came. These were rich and warm encounters at the table and over the Bible, which transcended social and racial boundaries. This drew the attention of the secret police, who sat in their cars outside their home watching the goings on.

Taking hospitality another step further, Annemie brewed a pot of coffee, poured it into a thermos, and sent her son outside to give it to their would-be enemies. Handing the thermos through the widow he said, "It is cold, here is some coffee to help you stay warm. By the way, we're having a meal and a Bible study inside. Please, you're welcome to join us. Come in!" The secret police declined the invitation to come into the home, but they did accept the coffee.

When the secret police were offered coffee and invited into the Bosch's home, their goal was that of observer, of spy. They intended to be a shadow and a threatening presence; they were meant to intimidate from afar. Offering coffee did a couple of radically insubordinate things. First, it openly demonstrated recognition of their presence. Suddenly they were within the circle of engagement. They were no longer the looming, lingering threat they intended to be. They were human, with human faces and human needs. Second, it demonstrated total transparency on the part of the Bosch's and those in their home as well as the flagrant law breaking they were perpetrating within. They were acting outside of the social order dictated by apartheid law, and they had nothing to hide; thus, there was no reason for the police to hide. Moreover, it dared the police to respond with the force and brutality for which they were so well known. However, when the door was held open rather than beaten down, the balance of power shifted greatly. Whether explicitly or intuitively, the police knew that no matter how they responded, the principalities and powers for which they stood would be exposed and made public (Col. 3:12).

Sam and Morag Ross also embodied amazing hospitality. A medical doctor and professor in Durban, Professor Ross quickly noticed a housing problem for the students of color studying at Howard College and the Medical School. These places of learning and the Ross's home were classed in a "whites only" area under the Group Areas Act. The students attending these schools had a long and costly commute every day if they were to live in their "designated" area and still attend classes. Disregarding the law and acting insubordinately, Sam and Morag, whose home was close the university, opened their doors to the students; as many as six at a time over the course of approximately fifteen years lived in the Ross household while they studied. Letters written from the students describe that they felt the Ross's home was "hospitality, love, humility and generosity exemplified."[12] The students were given a home and family at a time when they needed it most. The effect has been profound and lasting.

---

[12]Sam and Morag Ross, *Memoirs of Sam and Morag Ross* (Pietermaritzburg, South Africa: printed by the author, 2000), 47.

Such acts of hospitality demonstrated a powerful and subversive peace in a system that fed on acts of hatred and violence. The Mamas and the Ross and Bosch families offered authentic recognition of those who were deemed "less" by apartheid law. As well, they recognized and engaged the secret police in such a way that put the authorities in a difficult position. The police were seen, acknowledged, and engaged as full human beings in need of a place of belonging, when what they were seeking most was to be unseen and threatening.

In her book *Making Room: Recovering Hospitality as a Christian Tradition*, Christine Pohl notes that acts of hospitality such as these resist "boundaries that endanger persons by denying their humanness. [Hospitality] saves others from the invisibility that comes from social abandonment. Sometimes, by the very acting out of welcome, a vision for a whole society is offered, a small evidence that transformed relationships are possible."[13] Hospitality offered by Mamas and the Bosch and Ross families, along with many others, gave a creative glimpse of and spread hope for what many wanted South Africa to become.

Continuing the Revolutionary in-Subordination

While hospitality had a key role to play during the struggle against apartheid, its role is just as crucial in a postapartheid context. While the apartheid laws and boundaries ceased to exist in 1994, the apartheid imagination remains strong. Still more acts of revolution in-subordination are required to struggle against the pervasive, insidious, race-based power dynamics that still exist.

Throughout our seven years of service in South Africa, hospitality and sharing the table were fundamental roles in which we found ourselves. I often quipped that while the head of my work was in the library I created, the heart and soul of my work were based in the kitchen and at the table. During the last four years of our life and service in South Africa, we had the pleasure of hosting over

---

[13] Christine D. Pohl, *Making Room: Recovering Hospitality as a Christian Tradition* (Grand Rapids: Eerdmans, 1999), 64.

1,600 people. It was an immense gift to share food with many across South Africa's racial and socioeconomic spectrum, both in our home and in other settings. These shared meals began and sustained the relationships we so deeply value; as well, they gave everyone seated at the table the physical and relational sustenance needed to do the work to which we were called.

We learned the power hospitality has to bring together unlikely groups of people in a peaceable way. During our time in Pietermaritzburg, a group of people emerged from a study on Jesus and Politics that my husband, Andrew, led at a local seminary. After the workshop, this group approached Andrew and informed him that they were not content to end the discussion. They wanted to engage further. Over the next two years, an intentional community formed. We gathered together on a monthly basis to share a meal and study the Bible. This gathering would have been illegal during apartheid and continues to be unusual today. Tribes, races, socioeconomic statuses, religious denominations—all of the physical and ideological boundaries meant to keep us apart—melted away when we came together. Mainline and Independent Church expressions, black and white, foreign and South African—we all came together sharing the common need for companionship and food for both physical and spiritual journeys. This was a group of people who cared deeply for each other and valued the gifts, insights, and opinions of everyone present. Everyone took turns leading discussions, overturning common notions of power and leadership.

Hospitality also served as a tool to challenge understandings of gender roles and one's place in the home or within leadership. Gender roles in South Africa are still prescribed, especially in rural areas. The general expectation was that I would prepare meals and do most of the work while guests were in our home. For my husband, the cultural expectation was that he would sit with our guests while I served food and refreshment. Most importantly, *he* was expected to give thanks for the meal. These, too, were opportunities we took to demonstrate an alternate way of operating. When people arrived at our home, I would go and sit with our guests while Andrew served refreshments. When time came to give thanks for the meal, Andrew would either refer to me to pray or, more subversively, would ask one of the younger members of the group to give thanks. In a culture where the oldest male is often treated with most deference, giving the youngest—often female—the honor of giving thanks for a meal turned cultural notions of power on their head. This was yet another way in which we used hospitality to demonstrate an alternative way of being and, hopefully, the upside-down politic of the Kingdom of God.

Simultaneously disarming and deeply subversive, hospitality possesses the power to gently reshape the postapartheid South African imagination. Assuming a hospitable stance takes constant mindfulness in a space where pain, suspicion, and the deep seeded habit of apartheid still challenge the practice. Beginning in small pockets as we participated with our South African sisters and brothers, we witnessed and experienced how attitudes and assumptions can radically transform when a table is shared. Time and commitment are required to see and experience such transformation. Sharing one meal is not a miracle antidote to centuries of segregation and oppression, but it is a beginning.

Living in Revolutionary in-Subordination: A Return to Jesus's Motto

The notion of revolutionary in-subordination opens up the understanding or a re-understanding of Jesus's model as "willing servanthood in the place of domination." As acknowledged above, this understanding could be limited to those who have the ability to choose; however, it seems that a second segment to the phrase ought to be added. Jesus demonstrated willing servanthood both in the place of domination and in the *face* of domination. In other words, revolutionary in-subordination at its base requires defiance of unjust orders and powers, whether one is choosing servanthood rather than domination or using one's place as a servant to expose the powers for what they are. Jesus demonstrates both choice and defiance.

The point of revolutionary in-subordination is not the humiliation or defeat of either the superordinate or the subordinate; the goal is not to prevail or be destroyed. It is a third option: to expose the powers for what they are and open the possibility for an alternative route that creates space for another type of relationship.[14] It creates

---

[14]For a similar approach, see Walter Wink, *Jesus and Nonviolence: A Third Way* (Minneapolis: Fortress, 2003).

the chance for a new humanity and new humanness for both. This ultimately is what the Mamas and the Bosch and Ross families were doing. In recognizing their own position as subordinate to the apartheid regime—be it in the ideological manifestation of the innumerable laws or in the physical manifestation of the corporeal presence of the police and their brute force—each of these people used their position as "underling" to redefine what was possible.

Hospitality functions as an excellent proving ground to hone the skills of revolutionary in-subordination. In her book *A Christian View of Hospitality*, Michelle Hershberger rightly suggests, "Hospitality is an effective vehicle for stopping injustice and confronting racism."[15] Striking a balance between receptivity and confrontation, hospitality simultaneously demonstrated authentic openness and love to those who were deemed "other" in the apartheid system and openly challenged the apartheid system with potently peaceful defiance.

The lesson that South Africa teaches so well is how to be schooled and trained in the art of revolutionary in-subordination. Using one's power, whatever it is, to completely alter the dynamics of the situation is the point of the revolutionary in-subordination. It is by no means unequivocal and uncritical acceptance of one's position, but it is the clear understanding of one's position and the power within that role. Having a realistic view of the limitations of one's situation and position—but also of the loopholes, twists, and turns—is key to living life in revolutionary in-subordination. Close examination of any position will reveal many ways in which the role itself can play into the favor of the subordinate to upset the dynamic of power in any given situation. May we all as subordinates to principalities and powers seek to embody Jesus's example and, learning from our South African sisters and brothers, join the in-subordinate revolution.

---

[15]Michelle Hershberger, *A Christian View of Hospitality: Expecting Surprises* (Scottdale, PA: Herald, 1999), 164–5.

5

Women of Faith Advocating Peace in Colombia

Alix Lozano[1]

---

[1] English translation by Juan Sebastian Pacheco Lozano.

The participation of women in the peace processes and on the implementation of the agreements constitutes a fundamental prerequisite for peacebuilding in the midst of a democratic society based on the principles of equality and justice.

—JOHN PAUL LEDERACH[2]

What is the role of women of faith in a society in crisis—amid armed conflict and both structural and social violence? This question requires women of faith to overcome a double conditioning. First, we must transcend an assigned image—influenced by literalist and spiritualized interpretations of the biblical text and established as dogma by some fundamentalist churches—of the female gender as representing passivity, weakness, and receptivity, implying a lack of engagement with sociopolitical realities. Second, we must show that Christianity is not compliant with injustices but rather supports the liberating message of Jesus, set forth by a gospel of peace. Thus, as a Colombian woman, Mennonite, and pastor—a practicing theologian with a spirituality based on an Anabaptist tradition founded on principles of peace and nonviolence—I affirm in every woman, as in every human, multiple facets that can make her the main character of various roles in history. Women act as managers, animators, artisans, architects, and builders of paths of peace and reconciliation—including the role of political activist.[3] The commitment to peace and reconciliation in highly divided and violent societies is the responsibility of both men and women, necessitating political will and a faith perspective.

To illustrate faithful political engagement in the midst of a particular social, political, and economic context, this chapter describes the role of women in a Peace Process began in 2012 between the Colombian government and the Revolutionary Armed Forces of Colombia–People's Army (FARC–EP), a guerrilla group

---

[2]John Paul Lederach, Presentation at the Peace Summit at Javeriana University, Bogotá, Colombia, July 2017.
[3]Political activists are persons who raise awareness, defend, and promote human rights in the different spheres of society. Political activism is a way to advocate for and generate change.

active since 1964. The first phase of this process culminated in a Peace Agreement in 2016, reached after fifty-three years of a painful and brutal armed conflict.[4] This happened despite significant opposition from conservative religious sectors.

This chapter presents, first, the political reality of the country and its impact on women; second, the role that women have played in the internal conflict, the peace process, and the guarantees on the implementation of the Final Agreement; third, an examination of faith and politics exploring theological and religious obstacles to believers' advocacy during the Peace Agreements; and, last, the case study of the Ecumenical Group of Women Builders of Peace (GemPaz). I write as a founding member and part of the General Committee, arguing that GemPaz's political commitment from a perspective of faith emerges from biblical hermeneutics and a contextual community approach.

Peace Has a Woman's Name

Colombia, a country with approximately forty-eight million inhabitants, has experienced what academics call "prolonged conflict."[5] Since the 1940s, it is estimated that 350,000 people have died as a result of internal armed conflict, and Colombia now has 5.3 million internally displaced persons, more than any other country in the world.[6] Different forms of violence have accompanied four generations of Colombians: confrontations between different armed actors, forced displacement, violation of general human rights (including the right to live), loss of lands, family disintegration, and loss of social fabric. In the various

---

[4] "Después de medio siglo, Colombia y las FARC concluyen un acuerdo de paz," *20minutos*, August 25, 2016.

[5] John Paul Lederach, *The Moral Imagination: The Art and Soul of Building Peace* (Bogotá: Norma Editions, 2009), 75.

[6] According to Justapaz, as cited by Claudia Dary Fuentes, "Las iglesias ante las violencias en Latinoamérica: Modelos y experiencias De Paz en contextos de conflicto y violencia" (Churches in the Face of Violence in Latin America: Models and Experiences of Peace in Contexts of Conflict and Violence), CLALS Working Paper Series No. 3, rev. August 6, 2014 (Washington, DC: Center for Latin American & Latino Studies, American University), 6, http://ssrn.com/abstract=2412771.

peace processes that have taken place in Colombia, women rarely have had a formal role in the negotiation delegations. In spite of that, with each new process, they have found ways to exert influence, putting pressure on peace talks and advocating for their interests.

From civil society and the women's social movement, women have accompanied and promoted the peace process, shaped public opinion, and reaffirmed a negotiated solution to the conflict. During many critical moments of the process, women's organizations insisted on the importance of the parties not walking away from the negotiation table until they had reached an agreement to end the conflict. Women advocated for a ceasefire and increased citizen participation, among other things. Recognizing that the forms of violence used against women during the conflict were drastically different from those used against men and understanding that female bodies have been used as a weapon of war, the national Victims Unit advocated for and empowered women during the peace process, including a campaign, *La Paz tiene Nombre de Mujer* (Peace Has a Woman's Name).[7]

Women from different sectors, including women of faith, supported and reaffirmed the dialogues and final agreement and are currently overseeing what was agreed on by the two parties through verification, implementation, and follow-up, with the purpose of guaranteeing durable and stabilized peace for the transformation and restoration of the social fabric in Colombia. For example, the Victims and Restitution of Land Law established that "women victims of dispossession or forced abandonment will enjoy special protection of the State in the administrative and judicial procedures related to this law."[8] As a result, the restitution processes for women must be accompanied by measures to secure social security for them

---

[7] Unidad para la Atención y la Reparación Integral a las Víctimas, "Planes de acción para mujeres," 2018, http://www.unidadvictimas.gov.co/es/la-paz-tiene-nombre-de-mujer/9027.

[8] Agencia Presidencial para la Acción Social y la Cooperación Internacional, *Ley de Víctimas y Restitución de Tierras* (Bogotá: 2011), article 114, p. 55, http://www.cent rodememoriahistorica.gov.co/descargas/ley_victimas/ley_victimas_completa_web.pdf.

and their families and to create a real path to ownership of land forcibly abandoned or stripped away during the conflict.[9]

Women exhorted the Colombian government to fulfill the agreement and monitored the political will for compliance and implementation. The challenges that women continue to face in regards to the implementation of the Final Agreement relate to the lack of guarantees for secure living and work for female community leaders; inclusion in the process regarding the integral reincorporation of female ex-combatants; pedagogy of the Agreement in the territories; clarity related to the sources of funding; political will from the ruling class; and urgency to strengthen the institutional architecture to respond to these challenges and to insist on the cultural transformations that will enable a path toward reconciliation in Colombia. The Kroc Institute reported that, as of June 2018, "51% of the 130 gender-based provisions identified by the Kroc Institute had not started; 38% were in a minimum state of implementation; 7% had reached an intermediate level of implementation, and 4% had been fully implemented."[10] This shows that while there is progress, there is still a lot to be implemented.

Faith and Politics

Structural conflict was rooted in social disparity and the absence of the state in certain regions. Disparity is due to the way in which resources, such as wealth and land ownership, are redistributed in Colombia. The unequal distribution of the state's resources regarding employment incentives, provisions of public services, housing, access to proper health care, education, and recreation contribute to the already significant gap between wealthy and impoverished people. The absence of the state correlates with the rise of various

---

[9] Adriana Benjumea Rua and Natalia Poveda Rodríguez, "El derecho a la tierra para las mujeres: Una Mirada a la ley de víctimas y restitución de tierras" (Corporación Humanas, n.d.), 70, https://www.humanas.org.co/alfa/dat_particular/ar/Articulo_Tierras_AB_y_NP.pdf.

[10] "Inclusión de medidas para garantizar los derechos de las mujeres en el Acuerdo de Paz es innovadora, aunque presenta retrasos en su implementación, revela informe," https://kroc.nd.edu/assets/294959/definitivo_comunicado_de_prensa_31102018.pdf.

guerrilla groups, the FARC–EP among others, and also common delinquency groups and drug traffickers. Consequently, the history of regional conflicts in Colombia is multidimensional,[11] as is the relationship between faith and politics.

Colombia is a highly religious country, predominantly Christian, with Catholicism representing the majority. There is also ethnic and cultural diversity of Amerindians and African immigrants as well as Hispanic immigrants, indigenous peoples, and Romani peoples. As in many religious contexts, a dualism between faith and politics has put churches in "silent mode," legitimizing dictatorial governments, wars, and violence. Below I discuss the origin of this doctrinal position and how can it be overcome.

The Doctrine of the Two Kingdoms

Martin Luther distinguishes two kingdoms in his most political work, "On the Secular Authority."[12] Luther's thinking on authority is based on Rom. 13:1-7: "Let everyone be subject to the governing authorities, for there is no authority except that which God has established" (Rom. 13:1a NIV).[13] Such interpretation assumes that the world and its inhabitants must blindly obey and not resist the arbitrariness and injustices of a system whose violent authority excludes because they are authorities placed by God. According to this logic, resisting, claiming rights, and drawing attention to corrupt governments, feeders of war, facilitators of arms races, or structural violence would be to resist divine authority. Citizens of this earthly kingdom are thereby discouraged from exercising social and political responsibility.

There are some misconceptions and classic deformations in this bond of faith and politics. On the one hand, there are those who understand faith and politics to be separate entities and live by that

---

[11]For a brief discussion, see Alix Lozano, "Being a Peach Church in the Colombian Context," trans. Rebecca Yoder-Neufeld, in *Seeking Cultures of Peace: A Peace Church Conversation*, ed. Fernando Enns, Scott Holland, and Ann Riggs (Geneva: World Council of Churches, 2004), 148–9.

[12]Marco A. Huesbe Llanos, "Reforma Política Luterana en el siglo XVII de Martín Lutero a Henning Arnisaeus," *Revista de Estudios Histórico-Jurídicos* (Ediciones Universitarias de Valparaiso, 1999): 358.

[13]Huesbe Llanos, "Reforma Política Luterana," 363.

understanding. This would be to ignore the social and relational implications of faith. Another deformation would be to subordinate one to the other: politics is more important than faith or faith is more important than politics. There have been competitions at certain periods in history to see which subdued which. The church-state tension was brought to our continent and was incorporated into the conquest of the New World where the authority of the Catholic kings of Spain was incorporated through the sword and the cross.

The Anabaptist Movement of the Sixteenth Century

Anabaptism was a populist movement. As such, the participation of women was broad, and they played a special role. Their actions and responses to the Reformation movement in relation to baptism and the church-state relationship were political acts. Unlike the Lutheran theory of the two kingdoms, the Anabaptists' understanding of the dichotomies of faith and politics, also affirmed in the Bible, was that all people were subjects to the action of the Holy Spirit and an active part in communities through the exercise of the ministry of all believers, men and women alike, which implied mutual responsibility and care.

Anabaptists emphasized the action of the Holy Spirit as the central agent in the interpretation of the Scriptures, which scandalized the circles of political and religious establishments. Consideration was given to how common men and women, but especially women, had the audacity to face well-prepared theologians, scholars, and powerful lords. Women's responses to questions such as whether they rejected the baptism of infants and practiced the Lord's Supper with two items, bread and wine, in their home gatherings were documented in legal prosecution transcripts. They affirmed these acts when they were held accountable for their disobedience to the authorities and their ordinances. Above all, they simply quoted sections of the New Testament to affirm that their obedience was owed to Jesus and his teachings.[14] Members of these

---

[14] Carlos Martínez García, "Las Mujeres en el Movimiento Anabautista del Siglo XVI (I)," *ProtestanteDigital.com*, May 15, 2016, http://protestantedigital.com/magacin/39372/las_mujeres_en_el_movimiento_amabautista_I.

radical communities submitted to the practices of Jesus and not the authorities of the state and official church.

Women found that Anabaptist teachings provided them with principles for voluntarily exercising their beliefs in defiance of those imposed by the official church-state symbiosis or by their family clan. Anabaptism emphasized personal conversion, baptism as a public expression of the commitment to follow Jesus, and the reality of the church made up of believers. Strengthened by their faith, women chose torture and death rather than evading capital punishment when given the opportunity of retracting their beliefs. In their book *Profiles of Anabaptist Women*, C. Arnold Snyder and Linda A. Huebert Hecht are quite right to indicate that "making visible the lives of women from the past benefits us all by bringing necessary balance to the historical memory of humanity."[15] It is essential to rescue the accounts of women who decided to join the ranks of a persecuted movement.

Faith and Politics Today

Politics is a dimension of a person's concrete faith to the extent that life is a divine extension in every human. The person is a social being or *polis*, and an integral component of that being is socialization with other people. God believes in humanity, has hope in it, made it, and is one with it—that is the reason for God's incarnation. Humans need to recognize from their faith perspective their own role as a human in a violent society and before the state.

Faith includes politics because a Christian person, simply for being a Christian, must commit to justice and to social and integral well-being. Christians must work for transformation and universal salvation through becoming one with all people through love of life, translated into living righteously and through their own well-being. They should also opt for programs and people that come as close as possible to what they have understood to be the project of Jesus, God's project in history. As most churches are thinking

---

[15]C. Arnold Snyder and Linda A. Huebert Hecht, introduction to *Profiles of Anabaptist Women: Sixteenth-Century Reforming Pioneers*, ed. C. Arnold Snyder and Linda A. Huebert Hecht (Waterloo, ON: Wilfrid Laurier University Press, 1996), 1.

about morality issues, they must jointly participate in proposals for structural change that will lead to the idea of a just and sustainable peace over time.

Women and men, followers of Jesus, cannot be mere spectators to these social changes. They must be forgers of history, prophets who announce and denounce, who participate in the processes of claiming their rights, such as the right to life, work, and access to land—in other words, to promote "righteous living" among all people. Righteous living tries to represent the recovery of an idea of well-being based on a harmonious relationship with nature and the recovery of traditional knowledge.[16] To do otherwise, to do nothing, is to be complicit with the structures of evil. To be engaged in social action, it is necessary to be aware of the signs of the times, the moments, the contexts, and the social and political realities that society is experiencing at that moment and through time.

In Colombia there are countless women's groups and grassroots organizations that move within the ecofeminist paradigm and the pacifism of nonviolence based on the vindication of freedoms and the defense of human rights. Betsabé Espinal is an example of a woman with religious roots, who was one of the union leaders who led Colombia's first workers' strike at the Bello Fabric Factory in Antioquia in March 1920. This was not the first Colombian strike, but it is considered to have been the first time women had organized to claim their labor rights.[17] Advocating from a faith perspective requires engagement in the public sphere without shyness or shame. Advocates interact with those around them—not to overwhelm, conquer, or colonize but to create better worlds, people, and leadership.[18]

---

[16] Koldo Unceta, *Desarrollo, Postcrecimiento y Buen Vivir: Debates e Interrogantes*, ed. Alberto Acosta and Esperanza Martínez (Quito, Ecuador: Ediciones Abya-Yala, 2014), 103, http://filosofiadelbuenvivir.com/wp-content/uploads/2015/02/Desarrollo-postcrecimiento-y-Buen-Vivir-2014.pdf.

[17] Cindy Borrero, "Betsabé Espinal, Mujer Valiente y Luchadora: Pionera en la Defensa de los Derechos Laborales en Colombia," CEDESIP: Centro de Estudios Sindicales y Políticos, March 7, 2019, http://www.cedesip.org/betsabe-espinal-mujer-valiente-y-luchadora-pionera-en-la-defensa-de-los-derechos-laborales-en-colombia/.

[18] Leonardo Boff, "Fe y Política," *Koinonía*, Agenda Latinoamericana 2008, http://servicioskoinonia.org/agenda/archivo/obra.php?ncodigo=613.

The Ecumenical Group of Women Builders of Peace (GemPaz)

The Ecumenical Group of Women Builders of Peace (GemPaz) provides a case of a group of women of faith who assumed their commitment to their country. GemPaz is an ecumenical collective of Colombian women (Catholic, Evangelical, Protestant, and Anabaptist) who were born and have lived amid a context of violence. They are mestizo, Afro, indigenous, and *campesinas* (farmers). In practice, they understand their role as women of faith in a society in crisis, amid an armed conflict and with multiple forms of social and structural violence. GemPaz includes women of different professions and functions—religious, pastors, social workers, psychologists, theologians, managers, directors of institutions, and housewives—all of whom are leaders committed to building a stable and lasting peace as a practical expression of their faith through social justice and the protection of people who have been violated, impoverished, and excluded from society. This commitment prompted them to start a path toward peacebuilding in 2007. In their commitment to peacebuilding, they supported and promoted the peace process, including the Final Agreement, as a way of understanding that the liberating politics of Jesus and his praxis go far beyond theoretical concepts.

Through spaces called Ecumenical Circles, women meet once a month (in five regions of the country), where they cultivate a celebratory ecumenical spirituality of formation and praxis, including:[19]

- Promoting through ecumenical, "facilitated dialogue"[20] an attitude of openness and willingness for the resolution and transformation of conflicts.

---

[19] Internal, unpublished document of GemPaz.
[20] Facilitated dialogue is a method to transform relationships in such a way that the parties can work together in a cooperative way to address the issues facing their communities. This process enables a new conversation on a different level of thought and attention, allowing participants to get to the root of things and imagine new possibilities in relationships. Facilitated dialogue is inspired by Democratic Dialogue. See Bettye Pruitt and Philip Thomas, *Diálogo Democrático: Un Manual*

- Beginning a process of reconciliation, recognizing that inherited historical resentments and division between Catholics and Protestants in Colombia had divided them and created misgivings and resistances, and also that this division has contributed to the internal conflict that the country has suffered.[21]
- Overcoming divisions, preventions, and suspicions by healing wounds, gaining trust, and becoming friends and sisters, thus uniting women of Christian faith in the common fulfillment of their mission, such as politically influencing their environment and contributing to the transformation of society.
- Rereading the biblical text using the method "contextual reading of the Bible"[22] through communal hermeneutics, discovering the liberating politics of Jesus framed in texts such as the Sermon on the Mount (Matt. 5–7).
- Training and working on approaches such as conflict transformation, social and political advocacy, psychosocial-spiritual accompaniment, mutual care, and self-care from a biblical and theological basis.
- Advocating in the social and public spheres by regaining the political, prophetic place of women as part of the ministry of the priesthood of all believers, in which a different world that ignites hope is possible.

---

para Practicantes (ACDI, IDEA, OEA, PNUD, 2008), https://www.oas.org/es/sap/dsd me/pubs/DIAL_%20DEMO_s.pdf.

[21] GemPaz, "Manifesto of the VIII GemPaz National," June 6, 2019, https://www.facebook.com/notes/gempaz/manifesto-of-the-viii-gempaz-national-encounter-peace-is-a-matter-of-humanity-an/2729822120424823/.

[22] "Contextual reading of the Bible" is "a method of approaching the text of tradition that begins with an analysis of the living conditions of the communities and then links them to the liberation yearnings expressed in the Scriptures." Miguel Estupiñán, "Creer en la Reconciliación: Un Proyecto de los Menonitas y la Iglesia Protestante de Holanda," *Vida Nueva Digital*, September 6, 2017, https://www.vidanuevadigital.com/2017/06/09/creer-la-reconciliacion. This method was developed in Inge Landman, *Creer en la Reconciliación. Herramientas Prácticas para la Lectura Contextual de la Biblia* (Bogotá: Alen Impresores, 2017).

Their method has been to continue with the deconstruction of a patriarchal biblical reading and rereading in the light of a new moment in the depths of being and practicing, the effects of which transcend the lives and practices of each woman.[23]

Ecumenism encounters multiple resistances. Despite seeking unity, practicing inclusion, and promoting a good cause, it provokes fears. It is felt as a threat to the ecclesial identity. It suffers under the suspicion of promoting syncretism or even the relativity of truth. Fundamentalist biblical interpretation has been one of the causes for not making deep transformations. The biblical standpoint of resistance toward addressing sexual diversity and women's rights remains an obstacle to progress, as well as social and political responsibility at its fullest.

Distrust and suspicion are also present because, in one way or another, all people in Colombia, directly or indirectly, have been victims of the internal armed conflict. This causes resistance to a process of reconciliation and healing of wounds. This is especially challenging when welcoming female ex-combatants who are re-entering civilian life. There is also tension in a fluid structure, in which the way of doing and leading should be from an assertive standpoint of women, from its feminine essence, because the tendency is to repeat models or patterns that have historically been oppressive. These challenges necessitate strengthening the next generation, allowing for continuity of GemPaz's contribution and reason for being.

It is necessary to continue the ecumenical commitment between women and to continue to find paths and bridges that allow us to bear witness to unity during times of division and to expand its boundaries to enable interreligious dialogue. It is important to continue to cultivate a critical voice toward what is called and framed as "Christian" and "non-Christian." Is the voice of women of faith oriented in segregation, exclusion, and polarization? Or is it anchored in a constant search for God's vision? It is necessary to continue to cultivate a spirituality that does not close in on itself but rather opens itself to act differently in this world, to actively seek to transform the realities of injustice and inequity. For this to

---

[23]GemPaz, "Encuentro Nacional de GEMPAZ 2016," http://www.gempaz.org/index.php/noticias-gempaz/encuentro-nacional-de-gempaz-2016.

be possible, we must cultivate a spirituality based on God's vision of universal restoration, where all people can belong. Above all, the role of women of faith is to be vigilant and critical enough to know when the mission and vision are being clouded by moralisms or fundamentalisms. The appropriation, internalization, and practice of sorority goes beyond being a theoretical conceptualization to be a praxis between sisters and friends, who accompany, admire, and respect each other and "rejoice with those who rejoice" (Rom. 12:15). There are still political projects and affinities that are developed in the name of Christianity.

It is urgent to continue to make visible the work of GemPaz publicly and without shyness. This implies continuing to work with other professionals in the educational, political, and even economic decision-making spheres. As Fabián Salazar, coordinator of the Center for Theological and Religion studies of Rosario University asks, "What is the use of a theology of the afterlife if the problems and the 'hells' are being lived here on earth?"[24] A change of mindset is required regarding the role of women of faith in regional and national levels. They need to be reading the signs of the times (Luke 12:54-56).

A Liberating Politics

Anabaptists have inspired and challenged the work of collective groups such as GemPaz. Our participation has strengthened the community and female citizen participation as part of the ministry and responsibility of all people, through rereading and reinterpreting the biblical text. If the biblical text has been a colonizing instrument, including the patriarchal system that has controlled the role of women, it is necessary for women to have a say in ecclesial spaces, academia, and theology. It is necessary to learn from women who lead and write not only from academia but also from their essence, practice, and feminine perspective—women who can think and create with their words a practical liberating theology for others

---

[24]Fabián Salazar, "Desafío a los teólogos en Colombia," *El Tiempo*, September 4, 2007, http://blogs.eltiempo.com/confesiones/2007/09/04/desafio-a-los-teologos-en-colombia/.

and for the world. This is an Anabaptist theology that intentionally recognizes and includes women and values the role they have been playing throughout history in the midst of oppressive contexts.

Experiences and praxis, such as those of GemPaz, are helping to rebuild an Anabaptist theology and practice in which it is necessary to humanize the human, where the ethics of loving co-responsibility and where mutual care and protection guide us toward a liberating salvation. Understanding discipleship or following Jesus as a way of life, rather than a doctrinal method, has prevented proselytizing. Understanding that the other person is not the enemy but the brother or sister to be cared for is an extension of tradition. Peace implies the integral well-being of others, regardless of religion, race, gender, or sexual orientation. Today, women and men of faith must agree to advocate for liberating politics that favors the most disadvantaged in society. Today, it is vital that religions are allowed to structure new human identities, which enable the recovery of the political and prophetic place of women to build other possible worlds, where righteous living is the roadmap or navigational chart.

6

Nonviolence and the Assault on Marginalized Bodies

Regina Shands Stoltzfus

On a Sunday morning in 1963, the people of the 16th Street Baptist Church congregated in deeply segregated Birmingham, Alabama. An important gathering place for planning and praying for civil rights for African Americans, 16th Street was one of the largest African American congregations in the city. Several days earlier, a federal court ordered the city's school system to integrate. This Sunday morning, however, the city was somber. At 10:19 a.m., fifteen sticks of dynamite planted in the church basement detonated. The explosion, right under the girls' bathroom, killed Cynthia Wesley, Carole Robertson, and Addie Mae Collins—all fourteen years old—and eleven-year-old Denise McNair.

Fifty-two years later, on a Wednesday evening in June, congregants gathered for Bible study and prayer at the Emmanuel African Episcopal Church in Charleston, South Carolina. Dylann Roof, a self-proclaimed white supremacist, shot and killed six women and three men at the church, including the congregation's pastor. Their names were Clementa Pinckney, Cynthia Graham Hurd, Susie Jackson, Ethel Lee Lance, Depayne Middleton-Doctor, Tywanza Sanders, Daniel Simmons, Sharonda Coleman-Singleton, and Myra Thompson. Those who died that night were between the ages of twenty-six and eighty-seven.

Through these and other racialized acts of violence, Black bodies are physically harmed and deemed unlovable, even by people who inhabit those bodies. People who endure constant assaults on their personhood learn that their bodies are wrong in myriad ways. Under the rules of white supremacy, Black bodies are perpetually in the wrong place at the wrong time—hence segregated schools, neighborhoods, workplaces, and professions. The choices are to acquiesce or resist. An understanding of American racial history is needed to provide text and context for faith communities that see racial justice as part of their call.

The history of racially segregated churches in America reveals a history of segregated bodies, influenced by the wider culture and bolstered by teachings on who gets to be seen as fully human, with according human rights and responsibilities. Thus, a church committed to anti-racism must go beyond the "racial reconciliation" model of Christian race relations. Such models are concerned with forming interpersonal relationships across the boundaries of race but do not deal with the deep systemic roots of racism. Instead, churches must begin by recalling stories of racialization. How did people become "raced," and what does that mean in the US context? What does it mean for Anabaptist Christians and the way they perceive the power of the gospel in the aftermath of segregation? Such questions begin the necessary introspection for a racially homogenous congregation that is exploring intentional change or trying to deepen conversations within a racially diverse community. Therefore, it is crucial that members of marginalized communities and those from the center be in critical conversation with one another in order to build relationships before beginning the task of a new imagined future with others.

In this chapter, I draw upon critical race theory and narrative theology to identify how American racial history is a text that counters and competes with historic peace church theology, a theology that has greater potential than has thus far been realized to address systemic racism in a sustained manner. I begin by interrogating traditional peace theology. A wide gulf exists between theorists and practitioners. Christian ethics should "not only . . . analyze existing practices that inhibit and assault the social and spiritual well-being of persons" but also consider and give leadership to the transformation of those practices, primarily within the Christian community but ultimately for the sake of transforming oppressive practices that harm all marginalized peoples.[1] Then, I present a narrative of the Black church tradition essential for understanding the work of race relations. Black churches, historically an important center of resistance, continue to be a seedbed for community organizing and education as well as a place to craft a theology of liberation.[2] Indeed, the institution of the Black church is a result of imperialism, racism, and capitalism. Christianity itself is indicted as a chief agent in the transatlantic slave trade, not only by justifying the trade but also by functioning as a "civilizing" agent for the enslaved people.[3] Next, I discuss the ambiguous history of Mennonite urban missions—white Mennonites sent to Black communities—within the context

---

[1] Traci C. West, *Disruptive Christian Ethics: When Racism and Women's Lives Matter* (Louisville: Westminster John Knox, 2006), 38.
[2] Katie Geneva Cannon, *Black Womanist Ethics* (Atlanta: Scholars Press), 51–2.
[3] Katie Geneva Cannon, "Christian Imperialism and the Slave Trade," *Journal of Feminist Studies in Religion* 24, no. 1 (Spring 2008): 128, https://www.jstor.org/stable/20487919.

of American racial history. Given this history, Black people have had every reason to look on the intrusion of white people into their communities with suspicion. I conclude by pointing toward the kind of transformation possible when working to create a historical consciousness while working against racism.

Interrogating Traditional Peace Church Theology

Our scriptures are the foundational narratives that shape and order our traditions. In the biblical creation story, God creates and orders the universe by the power of a word. We confess our faith, we pray, we preach, and we sing. In this way, our words knit us securely to the people, places, and traditions of the past, all the while creating something new. Just as biblical scholars are becoming more adept at mining Scripture for marginal narratives that disrupt, scholars of religious history are increasingly using narrative as a method for listening at the margins. The narratives of racialized violence must be reckoned with if we take seriously the assault on Black bodies as antithetical to God's vision and call to God's people of shalom.

In the creation narratives, God declares creation good and establishes a relationship with the created order, including a distinct relationship with humanity. Humans are created in God's image, and then God images God's self after humanity in the person of Jesus: God with us, a member of the Trinity born of a woman, enfleshed, and suffering earthly pain and death at the hands of other humans. This death is memorialized in ritual—as Christ has taken on human form, human flesh, Christians ritually enact the taking on of Christ's body. It is a visceral, embodied reality from beginning to end, over and over again.

To glorify Jesus's death is to glorify suffering in a way that is ultimately problematic for those in marginalized bodies. It negates the Jesus we meet in the gospels, who heals and liberates.[4] In a broken world, those who seek to set things right are rewarded with

---

[4] Jacquelyn Grant, *White Women's Christ and Black Women's Jesus: Feminist Christology and Womanist Response* (Atlanta: Scholars Press, 1989), 212.

destruction, because the powers demand satisfaction. The ministry of Jesus and his death expose the violence of the world and the way it ultimately seeks to destroy that which would bring peace. Jesus walks into the suffering of the marginalized, not as a sacrifice but as one who walks with us even to the end. According to James Cone, Jesus's death is experienced over and over again in Black bodies.[5]

The church believes in the embodied Jesus as one who was conceived, was born, lived, and died. Belief rooted solely in the resurrected Jesus only negates the work of incarnation. The incarnate Jesus was the one promised to marginalized Jews in the Roman Empire. Therefore, it matters that the narration of Jesus's birth focuses on complication after complication. Jesus as enfleshed offers a relationship with a divine being who does indeed understand what it is to be frailly and complicatedly human.

The church needs to consider the humanity of Jesus but not at the expense of his divinity. For Mennonites, Jesus's Sermon on the Mount (Matt. 5–7) is the core of biblical teachings on nonviolence. It is the framework on which the radical call to an ethic of nonviolence is built, an ethic that necessitates rejecting all violence, including the state-sponsored and state-sanctioned violence of warfare. Mennonite identity is firmly entrenched in this ethic. However, for Jesus to be understood as savior raises the question: From what do we need to be saved? We need to be saved from the idea that we are unlovely and unloved—that we are, in the economy of the world, loveless. What does it mean to understand Jesus as the savior of humanity when death stalks your people?

The Black Church Tradition

For generations that go back to the time of Black enslavement, Black churches have held and tended to the Black community's core values—these values are a sustaining force for the Black church and represent a unique contribution to the nation and the world.[6] Moral, religious, social, and political agency on the part of the

---

[5] James H. Cone, *The Cross and the Lynching Tree* (Maryknoll, NY: Orbis, 2011), xv.
[6] Peter J. Paris, *The Social Teaching of the Black Churches* (Philadelphia: Fortress, 1985), xii.

oppressed, in spite of their circumstances, is a hallmark of the Black church tradition. Such agency provided a faith-based foundation for several iterations of Black liberation movements, whether they were rebellions, such as the ones led by Nat Turner[7] and Denmark Vesey,[8] or nonviolent resistance campaigns. The birth of the independent Black church in the United States, which resulted from Richard Allen's refusal to accept second-class citizenship in the Methodist Episcopal Church, represents a theological, sociological, and political stance that characterizes the social teaching of the Black church—the understanding that social and political engagement are part of one's Christian responsibility if one is Black. This partially explains the profound dedication Black people have to Black churches, and it highlights the significance of racially aware and racially conscious Black people in predominantly white churches and denominations. They risked being in relationship with white Christians when the historical context of Black and white Christian cooperation had not been sustainable because of the pervasive power of white supremacy and its infusion into US religious history.

Eric Lincoln and Lawrence Mamiya identify the civil rights movement, which was anchored in the Black church, as the catalyst for the Black Consciousness Movement.[9] While not monolithic in its message or approach, the Black church has identified and continues to identify Blackness, Black religion, and Black cultural production as positive. This explains why Black consciousness is important

---

[7]Nat Turner was born into slavery in 1800, and he led an armed rebellion in Southampton County, Virginia, in 1831. A deeply religious man who studied the Bible and preached to fellow slaves, Turner had frequent visions which he interpreted as messages from God. The rebellion was a response to the sin of the slaveholders who held people in bondage. Turner was captured and hanged two days after the rebellion.

[8]Denmark Vesey was an enslaved Black man who bought his freedom in 1799. In 1817, he joined the newly formed African Methodist Episcopal Church in Charleston, South Carolina. The church was constantly under the surveillance of white Charlestonians, who would intimidate and arrest members. As a leader in the church, Vesey studied the Old Testament and developed a theology of liberation, seeing himself and other enslaved persons as God's captive nation, who God would set free. Vesey and others planned an armed revolt, but he was arrested and hanged when plans of the rebellion were leaked.

[9]C. Eric Lincoln and Lawrence H. Mamiya, *The Black Church in the African American Experience* (Durham, NC: Duke University Press, 1990), 165.

to Black congregations within the primarily white Mennonite denomination; it gives such congregations a sensibility that is neither/nor—neither firmly grounded in Black church traditions nor understood or accepted as legitimately Mennonite.

The social teachings of the Black church had long affirmed a doctrine of human equality as authoritative in Christian faith, thought, and practice. In the Black church tradition (which includes historically Black denominations and Black congregations within predominately white denominations), correcting the social injustice of racism is a moral action. Opposition to racism is a primary component of the churches' moral code and is often paired with a rejection of violence as an act of justification.[10] The problem of racism is regarded as sin, a moral failing committed by humans.

Black denominations in the United States were grounded in their desire to worship freely without harassment and to care for their communities, and they often oriented toward politicized action and a quest for social change. From their inception, they demonstrated the desire for all Black people to be treated with dignity, as humans, and to not be relegated to second-class citizenry in white churches. This liberation tradition undergirds Black Christian ethics and highlights the cognitive dissonance of white US Christianity and the oppression and exploitation of Black people.[11] African American Christianity is well-rooted in its African past, as enslaved Africans retained portions of their own religions and also accepted Christianity, the "white man's religion," and made it their own.[12] Contextualization, reshaping, and recreation formed a significant part of the African American religious experience: "The black religious experience is something more than a black patina on a white happening. It is a unique response to a historical occurrence that can never be replicated for any people in America."[13]

The Great Migration of the early twentieth century saw nearly two hundred thousand African Americans move from the South to the North, while the onset of the First World War in 1914 stemmed

---

[10] Paris, *Social Teaching of the Black Churches*, 14.
[11] Cannon, *Black Womanist Ethics*, 1.
[12] C. Eric Lincoln, "Foreword," in *Is God a White Racist? A Preamble to Black Theology*, ed. William R. Jones (Garden City, NY: Anchor, 1973), vii.
[13] Lincoln, "Foreword," viii.

the flow of European immigrants to the United States just as demand for US industrial production increased. Factories that had depended on European immigrants began to actively recruit Black people from the rural South to keep up production.

While industries competed for Black workers and used various strategies to entice them to move north, the larger white society was not ready to live with African Americans. While the history of racial conflict and violence in the North has not been given as much attention as events in the South, in city after city, both Northern and Southern white homeowners and white-owned institutions colluded with one another to preserve all-white neighborhoods.[14] In 1910 Baltimore, for example, the need to address the growing population of African Americans and the corresponding white panic resulted in the city's legislation that established separate white and Black neighborhoods. The law sought to quell the "Negro invasion" of middle-class African Americans leaving the slums.[15] This legal enforcement did not last long but was followed by years of other forms of segregation that emerged in a number of municipal institutions. These were not uniquely Southern responses; as African Americans migrated, so did opposition to Black bodies in previously white spaces across the nation.

By 1930, most large cities with a significant Black population had established exclusive areas where Black people could live. The machinery of segregation became more sophisticated. Restrictive covenants were developed. These were contractual agreements among property owners that bound them to agreements stipulating they would not sell or lease to a Black family or allow a Black family to occupy the property for a specified period, usually ninety-nine years.[16] Such practices depended on a racial hierarchy in society that positioned African Americans at the bottom. By the 1940s, residential segregation in the North began to be increasingly

---

[14]Thomas J. Sugrue, *Sweet Land of Liberty: The Forgotten Struggle for Civil Rights in the North* (New York: Random, 2008).
[15]Garrett Power, "Apartheid Baltimore Style: The Residential Segregation Ordinances of 1910–1913," *Maryland Law Review* 42, no. 2 (1983): 299.
[16]Stephen Grant Meyer, *As Long as They Don't Move Next Door: Segregation and Racial Conflict in American Neighborhoods* (Lanham, MD: Rowman & Littlefield, 1999), 36.

justified by the language of the free market and by the rights of white citizens to protect the value of their property.[17]

This system of segregation was held in place by customs, policies, and procedures and enforced through the threat of violence against African Americans. Riots along the East Coast and throughout the Midwest accelerated the push of Black people out of white neighborhoods and helped Black neighborhoods become firmly entrenched ghettos by the Second World War.[18] This was the climate of the country when some Mennonites began their urban missions projects in earnest as they attempted to live out their commitment as a peace church.

Mennonite Urban Missions

One might suppose that Mennonite Christians, because of their anti-violence commitments, would be on the front lines of resisting the violence of racism. However, as a predominantly white denomination, Mennonites experienced the same pressure to become "American" as other immigrant groups, either by morphing into whiteness (if enough of a white pedigree could be determined) or assimilating into white culture. Early Mennonite immigrants to the United States during the eighteenth and nineteenth centuries were faced with fitting themselves into the nation's racial hierarchy. Like other European immigrants, they did not initially understand themselves as "white."[19] Whiteness developed as a political identity attached to citizenship and its corresponding privileges, such as owning property and voting.[20] Although they did not conceptualize themselves as white, they received benefits based on white skin.

The policing of race mixing in the United States is primarily about keeping Black people away from whites (with the broad exceptions of providing services or entertainment). This country has lived with

---

[17] Meyer, *As Long as They Don't Move Next Door*, 14.
[18] Meyer, *As Long as They Don't Move Next Door*, 31.
[19] Matthew Frye Jacobson, *Whiteness of a Different Color: European Immigrants and the Alchemy of Race* (Cambridge, MA: Harvard University Press, 1998), 23.
[20] Ian Haney-Lopez, *White by Law: The Legal Construction of Race* (New York: New York University Press, 1996), 1.

legislated segregation for more of its history than it has not. From the period of enslavement on, the Black body is highly desired to cook and clean, to care for and even nurse white babies and raise white children. At the same time, Black bodies were criminalized should they deign to take the wrong seat on a bus or train, to sit at a lunch counter, or drink from a water fountain designated "white only" and keeping white people white (hence laws against miscegenation). The collective understanding of Blackness as a negative identity that tainted with mere proximity is the undercurrent of how racial identity and race relations have played themselves out over the five hundred years of the Black presence in the Americas. Other ethnic and racialized groups quickly learned that consorting with Blackness would cost them the higher ranking within the hierarchy of races.

During the mid-twentieth century, Mennonites experienced sociological and theological shifts prompted in part by their increasing acculturation into mainstream white culture. For some, evidence of Mennonites conforming to the values of the larger society represented a dissipation of the distinctive witness that had previously been understood as their separation from mainstream culture. An alternative view to dissipation sees this instead as a new form of distinctive witness that was not possible as a geographically set-apart community. For some white Mennonites, living and worshiping in Black communities with Black congregants was indeed a way of living into their witness; this is evidenced by a number of Black and integrated Mennonite churches planted during that time, with support from mission boards and service organizations. Many of the church planters interpreted the Anabaptist distinction of being separate from the world to include a rejection of racially segregated Christian communities. In the American context, this was a countercultural vision of church, and within these congregations, new Mennonite identities developed. However, the experiences of people within these congregations were unique to their specific settings and went largely unnoticed and unknown by the denomination. In their local congregations, they embodied a visible resistance to structural racism by being church together. Yet this means of resistance did not carry over to the denomination and its institutions as a marker of identity of what it means to be Mennonite. Those who encountered the larger Mennonite Church at church-wide gatherings or as students in Mennonite schools or as employees of the denomination's agencies found themselves treated as strangers and outsiders.

When mid-twentieth-century white Mennonites entered Black communities as voluntary service workers and church planters, they did so without fully understanding the racial dynamics they would encounter. Coming from white Mennonite communities, their own racial identities did not have salience for them. Yet they encountered people who were fully aware of the meaning of whiteness, especially vis-à-vis Blackness. The navigation of interracial space took place on two levels. The most visible level was seen in the individualized one-on-one encounters with the local congregations and neighborhoods. Less visible were the ways in which Black people encountered and navigated spaces within the denomination's institutions. These encounters did not exist apart from the long history of interracial contact situated within the framework of white dominance and Black marginalization. For Black families in these congregations, racial consciousness and the corresponding racial etiquette[21] were part of their socialization and survival as they moved about in their neighborhoods, migrated to new areas of the country, and sought employment and housing and schools for their children.

For white Mennonites, the encounters themselves were new, but even if they did not have a history of personal encounters with people of color, especially African Americans, they were informed by the racial context of the times and indeed had some knowledge of what was being called "the Negro problem" or "the racial revolution." They were also socialized into the understanding of whiteness at the top of the racial hierarchy, even if they did not understand themselves as white. Despite their best intentions, they participated in the work of mission agencies and voluntary service organizations with the unspoken but real perspective now identified as the "white savior complex."[22]

---

[21] Michael Omi and Howard Winant define racial etiquette as a set of interpretive codes and racial meanings that operate in the interactions of daily life, a continual recognition of one's place in the racial hierarchy and the corresponding appropriate behavior in shared space. Michael Omi and Howard Winant, "Racial Formations," in *Race, Class, and Gender in the United States: An Integrated Study*, 9th edn, ed. Paula S. Rothenberg with Kelly S. Mayhew (New York: Worth, 2014), 16.

[22] There are numerous pop-culture references to the white savior complex, especially in movies that perpetuate the myth that white people, particularly men, are the only

African American Mennonite churches became settings where Christian, Mennonite, and African American identities had the possibility of being simultaneously nurtured and celebrated. They illustrated the vision of multiracial church contexts that could be dwelling places for people who assume and expect that part of Christian identity is living with diversity (racially, culturally, politically, etc.) and who choose to be together because they value inclusion and working at ending death-dealing oppression. This kind of diversity is not simply surface-deep and only based on colorfulness that looks good on brochures but instead is an intentional living out of a compelling gospel imperative: breaking down dividing walls and the systemic liberation of oppressed groups. The walls that divide are not only about skin color, and breaking them down does not mean simply (and perhaps grudgingly) sharing the same space for a couple of hours each week. Rather, this is a way of being church together that is the intentional coming together of the marginalized and the privileged and a reshaping of an understanding of what it means to be followers of Jesus and members of a church community. This way of being community means defying the norms of larger society.

The founders and early members of these churches came together without a blueprint of what these communities would become. James and Rowena Lark, who would become prominent African American leaders in the Mennonite Church, deserve much credit for nurturing connections between white Mennonites and Black communities. James Lark was the first ordained Black pastor and then the first Black bishop in the Mennonite Church. Amid many frustrations, he and Rowena helped the denomination learn to serve and include African Americans appropriately.[23] These unique constellations emerged out of the convergence of people responding to their respective histories that placed them in the same communities at the same time. Each group, from their respective historical vantage points, represented an otherness. White Mennonites had their remembered past as persecuted religious nonconformers who,

---

true heroes and that white people are the ones who can solve problems of people of color across the globe.

[23]Le Roy Bechler, *The Black Mennonite Church in North America, 1886–1986* (Scottdale, PA: Herald, 1986), 48.

in their rejection of the military, were not good citizens and had learned to be "the quiet in the land." African Americans had known rejection and discriminatory treatment since their enslaved ancestors had been brought to the Americas. Each of these historical contexts emphasized community as a central aspect of identity.

The whole of this history and context is the stuff of identity-making for white people and for people of color. Black and white Christians alike had to resolve the cognitive dissonance created by two factors. On the one hand, they lived within a society that clearly identified the relative worth or worthlessness of individuals based on their membership in a racial group and treated them accordingly (and taught them how to treat and think about one another). On the other hand, their religious identity taught them that all people are created in the image of God and that societal barriers that separate people and treat some people unjustly are acts of institutionalized violence that go against the very core of the message of the Bible—and most particularly the teachings of Jesus.

Toward Transformation

Christians working on race relations would do well to acknowledge the continued necessity to have church be a place of sanctuary, healing, and rebuilding. To do this, a faithful peace church perspective must go beyond the "racial reconciliation" model. Part of the healing work is bearing witness and telling the truth. After the lynching of fourteen-year-old Emmett Till in 1954, his mother, Mamie Till, held an open casket funeral. The funeral was televised, and millions of people around the world were able to bear witness not only to a mother's grief but to a nation's sin. Present-day technology means that the world can immediately bear witness to continued violence against Black bodies.[24] Witnessing Black injury and death on screens has become harrowingly commonplace and is a cause for increased and repeated trauma. Many who once had faith in the church's response have lost it; much of mainstream evangelical Christianity has not provided holistic care—care of

---

[24]For example, the immediate aftermath of the 2016 death of Philando Castile was livestreamed by his traumatized partner.

the mind and body as well as the soul—in the face of unremitting racism. Instead, many refuse even to bear witness.

The animosity and hatred that fueled the deaths of the four young girls in Birmingham in their house of worship was not accidental, incidental, or isolated. Those four African American girls, like their parents and grandparents before them—indeed like their enslaved grandparents and the ancestors of all of those who are descended from victims of the Transatlantic slave trade—were part of an othering project that is systematic, intentional, and aided by theologies that bolster white supremacy. Challenges to the tactics of the civil rights movement in the 1960s and the current Black Lives Matter movement reflect the ongoing discomfort of middle-class white Christians to face societal and religious complicity with racial oppression. At best, the discomfort and distancing feeds the cycle of divisiveness, and at worst, it solidifies racist systems and structures. This belief system killed Cynthia, Carol, Addie Mae, and Denise in 1963. It killed the nine worshipers in Charleston in 2015. It is the same system that led a Georgia councilman to declare to the press that because of his Christian beliefs, the sight of an interracial couple made his "blood boil."[25]

Churches carry on the tradition of segregation in part because of the legacy of residential segregation but even more so because of the history of Christianity's participation in the oppression of African Americans. To seek "diversity" without facing this history is futile. When faced with the issue of their violent racist past, Christians too often succumb to the impulse to go directly to biblical texts that teach love and forgiveness, with an implicit message of "forget and let's move on." People of color are urged to forget, to sacrifice themselves for the sake of unity. But any unity that results from such a formula is false; it is the illusion of unity that comes when one party is forced to pretend that their experience and their way of knowing does not matter or, worse, is disruptive. It is telling that in Geraldo Marti's extensive study of "successful" multiracial churches (success measured in part by maintaining a balance such that no one racial category is more than 80 percent of the total population), African Americans are

---

[25] Nicole Goodkind, "Georgia Mayor Reportedly Won't Hire Black Administrator Because 'City Isn't Ready,'" *Newsweek*, May 6, 2019, https://www.newsweek.com/georgia-mayor-atlanta-race-relations-1416577.

not part of the equation. Marti admits that racially conscious African Americans who bring their Black realities and concerns are dissatisfied and often do not stay.[26] This is because many efforts for multiracial and diverse communities require people to "transcend" race, which is not an option for Black people in the United States.

Christians must face head-on what it means to live as Christ's body—a body that is broken, battered, and bruised and calls out those that do the battering. Once again, the work of creating a historical consciousness is vital. Christian community must not only preach love and justice; it must embody it. As the body is made of many members, so the many members bring with them different viewpoints and perspectives that reflect a variety of social locations and the experience that brings. For a sustained movement to take hold, learning to be a diverse community that together resists evil and oppression must happen repeatedly within local congregations and across institutions.

Black and white church folk must stand together in uncomfortable spaces. This assertion recalls the challenge of Fannie Lou Hamer, a veteran of the movement who assuredly tied her own activism to her Christian commitment:

> But this white man who wants to stay *white*, and to think for the Negro . . . is not only destroying the Negro, he is destroying himself, because a house divided against itself cannot stand and that same thing applies to America. America that is divided against itself cannot stand, and we cannot say we have all of this unity they say we have when Black people are being discriminated against in every city in America I have visited.[27]

Hamer challenged the church to live up to its mission:

> To me, the 1964 Summer Project was the beginning of a New Kingdom right here on earth. The kinds of people who came down from the North—from all over—who didn't know anything about

---

[26]Gerardo Marti, "The Religious Racial Integration of African Americans into Diverse Churches," *Journal for the Scientific Study of Religion* 49, no. 2 (June 2010): 212, https://doi.org/10.1111/j.1468-5906.2010.01503.x.

[27]J. H. O'Dell, "Life in Mississippi: An Interview with Fannie Lou Hamer," *Freedomways* 5 (1965): 235–6, quoted in Rosetta E. Ross, *Witnessing and Testifying: Black Women, Religion, and Civil Rights* (Minneapolis: Fortress, 2003), 113.

us—were like the Good Samaritan. In that Bible story, the people had passed by the wounded man—like the church has passed the Negros in Mississippi—and never taken the time to see what was going on. But these people who came to Mississippi that summer—although they were strangers—walked up to our door. They started something that no one could ever stop. These people were willing to move in a non-violent way to bring a change in the South. . . . If I had to choose today between the church and these young people—and I was brought up in the church and I'm not against the church—I'd choose these young people.[28]

Community building is an integral component of sustaining anti-oppression work. However, this is community that builds the capacity to sit together in uncomfortable places, dares to ask difficult questions, insists on holding one another accountable, and, in the spirit of Jesus and the prophets, holds those with the most power to learn to be accountable to those without power.

A theological ethic that moves toward transformation must involve the presence and voices of Black people, especially Black women. Black men and women are not exempt from believing and perpetuating the myths that continue assaults against the bodies of Black women. Sexism and heterosexism, grounded in the belief that God created strict binaries and blesses hierarchies, continue to perpetrate the same violence against people. Thus, people who are working against racism need to understand how to do so within communities that are also committed to doing this work in anti-sexist, anti-classist, and anti-heterosexist ways. Learning to love the Black body is a critical step.

---

[28]Fannie Lou Hamer, "Foreword," in *Stranger at the Gates: A Summer in Mississippi*, ed. Tracy Sugarman (New York: Hill and Wang, 1967), viii, quoted in Ross, *Witnessing and Testifying*, 114.

PART THREE

Salvation, Redemption, and Witness

7

Salvation for the Sinned Against

Linda Gehman Peachey

For many Mennonite women, the journey toward salvation includes searching for a faith that is truly life giving. Often this means searching for a loving God and release from oppressive systems that have caused deep insecurities, shame, and anxiety. In short, Mennonite women seek an Anabaptist theology of salvation that takes them seriously as women and addresses their experiences of silencing, oppression, and violation, both in the church and in the world at large. Such a liberative theology would offer healing and wholeness in communities where all are treated with respect and dignity. It would also deal with the ways in which our systems—our accepted norms, decisions, and actions—cause harm and violate others, ourselves, and God's good creation. And it would never justify or promote suffering as the way to deal with sin and find salvation. In this chapter, I survey Mennonite writings on salvation and atonement, along with observations and contributions from Mennonite women. I conclude with my own understanding of how God brings salvation, life, and wholeness to those who have been violated and disregarded—those who have been sinned against.

While I speak out of my own journey, as a white, middle-class, Mennonite woman of Swiss-German ethnic background, I have also had opportunity to interact with and learn from women across the Mennonite church, including structured conversations through a research focus group of eight women from my congregation.[1] Together, we shared deeply about our understandings of salvation, where we find consolation and desolation, and how we understand Jesus's life, death, and resurrection. In this chapter, I have included some of this group's insights and perceptions, identified anonymously as from a focus group participant. Other relationships have been less formal but nevertheless profoundly significant in terms of the wisdom women have shared with me over the years, at times in the circle of intimate small groups, as well as through meaningful work and collaboration with women from a variety of ages and racial and ethnic identities. I also draw on the writings of Mennonite women

---

[1] The focus group met with me for two-hour discussions five times in 2017. In terms of demographics, all of these participants are white women, ranging in age from thirty-five to eighty-one. Five grew up in ethnically Swiss-German Mennonite communities, and three joined Mennonite congregations as adults. Institutional Review Board protocols for human subjects were followed for these sessions.

over the past thirty years, found in articles, blog posts, newsletters, dissertations, and books.

Mainstream Anabaptist Theology

Currently, our salvation theology primarily reflects the perspectives and questions of white men. In surveying Mennonite authors who have written books specifically about salvation and the atonement over the past three decades (Mark Baker, Palmer Becker, Darrin Snyder Belousek, Ted Grimsrud, J. Denny Weaver), all are from this demographic.[2] In these texts, there is great emphasis on the need for forgiveness, peace, reconciliation, and love for our enemies but little attention to justice or the voices of those who have been violated and oppressed. In his 2017 overview of Anabaptist theology and practice, for example, Palmer Becker identifies reconciliation as a primary theme, indeed "the center of our work,"[3] but makes few references to justice. Even in Ted Grimsrud's text, which argues for restorative justice as a framework for salvation theology, the emphasis is on offenders rather than on the needs of those who have suffered harm.[4]

The themes of peace, forgiveness, and reconciliation are important tenets of Anabaptist faith. They have enabled a courageous witness for peace and a refusal to participate in military service during times of war. They have encouraged loyalty first to the worldwide body of Jesus's disciples rather than unquestioning allegiance to the nation-state. Nevertheless, when these teachings are divorced from the experiences of those who are oppressed, the message can be turned upside down and become bad news for those who are vulnerable to exploitation and violence.

---

[2] Although Mennonite women have written articles and organized conferences, few have had the opportunity to write full-length books, so their thoughts and experiences are more difficult to access and rarely used in congregational, college, and seminary classes. Consequently, they have had less influence in shaping the discourse of Mennonite and Anabaptist theology.
[3] Palmer Becker, *Anabaptist Essentials: Ten Signs of a Unique Christian Faith* (Harrisonburg, VA: Herald, 2017), 109.
[4] Ted Grimsrud, *Instead of Atonement: The Bible's Salvation Story and Our Hope for Wholeness* (Eugene, OR: Cascade, 2013).

This dynamic of neglecting marginalized voices also shows up repeatedly in the influential 1995 *Confession of Faith in a Mennonite Perspective*.[5] Even though Jesus spent most of his ministry working to heal and save those who were poor and oppressed, this *Confession of Faith* follows a Western, male emphasis on God's efforts to save rebellious sinners. For example, the commentary on "The Church in Mission" emphasizes, "The power of the gospel is so strong and God's mercy is so wide that it is possible for any person to repent and be saved. No enemy is so evil as to be beyond God's love."[6] Certainly, we believe this to be true. But is the gospel also strong enough to save those who have been violated and desecrated? Do we believe God's love can also release and restore them? Sadly, the *Confession of Faith* barely addresses this reality, giving only scant attention to God's actions to redeem those who have been sinned against. Instead, the article on sin stresses that all people are sinners, who have chosen to disobey and turn away from God.[7] Although there is some recognition of powers that dominate and destroy people, we are all deemed responsible: "The more we sin, the more we become trapped in sin. By our sin we open ourselves to the bondage of demonic powers."[8] There appears to be no difference between those who use their power and privilege to manipulate and use others and those who experience this exploitation.

In his discussion of feminist and womanist writers, J. Denny Weaver acknowledges some differences between those who experience oppression and those who oppress them. However, he argues that oppressed persons are also complicit in sin when they "acquiesce in their oppression or accept the inferior identity foisted on them by dominators."[9] They need to acknowledge this sin, stop submitting to their oppression, change sides, and yield to God's

---

[5]Of the ten members of the "Inter-Mennonite Confession of Faith Committee," six were white men, three were women, and one a Latino. General Conference Mennonite Church, and Mennonite Church, *Confession of Faith in a Mennonite Perspective* (Scottdale, PA: Herald, 1995), 6.
[6]*Confession of Faith in a Mennonite Perspective*, 44.
[7]*Confession of Faith in a Mennonite Perspective*, 31.
[8]*Confession of Faith in a Mennonite Perspective*, 31.
[9]J. Denny Weaver, *The Nonviolent Atonement*, 2nd edn (Grand Rapids: Eerdmans, 2011), 213.

reign.¹⁰ While his intention may be to encourage victims to move away from passivity to become more active agents in the process of salvation, his words sound all too much like blaming victims for what they experience, with little apparent empathy for the defilement and violence that has been perpetrated on their bodies and psyches. He allows little space for recognizing that some people did nothing to deserve their situation, and it is not their fault when they are used and violated. Instead, Weaver insists that all of us "need to acknowledge our enslavement to the powers that killed Jesus, to confess our place on the side of those who opposed the reign of God."¹¹ He makes no clear distinction between those who ordered and carried out Jesus's death, for example, and the women who followed Jesus and mourned his death.

There is a second difficulty with much of current Anabaptist atonement theology: not only does it fail to address the needs of those who are oppressed, but it also communicates that the way to salvation is through suffering and even death. The *Confession of Faith*, for instance, underscores Jesus's willingness to suffer and forgive his enemies, including those who tortured and killed him.¹² The commentary on "Jesus Christ" points out explicitly that, coming from an Anabaptist Mennonite perspective, it stresses "Jesus' obedience and suffering in his work of atonement."¹³ And the article on "Salvation" asserts that "God sent his Son, whose faithfulness unto death on the cross has provided the way of salvation for all people."¹⁴ By contrast, there is little attention to Jesus's solidarity with victims, his work for justice, and his resistance to the exploitative practices of the religious leaders who had sided with Rome against the welfare of their own people.¹⁵ It does nothing to explain how Jesus led a renewal movement among

---

[10] Weaver, *Nonviolent Atonement*, 93.
[11] Weaver, *Nonviolent Atonement*, 93.
[12] *Confession of Faith*, 65–6. The words "suffer" and "suffering" occur thirty-one times in the *Confession of Faith*, along with the "cross" fifteen times and "loving enemies" eight times.
[13] *Confession of Faith*, 15.
[14] *Confession of Faith*, 35.
[15] *Confession of Faith*, 13–16. For example, while the article on "Jesus Christ" mentions Jesus's ministry of "preaching, teaching, and healing," it says nothing about why Jesus was such a threat to the powers of his day and why they crucified him.

the people, in opposition to the religious, economic, and political structures that contributed to and justified the people's suffering.[16]

Often overlooked is how Jesus's healing ministry contributed to this resistance movement. These healings were not just individual acts of kindness but "deeds of power" that reminded people of how they had experienced God's power in their history.[17] Just as Moses had worked to free people from slavery, Jesus used God's power to release people from their bondage to the oppressive systems that made them vulnerable to hunger, sickness, disfigurement, and disgrace. In freely healing people and empowering them to heal each other, Jesus liberated them from the costly demands of the temple-state as well as the internalized feelings of shame, guilt, and fear they had felt before God and the community.[18]

Jesus also sought to strengthen community life, urging people to reclaim the practices of the Mosaic covenant, which emphasized justice and well-being for everyone. This included caring for those who are poor and vulnerable, lending freely to one another, regularly releasing debts, giving rest to the land, and supporting relatives who fell into difficulty.[19] Provisions like these helped to sustain village life and maintain the dignity and viability of each household even as so many forces threatened to pull them apart.[20]

---

[16]Here I am drawing especially on the work of Elisabeth Schüssler Fiorenza, who argues that Jesus stood firmly in the prophetic tradition, acting to renew and restore those who had been marginalized and outcast by their rulers, both Jewish and Roman. Elisabeth Schüssler Fiorenza, *In Memory of Her: A Feminist Theological Reconstruction of Christian Origins*, 10th edn (New York: Crossroad, 1994), 105–59, especially 135–6. See also Elisabeth Schüssler Fiorenza, *Jesus: Miriam's Child, Sophia's Prophet: Critical Issues in Feminist Christology* (New York: Continuum, 1994), 140–2. I also use the work of Richard A. Horsley, who emphasizes the political and economic role of the temple institution in occupied Palestine, as well as Jesus's efforts to recover and reinstate the life-giving practices and traditions of Jewish faith. See, for example, Richard A. Horsley, *Jesus and Empire: The Kingdom of God and the New World Disorder* (Minneapolis: Fortress, 2003), and Richard A. Horsley, *Jesus in Context: Power, People, and Performance* (Minneapolis: Fortress, 2008).

[17]See Matt. 7:22; 11:20-21, 23; 13:54, 58; 14:2; Mark 6:2, 5, 14; 9:39; Luke 5:17; 10:13, 19:37; Acts 2:11, 22: 10:36-38; and 1 Cor. 12:28.

[18]Richard A. Horsley and Tom Thatcher, *John, Jesus and the Renewal of Israel* (Grand Rapids: Eerdmans, 2013), 108–11.

[19]For example, see Leviticus 25 and Exod. 21:1-23:11.

[20]Horsley, *Jesus in Context*, 215.

Warren Carter argues that a key aspect of Jesus's ministry was inspiring and supporting more inclusive and constructive household practices. The goal was to create "alternative systems and ways of being" that were nonhierarchical, weakened patriarchal power, cared for children, and encouraged the sharing of economic resources.[21] We see a glimpse of this in Jesus's relationship with the household of Martha, Mary, and Lazarus. Contrary to patriarchal assumptions, Martha and Mary appear to be the primary leaders in this home.[22] They also demonstrate a deep friendship with Jesus, which allows them to be comfortable in his presence, able to freely voice their thoughts and feelings without fear or pretense.[23]

Sadly, the church has neglected to teach and practice these aspects of Jesus's struggle for and with subjugated people. It has ignored the ways he instituted alternative political and religious practices in opposition to the powerful interests of his society. By emphasizing instead Jesus's unconditional love and forgiveness, it has silenced victims and fostered meek submission to their suffering. For example, one woman described her experience of her husband's violence this way:

> Growing up Mennonite, I was taught early in life that we were called to be peacemakers in the world. I came to believe that in following Jesus' steps, with God's love flowing through me, I could be a peacemaker and be instrumental in calming strife and conflict. . . . But in our house the problems would not be solved. . . . His anger and his criticism of me would grow. I would

---

[21]Warren Carter, *Matthew and the Margins, A Socio-political and Religious Reading* (Sheffield, UK: Sheffield Academic, 2000), 3, 10, 13; Warren Carter, *Households and Discipleship: A Study of Matthew 19–20* (Sheffield, UK: Sheffield Academic, 1994), 20, 191–2.

[22]In the Roman Empire, households were expected to mimic the imperial model of the husband/father ruling like Caesar, the supreme patriarch, over his wife, children, and slaves. According to Nijay K. Gupta, this pattern can be traced back to Aristotle, who argued that these hierarchical relationships were established by nature and should be upheld for the welfare of society. Nijay K. Gupta, *Colossians* (Macon, GA: Smyth & Helwys, 2013), 162.

[23]Both were able to express their disappointment and lament that Jesus did not arrive in time to save their brother. Jesus in turn did not rebuke them but responded to their concerns and freely expressed his own distress and tears. John 11:21, 32-6. Also see Luke 10:38-42.

try harder to please him but he would not be soothed. I was blamed for just about everything and I got so that I accepted that blame.[24]

Even when her husband beat her so badly that she did not recognize herself in the mirror, she tried to forgive him, as she had been taught since childhood: "How many times did Jesus tell us to forgive? Did he say to forgive only if it was a minor offence? Of course not! So, I would forgive, wanting desperately to believe that he wouldn't strike me again. I would try again, to be a better Christian, to be a better wife."[25] Sadly, the violence did not end until she finally sought help and refuge in a women's shelter.

Similarly, Leona Stucky found herself caught at the age of fifteen in a physically and sexually violent dating relationship. Despite her youth and the fact that she tried to leave the relationship, she ended up pregnant and was forced to confess sexual sin to her congregation as if she and this young man were equally guilty. Afterward, referring to a placard on her bedroom wall that read, "LOVE CONQUERS ALL," she wrote, "I went home to hate myself, to feel the emptiness of ritual forgiving, to understand, once and for all, that love did *not* conquer all."[26] Tragically, there was no redemption or safety for her in her community, as the only apparent option was to marry this brutally abusive man who raped her and repeatedly threatened to harm her family.

Clearly, these women needed salvation not primarily because of their own sin and rebellion against God but rather because of the sin and violence of others. They needed love and support in order to escape the violence and encouragement to contest the systems and beliefs that excused and protected those who abused them. Unfortunately, the church has often ignored these realities and failed to take women's experiences seriously. Rather than leading to salvation, it has often increased their suffering and sense

---

[24] Anonymous, "My story," Mennonite Central Committee (MCC) website Abuse: Response and Prevention, n.d., http://abuse.mcc.org/abuse/en/domestic/stories/change.html. (MCC discontinued most pages from this site, so this story is no longer available there; cf. https://mcc.org/learn/what/categories/abuse-prevention.)
[25] Anonymous. "My story."
[26] Leona Stucky, *The Fog of Faith: Surviving My Impotent God* (Santa Fe, NM: Prairie World, 2017), 98; italics in original.

of bondage and shame. Indeed, several women in the focus group acknowledged that their times of greatest desolation happened in the church. One participant said, "Most of the traumas in my life are connected to church."[27] She went on to share that when she was a little girl, she noticed that all the language and all the leaders in church were male, so when she went to church, she played a game in which she clicked the left side of her head in order to become a boy, "so she could belong to the words."[28] Then she would click back at the end of the service. At that time, she had "no concept that women were made in the image of God."[29] These realities deeply affect women's perceptions of God and themselves and their ability to find forgiveness, freedom, and wholeness.

Salvation, Sin, and Suffering

The biblical concept of salvation is not primarily about dealing with individual sin and guilt. Rather, as Justo González emphasizes, throughout the biblical story, salvation describes God's efforts to restore health and well-being and to provide safety and liberation from danger and cruelty.[30] This understanding of salvation was especially meaningful to one woman in the focus group: "I have really learned to appreciate the fact that in Greek, the word for salvation is the same as for healing: healing me, healing the world and the cosmos. Liberation is still important but there is the sense of going deeper, dwelling in God, dwelling in love."[31] One could also say that salvation is a comprehensive vision of God's will for life on earth, which embraces both peace and justice. It is the transformation of life that comes through a loving and true

---

[27] Focus group participant B.
[28] Focus group participant B.
[29] Focus group participant B.
[30] Justo L. González, *The Story Luke Tells: Luke's Unique Witness to the Gospel* (Grand Rapids: Eerdmans, 2015), 64.
[31] Focus group participant C. The *Confession of Faith* also mentions this fact in its section "The Church in Mission," 44. Unfortunately, it appears to limit the church's role in healing to prayer and anointing with oil, with no references to community organizing or any challenge to destructive public policies and practices.

relationship with God, oneself, others, and the earth. It is a journey toward just and right relationships in all these areas.

This understanding of salvation also acknowledges the corporate reality of sin and the way it binds and destroys human life and relationships and creation more broadly. Sin is not only personal and interpersonal but tends to grow into systems and structures much larger than the individuals involved.[32] This means that people not only participate in and perpetuate sinful actions, but they also experience being sinned against. People are oppressed by social systems and structures and often feel trapped. Too often, they are caught in systems that were not intended to protect them or enable them to flourish.[33] Rather, these systems were designed to benefit the few at the expense of everyone else. This makes it difficult to choose wisely or in a way that will bring change and movement toward what is life giving and good. One woman described it this way: "Sin is distortion, a twisting of God's will into something that serves the empire, or the family system, someone else, rather than who we were intended to be. We do this to ourselves, to others, to the world. The world, our families, do this to us. We all participate in distortion."[34] Another said, "Sin is the gulf between me and God. I need to come to an acceptance of my value and maintain that deep connection with God; anything that gets in the way of that connection is a result of the brokenness in me and in the world."[35]

In the midst of all this, we must never glorify suffering or talk of this lightly, separated from the realities of those who are experiencing pain, injustice, and violation. As one woman said very plainly, "It's very cruel to tell someone that your pain has some larger purpose. It's so horrible to do that to people, to make suffering into an addition

---

[32] James Poling explains that a "pattern of sinful decisions eventually creates institutions and ideologies that are enduring patterns of influence." Not only that, but these systems carry out evil, which are often reinforced by religion. James Newton Poling, *Rethinking Faith: A Constructive Practical Theology* (Minneapolis: Fortress, 2011), 34.

[33] Jenny Castro, Communications Associate and Women in Leadership Project Coordinator for Mennonite Church USA, provided this valuable insight during a lunch discussion, October 27, 2018, while we were reflecting on how women often experience life in church institutions.

[34] Focus group participant A.

[35] Focus group participant E.

problem, a formula: your pain plus this equal meaning."[36] Instead, we need to be able to confess that "things have happened that should not have happened; your pain should not have happened."[37] We need to be able to say that some things are wrong. This is not God's will. People should not be violated. They should not be hungry, dishonored, or shamed. They should not be tortured or raped. We must be able to say this about Jesus too. He should not have been crucified. No one should be crucified. No one deserves such a cruel and humiliating death. But these things happen. People do hurt each other in terrible ways, and there are real and devastating consequences. It is natural then to search for some meaning in this suffering, for ways to redeem and transform the pain and agony. But we must be careful not to be glib about this or insist on certain answers. We need to admit that too often our answers do not help others but are a way to get us "off the hook."[38] They are "a way to control, to make us feel that it won't happen to me."[39]

The Cross as Subversive Resistance

As we seek salvation, we need to insist that what redeems us is God's love. We are not saved by suffering but rather through God's solidarity and presence with us in creative resistance to the powers of evil that exploit and enslave us. Mennonite women have repeatedly emphasized these truths. Scholars such as Carol Penner, Carolyn Holderread Heggen, Elizabeth Soto Albrecht, Mary Schertz, Malinda Elizabeth Berry, and Susanne Guenther Loewen have all explored the harmful implications of linking salvation so closely to suffering and the cross. They have also offered crucial insights into the meaning of the cross, insights that can be life giving and strengthening to those who experience intense suffering.

Heggen, for example, challenges the widespread belief that "suffering is a Christian virtue" or that Christ's suffering is what

---

[36] Focus group participant D.
[37] Focus group participant A.
[38] Focus group participant E.
[39] Focus group participant D.

saves us.⁴⁰ As she insists, we dare not "idealize the results of suffering. Many victims of involuntary suffering come out of the experience with crushed spirits and profound emotional and spiritual pain."⁴¹ Similarly, Penner points out that for women experiencing violence, this constant call to endure suffering is not good news, as they "would find no encouragement to find safety, flee from suffering, or secure justice from their abusers."⁴² Soto Albrecht likewise insists that such suffering is not salvific. Instead, she echoes the insights of Latin American liberation theology, which understands Jesus's cross as a sign of "God's solidarity with the poor and oppressed."⁴³ Further, Jesus models a way of bringing salvation and healing that is communal, resists violence through love, and provides justice as well as peace.⁴⁴ Schertz also claims that Jesus's early mission did not dwell on suffering but rather on his choice to follow God's call at all costs. There may be suffering, but salvation involves much more than the cross. Based on her study of Luke's Gospel, she argues that Jesus's primary mission was to inaugurate God's reign on earth.⁴⁵ People are converted then "because Jesus preached, taught, healed, exorcised demons, suffered, died, and was raised—all to announce and bring about the kingdom of God."⁴⁶

For Berry, the cross shows God to be fully engaged with the world and life on earth.⁴⁷ Drawing on the work of Reinhold Niebuhr, Perry Yoder, Martin Luther King Jr., Toni Morrison, and

---

⁴⁰Carolyn Holderread Heggen, *Sexual Abuse in Christian Homes and Churches* (Scottdale, PA: Herald, 1993), 94.
⁴¹Heggen, *Sexual Abuse*, 95.
⁴²Carol Penner, "Mennonite Silences and Feminist Voices: Peace Theology and Violence against Women" (PhD diss., University of St. Michael's College, University of Toronto, 1999), 178–9. She notes that this teaching comes through not only in writings by prominent Mennonite theologians but also through hymns sung in worship.
⁴³Elizabeth Soto Albrecht, *Family Violence: Reclaiming a Theology of Nonviolence* (Maryknoll, NY: Orbis, 2008), 91.
⁴⁴Soto Albrecht, *Family Violence*, 96–7.
⁴⁵Mary H. Schertz, "God's Cross and Women's Questions: A Biblical Perspective on the Atonement," *The Mennonite Quarterly Review* 68, no. 2 (April 1994): 194–208.
⁴⁶Schertz, "God's Cross and Women's Questions," 206.
⁴⁷Malinda E. Berry, "'This Mark of a Standing Human Figure Poised to Embrace': A Constructive Theology of Social Responsibility, Nonviolence, and Nonconformity" (PhD diss., Union Theological Seminary, 2013), 137.

Doris Janzen Longacre, she insists that Christians must concern themselves with social justice, which calls us to nonviolent resistance to evil, not just a pacifism that maintains one's personal and moral purity.[48] Indeed, such pacifism can indicate a kind of power and privilege that allows one to stand detached from the suffering and exploitation of so many of the world's people.[49] By contrast, King's work of nonviolent resistance was deeply engaged with those realities and committed to authentic social change.[50] Berry then appeals to Morrison's claim that the cross is an early and universal human symbol, indicating a "standing human figure poised to embrace."[51] As such, the cross is a sign and act of solidarity that is both personal and political, that involves both justice and love.[52] Again, the goal is not purity but a world community built on a vision of just and loving relationships, such as Longacre articulated.[53] It is a world in which we "serve as God's midwives . . . to help Her give birth to the things that will turn the cosmos toward love, justice, and shalom."[54] God remains the mother and the one who will bring forth shalom, but we as humans have a role to play in assisting in this birth.[55]

Suzanne Guenther Loewen also uses this image of new birth. As both Mennonite and feminist, she explores these questions through careful attention to the writings of J. Denny Weaver and Dorothee Sölle. While she values Weaver's work, she observes that his first priority is proving God's nonviolence and the victory of the resurrection.[56] This ends up distancing God from the experiences of oppression. By contrast, she observes that Sölle

---

[48]Berry, "'This Mark of a Standing Human Figure,'" 128.
[49]Berry, "'This Mark of a Standing Human Figure,'" 196.
[50]Berry, "'This Mark of a Standing Human Figure,'" 24, 71.
[51]Berry, "'This Mark of a Standing Human Figure,'" 16.
[52]Berry, "'This Mark of a Standing Human Figure,'" 16.
[53]Berry, "'This Mark of a Standing Human Figure,'" 29; based on Doris Janzen Longacre, *Living More with Less* (Scottdale, PA: Herald, 1980). Longacre articulates a vision of nonconformity that includes living justly, learning from others, cherishing the earth, nurturing people, and freeing oneself from the norms and expectations of the American empire.
[54]Berry, "'This Mark of a Standing Human Figure,'" 29.
[55]Berry, "'This Mark of a Standing Human Figure,'" 197.
[56]Margreta Susanne Guenther Loewen, "Making Peace with the Cross: A Mennonite-Feminist Exploration of Dorothee Sölle and J. Denny Weaver on Nonviolence,

focuses on the reality of suffering, repeatedly emphasizing how the cross demonstrates God's ultimate solidarity with those who are poor and oppressed. God's willingness to suffer is helpful, then, for it demonstrates God's full and complete love, which will stop at nothing to respond to human pain and oppression.[57] As Loewen summarizes, God's presence can transform suffering, empowering us "to resist injustice and choose life."[58] The cross thus represents not only the pain of death but also the pain that comes from birthing new life.[59]

In all these ways, the cross represents resistance to the powers who seek to rule the world. It was not payment to an angry or offended God for our sins but rather God's willingness to enter fully into the sins of our world and reveal them for what they are. And the terrible truth is that the powers were so rebellious, so opposed to God's will, that they tried to destroy God. Jesus's death, then, was the result of his ministry of seeking life and wholeness for all God's people, even though this threatened the powerful leaders who benefited from the Roman occupation. This also means that Christian claims about the cross are subversive. To affirm that *God* was crucified means that God is present in and with those who are most rejected. As Wonhee Anne Joh argues so convincingly, this conviction means that God was not on the side of imperial power but rather with the abject, "those who have been repressed, expelled, persecuted, executed, oppressed."[60] Insisting on this truth can provide the courage to reclaim those despised parts of ourselves and our society that we need for our redemption.[61] It can encourage us to act for and with others on the margins who have the wisdom and insight needed to move toward healing and a better world.

Atonement, and Redemption" (PhD diss., University of St. Michael's College, University of Toronto, 2016), 45, 111, 139–40, 183–4.
[57] Loewen, "Making Peace with the Cross," 139.
[58] Loewen, "Making Peace with the Cross," 135.
[59] Loewen, "Making Peace with the Cross," 226–8.
[60] Wonhee Anne Joh, *Heart of the Cross: A Postcolonial Christology* (Louisville: Westminster John Knox, 2006), 114.
[61] Joh, *Heart of the Cross*, 113–18.

Finding Salvation

For those seeking salvation, God's presence in and with us can provide strength and empowerment. We can trust that God will go with us all the way through death and to new life. God holds all that we are and all that we experience in a strong and vulnerable embrace. We can experience salvation as we recognize that we do not have to be alienated or separated from God. As one woman summarized, "Communion with God already exists, but we need to become aware, reoriented, able to see the love that is already flowing toward us."[62] Another focus group participant observed that God can receive our pain: "God can hold it and transform it because of this endless flow of love. God doesn't run from our pain and this allows us not to run from each other's pain, or from our own."[63] Significantly, this image of being held by a loving presence comes up repeatedly in the stories of women from many traditions. For example, Rebecca Parker recalls a time when she was being orally raped as a child and thought she was going to die. Yet, in that moment, "I knew that there was a Presence with me that was 'stronger' than the rapist and that could encompass my terror."[64] She felt this presence had the power to save her and, indeed, believes this Presence did stop this man and saved her life.

Mennonite women also describe being held by a loving God. One focus group member described how she had always heard about the need to hold onto God. Yet, she found herself responding deeply to the idea that God was holding her: "Just be held. That's beautiful! That's what we need to hear when we are in pain, instead of those clichés like 'God needed a flower in his garden.'"[65] Another shared about a time when she was struggling with postpartum depression and not sleeping at night: "It was horrible—but then one night, I had this very strong impression

---

[62]Focus group participant D.
[63]Focus group participant C.
[64]Rita Nakashima Brock and Rebecca Ann Parker, *Proverbs of Ashes: Violence, Redemptive Suffering, and the Search for What Saves Us* (Boston: Beacon, 2001), 211.
[65]Focus group participant B. Some people use sayings like this when trying to offer comfort to those who have lost a loved one.

that Jesus was holding me like a baby. This is making me cry and it happened years ago. That is what I needed from God."[66] These experiences of God's presence are not a panacea. As Parker concedes, her rapist could have denied the Presence in the room and could have killed her.[67] Tragically, there are times when it appears God is absent, and love is not enough. And even when God is able to offer support and presence, the harm remains: nothing can erase the violence.[68]

We must also acknowledge that God's presence is often made tangible in and through human partners: people who offer loving attention and practical assistance, who speak up and courageously challenge those who cause harm, who work to change unjust policies and systems, and who build healthy communities based on respect and equal regard. They are people who give one another strength, vision, and energy as they worship and struggle together toward wholeness and life. God's partners are people like Leona Stucky who struggled long and hard to break free from her violent husband. Along the way, she needed practical help to leave her home and find shelter. She also needed and sought changes to policies and systems (police practices, laws, church teaching, mental health services) that too often failed to intervene or provide useful assistance. She pursued living arrangements based on respect and equality and worked hard to become a counselor, so she could offer a healing presence to others. Throughout, she maintained an honest, open relationship with God, demanding some account and explanation for all the pain she and her family members had experienced.[69] In the end, she does not claim ultimate answers but observes that as she is able, emotionally and spiritually, to hold her own life as well as what others share with her, she has found that somehow "a kind of confessing, knowing, loving, forgiving, and learning happens—and we mature enough to tackle the next step of our journeys."[70]

---

[66] Focus group participant D.
[67] Brock and Parker, *Proverbs of Ashes*, 212.
[68] Brock and Parker, *Proverbs of Ashes*, 213.
[69] Stucky, *Fog of Faith*, 301–2.
[70] Stucky, *Fog of Faith*, 311.

Conclusion

The God we meet in Jesus is always reaching out to embrace, empower, liberate, and vindicate those who suffer wrong. The goal is always to heal those who are broken and draw them into the circle of God's love and justice. This circle includes sinners and those sinned against. Indeed, everyone is both, at one time or another. But when people sin, they cannot find full healing without acknowledging the presence and challenge of those whom they have harmed. They cannot find true forgiveness and restoration unless they can admit that their actions and participation in unjust systems cause innocent people to suffer. They have to confess that these systems will sometimes even crucify God. Following Jesus means turning away from these systems and these harmful acts. It means turning instead toward the God of life and joining in God's saving, healing work in the world.

As Jesus demonstrates, this saving work especially seeks out those who have been violated, exploited, and oppressed. God does not control all things or solve all problems but continues this ministry of healing love and witness in and through those who have been sinned against. God invites us all to learn from their wisdom and perspective: to turn toward love, away from violence and domination; to support one another and engage in the practical steps that nurture and sustain life; to build just and peaceful communities that care for those who are most vulnerable; to actively challenge the individuals and systems that violate people and the earth and to hold them accountable; to develop and practice personal, social, corporate, and spiritual disciplines that join with God in bringing salvation and healing to us all.

Through it all, we can rest in the assurance that God holds us in a deep embrace. God is present with us, encouraging, loving, enlivening us even as we struggle against betrayal, sin, oppression, and death. Such love is strong and bold, which will never leave or forsake us, even in the midst of death. It is solidarity, both tender and just, that brings forth and supports new life.

8

Never Merely Victims

Erin Dufault-Hunter

"My stepfather is dying."

Helen's tone was neither fearful nor gleeful.[1] Rather, as she spoke about the death of a man who had sexually assaulted her for years, I could hear a puzzlement mixed with wonder.

"Would you be able to meet to talk?"

On that walk, we recalled the pain this man—a once powerful man who forced access to her body and whose own body now was frail, failing—caused her. He appeared unaware of the limited time in which he could repent of this evil, and he (along with all her family) continued in denial—not of the rapes but of the wrongfulness of them. She contemplated that though her perpetrator would soon be dead, his abuses infected her life, especially interactions with her family. But as we walked and pondered aloud about this, she made a shocking, beautiful statement that caught me up short. Simply and with a gentleness that stunned me, she said, "I pity him."

"Pity" can be spat at another, an accusation of their worthlessness or contemptibility. But Helen clearly meant this in its original intention: she saw him clearly, as a pitiable human—shriveled and shrunken. In a remarkable display of true liberation, Helen spoke and felt truthfully. She knew God judges all evil and rages at its dull but deep harm of her and so many girls like her. But God does not see her only as a victim, as someone disempowered by the ravages of sexual abuse. Rather, God frees her to take up her own life, to accept the honor and responsibility of one who participates in Christ's persistent and offensive compassion toward even the wickedest among us. "I pity him." What an astonishing freedom, a glimpse of how those seemingly damned to victimization escape the logic of violence and instead enact a humanity inaccessible and unimaginable to perpetrators.

Sexual violence against women—from harassment to rape—is a pernicious and ubiquitous sin that Christians must vigilantly name, unmask, and overthrow in every culture and in every moment in history.[2] In doing so, we actively proclaim a God who

---

[1] Name and identifying information have been changed to protect victim's anonymity.
[2] Walter Wink charges us to "name" and "unmask" the powers. Walter Wink, *Naming the Powers: The Language of Power in the New Testament* (Philadelphia: Fortress, 1984); Walter Wink, *Unmasking the Powers: The Invisible Forces That Determine Human Existence* (Philadelphia: Fortress, 1986). I understand this charge to resist

redeems women from sexual oppression. But we also presume that evil often appears unrelenting, and our longing for justice and liberation seems a distant dream amid "realities" easily confirmed in our social media feeds and documented by news outlets. It is at this juncture that Anabaptism offers hope to reshape the imagination and witness of the church amid rampant sexual violence. Anabaptists know the persistence of violence and are confident of God's judgment of it. Yet, Anabaptists also seek faithfully to embody an alternative power by taking up the way of Jesus amid this present darkness, because Christ currently reigns as victor over all the powers that be.[3]

In this chapter, I presume that the long-standing effects and pervasiveness of sexual violence present a unique challenge to those who seek to address these experiences from within a distinctly Christian vision. I argue that any attempt to address sexual violence must do so with eyes wide open, a double vision that holds together two truths in our present moment: we must (1) account for the perniciousness of such oppression while (2) holding the victim's life within the reality of God's unrelenting redemption. Anabaptism offers hope to reshape the imagination and witness of the church by reminding us that victims of sexual violence are never *merely* victims, even as we name the harm it inflicts. Because not even sexual violence overcomes God's redemptive power for and in the exploited, victims can come to love enemies by perceiving them truthfully. Victims can see victimizers for the pitiable creatures they are, stripped naked by the lens of the eschatological future as it meets us in the present, and can do so without becoming like them, refusing to disregard their humanity.

---

sexual sin to be biblical, beginning with God's intention for sexed humanity as partners in Genesis 1 followed by the description of ways this will become warped in Genesis 3 and beyond.

[3]Among many metaphors for comprehending the atonement, Anabaptists often utilize that of Christus Victor, the one who overthrows the powers that be. Mennonites among others also use the symbol *agnus dei*—the Lamb of God—who is offered as a sacrifice and also holds a scepter as ruler. This points to the character of Jesus as one who reigns with humility and who comes into his power through noncoercive measures, another emphasis among Anabaptists.

A Primer on Trauma, Abuse, and Harassment

One of the remarkable if distressing realities of sexual violence is its effect on us, infecting our minds and bodies in exceptional ways. Speaking honestly about this violence requires attending to its distinctive features and forms in order to honor the singularity and extremity of individuals' experiences as well as its shared effects on victims.

Helen's experience of incest is clearly an incident of sexual *trauma*. Theologian Shelly Rambo has written extensively on trauma and notes that it is variously defined by clinicians. But she notes that virtually all agree that trauma refers to an experience or set of experiences that overwhelm a person's capacity to respond effectively to a threat: the traumatized person feels continually endangered, even when safely removed from the situation.[4] But it is trauma's unique capacity to sever mind from body and past from present that renders it particularly confounding and severe for victims and those around them. A marker of post-traumatic stress disorder (PTSD), for example, is the occurrence of flashbacks in which the past invades the present: a person can completely shut down or become agitated and hyper-aroused.[5]

Rambo identifies three interlocking, characteristic problems that mark off trauma as a uniquely difficult embodied response:

---

[4]See Shelly Rambo, "Trauma and Faith: Reading the Narrative of the Hemorrhaging Woman," *International Journal of Practical Theology* 13, no. 2 (2009): 235, https://doi.org/10.1515/ijpt.2009.15; and Charles Manda, "Re-Authoring Life Narratives of Trauma Survivors: Spiritual Perspective," *Hervormde Teologiese Studies; Pretoria* 71, no. 2 (2015). For careful definitions of trauma and its distinctives, see Bessel van der Kolk, *The Body Keeps Score: Brain, Mind, and Body in the Healing of Trauma* (New York: Penguin, 2014). Note that one-time events may or may not be traumatizing in the sense defined here, whereas repeated occasions of abuse, assault, or harassment often result in trauma that eventually manifests in PTSD, substance abuse, or other maladaptive behaviors. For a short, accessible book by a psychologist written with pastors and caregivers in mind, see Karen A. McClintock, *When Trauma Wounds: Pathways to Healing and Hope* (Minneapolis: Fortress, 2019).

[5]Rambo, "Trauma and Faith," 235. Some dub trauma a "special form of memory . . . experience that has affect only, not meaning." Manda, "Re-Authoring Life Narratives," 2.

the problem of *temporality* (one's brains cannot absorb what is happening to them and makes it impossible to situate what is happening chronologically, even in the future); the problem of *memory* (rather than recalling past events, memories "possess" the victim, unbidden and often incoherent as in flashbacks); the problem of *speechlessness* (terrorized by memories of the past that resist integration and orderly recollection, one cannot speak one's own experience, resulting in profound disempowerment).[6] Betrayed by their own bodies, trauma victims are rendered mute, isolated, and in pain.[7]

Even when not bearing all these distinctive problems associated with trauma, sexual abuse and harassment often result in some of these symptoms and can prove debilitating to victims. Particularly, if repeatedly encountered or endured, "lesser" types of sexual violence reside in our bodies in ways that similarly defy a (seemingly) reasonable response to current experience that can lead to what is termed "complex trauma."[8] Abuse and harassment can stubbornly resist healing and shatter a person's confidence in herself, her community, and her God. Here, sexual *abuse* includes forcing, manipulating, or exploiting someone to take part in sexual activities. Abuses can involve touching and penetration but also include showing pornography or forcing someone to watch—or be watched performing—sexual acts. Importantly, abuse includes emotional coercion and intimidation. Sexual *harassment* includes sexual comments, physical touch, requests for sexual favors, or inappropriate emotional intimacy, usually in contexts in which

---

[6] Rambo, "Trauma and Faith," 235-7.
[7] Rambo points to Simone Weil's discussion of affliction as not merely suffering but suffering characterized by degradation and severed relationship with others. As Rambo also comments, Elaine Scarry explored the uniquely isolating experience of certain kinds of pain in her classic work, *The Body in Pain: The Making and Unmaking of the World* (Oxford: Oxford University Press, 1985), 12. Rambo, "Trauma and Faith," 237-8.
[8] For an explanation of complex trauma and avenues for healing in religious contexts, see Jana Pressley and Joseph Spinazzola, "Beyond Survival: Application of a Complex Trauma Treatment Model in the Christian Context," in *Treating Trauma in Christian Counseling*, ed. Heather Davediuk Gingrich and Fred C. Gingrich (Downers Grove, IL: InterVarsity, 2017), 211-31.

power differentials or possibilities of retaliation or punishment make refusal difficult and costly.[9]

As trauma specialists describe, Helen's past erupted into her life without warning. She excelled academically and seemed to keep the chaos of home and family at arm's length, graduating from college and attending seminary. But a variety of circumstances triggered severe PTSD. In her twenties, she experienced flashbacks; she regressed in age, unable to function beyond a six- or seven-year-old child. I went through her home, removing anything that could be used to harm or kill herself; friends kept vigil, making sure she was not alone. It was a dark season and a vivid reminder of how the evil of sexual violence can lie dormant, only to rage, threaten, and assault victims later.

Sexual trauma pitilessly demands attention, whether it expresses itself as internalized shame or as chronic illness. Some victims wrestle with intimacy; partners struggle to support those whose sexuality has become fraught; and long-term physical and emotional connection can be difficult. They may be shocked by sudden, seemingly illogical weeping or by a disconcerting dissociation during sex or physical intimacy. The consequences of sexual violence arise unbidden and threatening. The invasiveness of initial sexual victimization lodges in our bodies and in psyches like a virus that manifests throughout a victim's life, a relentless and unpredictable "guest" that disrupts connection and intercepts joy.[10]

Gender Violence and Christian Faith

Particularly for those committed to nonviolence but also for all those committed to the offensive engagement that is Christian forgiveness, victims are necessarily burdened with having to figure out how to

---

[9]On power and consent in ministerial relations, see Darryl W. Stephens, "Fiduciary Duty and Sacred Trust," in *Professional Sexual Ethics: A Holistic Ministry Approach*, ed. Patricia Beattie Jung and Darryl W. Stephens (Minneapolis: Fortress, 2013), 23–33.

[10]An excellent source for comprehending trauma's effects on the body as well as some healing practices is Van der Kolk, *The Body Keeps Score*.

respond to violence without becoming like their victimizers.[11] Left to its own devices, violence creates more violence, and victims of sexual abuse and harassment often find ourselves fantasizing—or worse—about the damage we wish to inflict on perpetrators. Violence always desires to replicate itself, to lock humans in its vicious logic and render escape seemingly impossible. Thus, along with the usual psychological and physical burdens victims must bear, Christian victims also take on the weighty charge to "love our enemy." If such a command is not to become a cruel farce, a community must sustain victims (and perpetrators), holding them in the womb of uncomfortable truths about evil's effects, about the power of self-deception and warped perceptions, about the need for practices of lament, and about the cost of being restored in our humanity. For forgiveness to be Christian, it requires nothing less than this sort of honesty.

On the one hand, too often communities lack habits to bear the weight of this reality. Communal unwillingness to attend to victims or root out systemic sin becomes the contaminated soil in which sexual violence flourishes. Communities incapable of addressing the egregiousness of sexual violence abandon women to hopelessness, despair, or frustration. Some versions of Christianity (and perhaps particularly pacifist ones) suppress abuse or deny its effects. We can confuse pseudo-apologies from perpetrators, calls to "release" them or overlook their improprieties, with the hard work of forgiveness.[12] Some encourage victims to replace the possibility of the slow release of the perpetrator with a silencing or minimizing of the injury. Comments like "God works everything together for good" or "God never gives you more than you can handle" provide cover for the fear of facing evil's impact. Even for victims who escape the immediate situation of abuse, such communal minimizing surrenders the victim to its longer-term effects, unable

---

[11] For an accessible discussion of these dynamics, see Miroslav Volf, *Free of Charge: Giving and Forgiving in a Culture Stripped of Grace* (Grand Rapids: Zondervan, 2006); for a more academic examination, see Miroslav Volf, *Exclusion and Embrace: A Theological Exploration of Identity, Otherness, and Reconciliation*, rev. edn (Nashville: Abingdon, 2019).

[12] "Pseudo" here notes that Christians must note that our forgiveness enacts the thick, restorative justice of God. For a discussion of false forgiveness, see Volf, *Free of Charge*.

to find release from the residue of shame, humiliation, and rage. The wounded can become revictimized and bereft of antidotes for the chronic, underlying ache of victimization.

On the other hand, communities may grasp the horror of sexual sin and call for justice. Victims may sense comfort and courage from allies who share their anguish and name their rage. But without a commitment to the *redemption* of sexual sin, justice is often limited by secularized frameworks that stop at rage and punitive action. Stuck within this imaginative mold, the victim remains enslaved by violence, with their primary identity as victim or survivor. The wrong—the evil done and its fruit—remains dominant, the most decisive factor for comprehending what has occurred and what we can imagine in its wake.

A truthful proclamation of the gospel in word and action must affirm the real effects of victimization and thus offer comfort to victims. It must also offer a path for liberating victims from the shackles of sexual violence. Like all Christian freedom, our deliverance not only releases us *from* something but also frees us *for* something. In a seeming paradox of Christian freedom, we submit our lives to the crucified and risen Christ and, in doing so, become freed from the chains forged by sin—including those forged in sexual violence. Most notably, victims' participation in Christ reverses the shaming mechanism meant to incapacitate them, and sometimes God's future redemption breaks into the present.[13]

Theological Perspective

Especially after the public scandal of John Howard Yoder's sexual abuses, Mennonites have struggled with how our pacifist disposition and tradition provided a context for the continued, broadly known

---

[13]While painful torture, crucifixion was particularly aimed at shaming the victim. Rather than deny or ignore this shame, Jesus accepts it but not on its own terms. He renders it powerless by "despising" it, thus exposing the impotence of such cruelties against the power of God's love (see, e.g., Heb. 12:2). I have been deeply influenced by the work of Sarah Coakley, who asserts that we gain power through submission to Christ. But as a feminist, she notes the ways such language has been twisted to exploit or oppress women. Sarah Coakley, *Powers and Submissions: Spirituality, Philosophy, and Gender* (Oxford: Blackwell, 2002).

personal sin by its most articulate and persuasive theologian. But perhaps more puzzling is the church's spectacular failure to care for women abused by him. Many works have engaged in this discussion and analysis.[14]

Nonetheless, Anabaptism's unique resources and emphases highlight key elements for comprehending and addressing sexual violence as Christians. We commit to nonviolence and promote peace that includes forgiveness of enemies and hope for their rehabilitation. We seek to imitate Christ in enacting such offensive justice; we follow a Jesus often imaged as crucified Lord and sacrificial Lamb. One hears echoes of these dispositions toward sexual violence in some Anabaptist discussions of abuse. For example, in the issue of the *Mennonite Quarterly Review* dedicated to this topic, one author frames the crisis as one of enacting *shalom* for victims and victimizers while another explores the difficulty of a forgiveness that includes perpetrators.[15]

---

[14]The *Mennonite Quarterly Review* dedicated its January 2015 issue to sexual abuse and draws from these sensibilities. It includes a thorough history of John Howard Yoder's abuses, responses of others to it, the continued presence of sexual abuse in the Mennonite Church, the reassessment of Yoder's work in light of abuses, and clarification about Yoder's abuses (and that of others). See especially: Rachel Waltner Goossen, "Defanging the Beast: Mennonite Responses to John Howard Yoder's Sexual Abuse," *Mennonite Quarterly Review* 89, no. 1 (January 2015): 7–80; Rebecca Slough, "Congregational Responses to Abuse and Trauma: The Persistent Hope of Shalom," *The Mennonite Quarterly Review* 89, no. 1 (January 2015): 95–110; Gayle Gerber Koontz, "Seventy Times Seven: Abuse and the Frustratingly Extravagant Call to Forgive," *Mennonite Quarterly Review* 89, no. 1 (January 2015): 129–52; Carolyn Holderread Heggen, "Sexual Abuse by Church Leaders and Healing for Victims," *Mennonite Quarterly Review* 89, no. 1 (January 2015): 81–93; Linda Gehman Peachey, "Naming the Pain, Seeking the Light: The Mennonite Church's Response to Sexual Abuse," *Mennonite Quarterly Review* 89, no. 1 (January 2015): 111–28. For a list of other works on this topic, see MC USA, "John Howard Yoder Digest: Recent Articles about Sexual Abuse and Discernment," Menno Snapshots, http://mennoniteusa.org/menno-snapshots/john-howard-yoder-digest-recent-articles-about-sexual-abuse-and-discernment-2/.

[15]On *shalom*, see Slough, "Congregational Responses"; on the difficulty of forgiveness, see Koontz, "Seventy Times Seven." There have been numerous other articles and books in response to John Howard Yoder's abuses and corresponding institutional failures it exposed. As one long-standing voice of the Mennonite church, these frameworks in the *MQR* typify Anabaptist commitments to restorative justice.

But Anabaptists are also susceptible to thin theological reflection that abandons victims and victimizers to the ravages of unchecked violence and its bitter fruit. A reticence to acknowledge that we all seek (and need) to be powerful feeds denial—denial that perpetrators thirst for control, that victims struggle with chronic conditions, and that communities do not know what to do with either victims or perpetrators. Perhaps nowhere more evident than in its sexualized expression, violence boasts of its capacity to incapacitate and control others.[16] Like all sin, sexual abuse seeks to circumscribe another's identity and determine her destiny.[17] Yet the gospel proclaims that Christ liberates us from sin's control, binding the strong man and releasing us for an abundant life—one lived now amid a sometimes vicious world.[18]

Most strikingly, an Anabaptist vision must insist that victims of sexual violence cannot be *primarily identified as victims*. By leaning into the humiliated, tortured-yet-risen body of Christ, victims become free from the logic of violence and are released from the scripts that sexual violence (or that Christian realism) write for us.[19] Victims of violence, yes, but more importantly, children of a God who ransoms us from powers that would consume our life's energy to fuel their own. In a gospel at once offensive and attractive, Anabaptists affirm that God's compassion triumphs over coercive powers. So victims of sexual violence can come to love enemies by perceiving them as "pitiable" creatures seemingly securely wrapped in violence, minions of an already-defeated god who cannot withstand the hard, bright burn of Love.

---

[16]See notes above regarding trauma in particular and the ways it uniquely incapacitates us for response in time to what is happening to or around us.

[17]We do not have the space to explore how violence always circumscribes perpetrators as well, promising freedom to control others while making escape from abusing more and more difficult. All habits prove difficult to shake; violence develops its own particular addiction, with its promise to deliver perpetrators from fear or lack, only to catch them up in an endless cycle of self-protective assaults on others and, sometimes, on themselves.

[18]See Mark 3:27.

[19]Christian realism insists that human sin makes compromise inevitable, including at times utilizing violence to promote peace and justice.

"Show Me Your Wounds": The Ubiquity and Effect of Sexual Violence

One vivid example of the pervasiveness and pitilessness of sexual violence was the response of women to the Brett Kavanaugh hearings.[20] Women across the country (and around the world) reported how the hearings retraumatized them, disrupting their sleep; many found themselves alternating between rage and despair at the unrelenting, omnipresent, oppressive force of gendered violence.[21] While many of the women posting about Kavanaugh were victims of sexual assault, others noted that the hearings surfaced anxieties, fears, and long-term effects of sexual harassment more broadly. Whatever the sexual violence, women noted the repetitiveness of mechanisms of blaming and shaming, mechanisms that generally silence, stun, or otherwise imprison women in continuing patterns of gendered abuse.

Particularly striking is that the Kavanaugh hearings raised these tensions amid the #MeToo movement. In response to widely publicized abuses of film producer Harvey Weinstein, the #MeToo movement exploded. Women (and some men) came forward to press the industry about ways it consistently ignores or even promotes sexual harassment—if not assault. This emboldened women to challenge abuses in other industries and arenas. But it turns out his behavior was not secret. Weinstein's exploitation of women was widely known and ignored for decades; social media lit up with stories documenting his actions as merely typical of the industry's culture. In response, leaders issued calls for or promises

---

[20]As part of his nomination to the US Supreme Court, Kavanaugh faced accusations of sexual assault when he was seventeen by Christine Blasey Ford. A transcript of the hearing can be found at https://www.washingtonpost.com/news/national/wp/2018/09/27/kavanaugh-hearing-transcript. Kavanaugh denied any wrongdoing and was openly contemptuous and confrontational about Ford and toward the senators who questioned him about her. President Donald Trump stoked the fury of many, mocking Ford at a rally in Mississippi and on Twitter. Kavanaugh was confirmed and currently sits as one of nine Supreme Court justices.

[21]This was widely noted on social media streams—but see this letter to the New England Journal of Medicine by Eve Rittenberg, a doctor at Fish Center for Women's Health, part of Brigham and Women's Hospital: https://www.nejm.org/doi/full/10.1056/NEJMp1813497. She notes symptoms such as dread, cutting, and sleeplessness.

of change. Yet after two years of investigations, only Weinstein has been charged with a crime. In the end, two women charged him with criminal acts, and dozens of others who claimed abuse were told these were "uncomfortable, but not unlawful, encounters."[22]

Like an ever-doubting Thomas, society sometimes demands that women display our sexual injuries, stipulating that it will believe only when allowed to plunge careless hands into our sides, to poke around in our wounds. And when women find the courage to expose such intimate humiliations, these turn out too often to be exercises in "policy and procedure" that end with little systemic change or personal satisfaction.[23]

Occasionally, sexual violence extracts a public sacrifice, demanding that we offer up a symbolic "lamb" like Weinstein who soaks up our moral outrage, soothes our collective consciousness, and thereby affirms our belief that we have indeed "made progress." (I found it ironic that men who I know have harassed women or protected men who have done so were among the many who loudly professed distress at "those acts"; both progressives and conservatives doth protest too much, methinks.) As we have seen in the last several years, such public remorse and chest pounding often leave the guts of our structures unchanged and most perpetrators unrepentant and untouched. Simultaneously, the bodies of women and girls remain vulnerable.[24] While some communities offer

---

[22] Donna Rotunno, attorney for Weinstein, as quoted in *Newsweek*, July 27, 2019, https://www.newsweek.com/im-harvey-weinsteins-attorney-i-took-this-case-win-opinion-1451447.

[23] In making this observation, I am not saying that law and policies are irrelevant. Rather, I am noting that law turns out to be a blunt instrument for administering a justice able to enact God's just peace, perhaps most clearly in sexual abuse or harassment that are difficult to prove by legal standards and can be relationally complex. Weinstein's case highlights this, as do numerous cases that were initiated during this season (such as one against Kevin Spacey) but are ultimately dropped. Myriad difficulties arise in legislating and enforcing antidiscrimination and harassment law; see, for example, discussions of revisions to Congressional Accountability Act of 1995 passed after the Kavanaugh hearings by Congress in an attempt to better police its own abuses.

[24] Men and boys are also the victims of sexual violence and assault but at a much lower rate than women and girls. In the United States, one in five women versus one in seventy-one men will be raped in their lifetime, and 91 percent of rape and sexual assault are female. National Sexual Violence Resource Center, "Statistics

healing that comes through pursuit of God's just peace, many other women live in trauma's long shadow.

To put it bluntly, sexual violence seems to win. It wins by making this cycle of oppression seemingly inescapable, whether in the body intimate or the body politic. It wins by denying victims' self-worth, causing them to despair of their stake in God's good future and, overall, imprisoning them within the walls of violence's logic (e.g., victims fantasize about revenge on one hand while they inhabit a body whose pain and experience of trauma causes little to no disruption in business-as-usual, whether that "business" is a household, church, institution, or workplace).

The Problem with Powerlessness

Disrupting the seemingly irrefutable logic of violence, Helen's pity testifies to transformation of "mere" victims into God's powerful partners in a whole and holy reality, one often unimaginable to perpetrators addicted to coercion. Thus, Helen's compassion does not display powerlessness but instead enacts an authority to name reality, to see the present as refracted through the end of history. Yet Anabaptists in particular tend to laud "powerlessness"; this not only is unbiblical but also proves especially problematic for victims of abuse.

Quite rightly, Anabaptists warn against collusion with the mighty. Our shorthand: we release the need to make the world come out right and pursue faithfulness rather than effectiveness.[25] John

---

about Sexual Violence," 2015, https://www.nsvrc.org/sites/default/files/publications_nsvrc_factsheet_media-packet_statistics-about-sexual-violence_0.pdf. Because it is less common, it carries its own complexities and difficulties to unmask and heal. That then-candidate Donald Trump could be shown on tape bragging (among other crude comments) that powerful men like him can "grab 'em by the pussy and "do anything" and still go on to win the presidency underscores the vulnerability of women and our sexualization (and how our welfare is sacrificed to politics-as-usual). That these comments failed to impact his overwhelming support among "white evangelicals" remains telling about conservative Christians' commitment to protect the innocent, especially women and girls, from violence.

[25] Catholic theologian William Cavanaugh has written and spoken on this topic. See William Cavanaugh, "Don't Change the World." *The Table*, Biola University Center for Christian Thought, July 13, 2017, https://cct.biola.edu/dont-change-world/.

Howard Yoder famously articulated this Anabaptist distinction, insisting that Jesus does not take up the "handle" of history, and thus neither should we.[26] At first blush, this corrects Reformed theology's confidence in being able to take up this handle with firm and faithful hands. Our ethic must align ends (God's justice) and means (God's nature, seen most vividly in Christ). For Anabaptists, Jesus invites us to imitate his submission to the Lord who does have the handle of history, who takes up even the horrors of the past so they cannot hijack God's good future.[27] But if *only* this kind of imitation is encouraged—that of "powerlessness" or submission—victims are left at the mercy of the sick cycle of violence.

Instead, Anabaptist theology must be guided here not by the image of the sacrificial lamb but rather by the wounded-yet-risen body of Christ. Christ takes up all sexual victims into this same body, making them powerful by enabling an alternative to violence—one that makes even compassion for enemies possible. In the language of improvisation, Jesus "overaccepts" the violence of his enemies and in doing so transforms what was meant for humiliation into a sign of God's vindication of the vulnerable.[28] Even in the resurrection, past violence remains evident; God does not erase the past. But wounds become a means of power, the means of salvation, and all those women taken up into this same body—who lean into, release

---

Cavanaugh is particularly fascinating in this regard, as he has also advocated for close connections to global Christianity and has written extensively on importance of the church's witness to the powers that be, particularly in Chile during Pinochet. William Cavanaugh, *Torture and the Eucharist: Theology, Politics, and the Body of Christ* (Oxford: Blackwell, 1998).

[26]"Jesus was so faithful to the enemy love of God that it cost him all his effectiveness; he gave up every handle on history." John Howard Yoder, *The Politics of Jesus* (Grand Rapids: Eerdmans, 1994), 233.

[27]Such is the complicated promise of Rom. 8:28. One reflection on how naming the horrors while also believing in God's future is Miraslov Volf, *The End of Memory: Remembering Rightly in a Violent World* (Grand Rapids: Eerdmans, 2006).

[28]Borrowing from the practice of improv theater, Samuel Wells explains that Christian ethics rests not so much in blocking (saying no to what culture offers or what has occurred) or in accepting (saying yes to the same). "Overaccepting" depends for its power and sense on placing the interaction within a much larger, expansive story. For an explanation of overaccepting and its importance for re-envisioning Christian ethics, see Samuel Wells, *Improvisation: The Drama of Christian Ethics* (Grand Rapids: Baker, 2004), 131–40.

themselves to his crucifixion—are made free to take up their pasts (the cross is, still, an awful reality) and their present as those whose destiny is not determined by victimizers. Violence does not have the last word; coercion even of the most horrible sort does not finally tell women who they are or who they will become. The powerless become the powerful, liberated from the logic of abuse's dull and predictable patterns.

Like Christ, we do not seek out violence or believe we deserve abuse—this belief is something all too common, particularly for women in some Christian circles.[29] Rather, when we have no other option, we absorb it without responding in kind. Many girls and women have no other option; determination to survive may be their only means to protest abuse. Even in situations of "mere" harassment, constant resistance or multiple occurrences prove exhausting. This is especially true in spaces where people are unwilling to acknowledge the wrong or correct it because of the financial, personal, or social cost of doing so.

What is often unstated or unclear is the link between our desire for power and our desire for freedom. Understood within the grammar of the gospel, true power is not shaping others as we wish. Rather, the power we should seek is that of the capacity to perceive our lives truthfully and, so freed by truth, to script our lives accordingly. We recognize that the hunger to bend others to our will and thus satisfy our cravings (an impulse obvious in sexual violence) is a craven, defeated instinct judged by Christ. Like Christ, victims can choose to share their wounds not in humiliation but rather as powerful protest against being identified by them.[30]

---

[29] With remarkable fearlessness of its implications, Scripture records that Jesus wants to avoid torture and death (Matt. 26:36–43) and cries out in accusation by borrowing the psalmist's bare agony and sense of abandonment (Mark 15:34). But from the cross, Jesus also forgives his petty but vicious murderers (Luke 23:34). As recent translations of "Son of Man" remind us (e.g., Common English Bible), Jesus is the Human One who shows us what it means to live as a free human being. So, amid brutality, Jesus expresses a longing to escape execution as well as the loneliness and sorrow of abandonment. Yet in doing so Jesus remains free—free to act as one made in the image of the God of Israel who offers mercy. He does not devolve into the likeness of his abusers and perpetuate the violence that he could (seemingly rightly) wreak upon them (e.g., see Matt. 26:53).

[30] While Thomas likely issues his words as a challenge, Jesus takes these words and reworks them into invitation to a new reality: "Put your finger here and see my

In doing so, we enact Jesus's vindication of the vulnerable; allies attend to these wounds unflinchingly, knowing violence cannot trump God's redemption. By the Spirit who raised the wounded Christ, Christian victims receive power to live as those determined by the force of God's offensive grace.

Truths

Helen's sentiment enacts the gospel by viewing the abuser not through the power of his violence but rather through the force of the cross. She has been emancipated from shame and rage enough to see the abuser as the pitiable creature he is. When unmasked, sexual violence is exposed as incapable of usurping God's ultimate liberation of the oppressed. The pity expressed here is one that sees that while she was treated as an object, it is he who is the shriveled, less-human one. Facing his own mortality, he has thus far refused to submit to a truth that even still could set him free from the cycle of violence. Grace begins by accepting the fact of his pitiable state.

The offensiveness of the gospel lies here, in the crux where truth strips us naked in our need (for forgiveness, for redemption) and beckons us to enter the body of Christ. As recorded in the *Martyr's Mirror* or as enacted by ordinary saints, Anabaptists have consistently proclaimed the cross in this way, declaring that victims can hope for the redemption of their enemies and thus be freed from the way violence skews our vision not only of ourselves but also of our enemy's humanity. This imitation of Christ amid violence becomes possible not because the abused muster up some extraordinary moral willpower. Rather, like Jesus, victims commend themselves not to defeat by evil but rather to the Spirit. They simultaneously admit their inability to overcome evil but also deny evil's pretention to control their history, their story. Admission of vulnerability opens us to God's Spirit—an unstoppable force that brings goodness from chaos. The Spirit exposes and disrupts the dull but vicious cycle of violence, and victims see victimizers for what and who they really are.

---

hands. Reach out your hand and put it in my side. Do not doubt but believe" (John 20:27).

True liberation from an Anabaptist perspective insists on this offensive grace, extended to others through bodies still aching for their own full redemption by that same grace.[31] Too frequently, we forget that "redemption" comes from the world of slavery and indentured servitude, a social context that recognized that persons (especially vulnerable ones) needed someone to avenge wrongs and restore right relations. While some Christians associate redemption with our need to be forgiven personal sins, this is secondary to its primary meaning as the state of having been released from bondage into a justice that avenges, repairs, and liberates. Notice the implication: to speak of the redemption of sexual violence presumes its deep wrongness, notes its real power to harm and entangle us in the mire that all harassment and assault leave in their wake. If we understate or forget that redemption always implies this reality, we undercut the arc of the biblical drama and its unblinking, brutal honesty about consequences for those who prey upon the weak.[32]

Taken within this larger context of truthfulness, words of compassion or forgiveness do not mock victims but rather testify to victims' humanity that resists both hate and humiliation. An insult lies at the core of an Anabaptist vision and our determination to perceive in even the most heinous person—those who truly deserve the appellation "enemy"—the wretchedness of their state and need for God's redemptive grace. To see a perpetrator in this way is to defang violence, to throw a wrench into the grinding monotony of coercion and the suffocating dissociation, shame, and rage that sexual violence fosters. It reveals how impotent such violence is and unmasks its fragility and its ultimate impermanence.[33]

---

[31] This understanding is not unique to Anabaptists. While a hallmark of our tradition, it is also affirmed by many other Christians. As Anglican and former archbishop of Canterbury remarks about the Sermon on the Mount, "When I am injured . . . I have, as a believer, the freedom to alter the terms of the relation: I can decline to see it as a challenge to equalize the score, and opt to display positively the sovereign liberty of God not to retaliate or defend an interest. In other words, I can either attempt to close off my vulnerability or I can work with it as to show the character of God." Rowan Williams, quoted in Wells, *Improvisation*, 134.
[32] See, for example, Isa. 43:14-15.
[33] Augustine commented on what he dubbed the "privation of evil." Rowan Williams, "Insubstantial Evil," in *Augustine and His Critics*, ed. Robert Dodaro and George Lawless (Oxfordshire, UK: Routledge, 2000), 105–23.

Such liberation will also always be insulting because freedom from abuse belies the falseness of raw power and exposes its weakened, shallow roots. Yet unlike the scarcity economy of worldly strength, submission to the ways of Christ never negates women's pasts, never silences violations. Rather, Christ wipes away every tear of the saints who follow him into the new creation.[34] The seeming paradox of the Anabaptist vision lies in this: in our release of control and our obedience to the wounded-yet-risen Christ, we become free to live as those given power beyond mere violence because the just peace of the city of God is already here—in and among us.

A crucial caveat must be noted about the embodiment of this grace by Helen and others like her: she might never have been able to come to this. Indeed, she may again retreat from this space, unable to tend the complexities of her life's wounds while extending grace to her offender. Anabaptists frequently comment that faith is a communal virtue, never a burden placed on the shoulders of an individual. Like the friends who tore away the roof that kept a man from Jesus's healing presence, communities must stubbornly demand God's justice for those held in the chokehold of abuse.[35] The noncoercive gospel we proclaim means even a victim's own incapacity to yet imagine or enact such pity cannot block God's redemption of her woundedness.

Thus, a Christian response to sexual violence must take into account three basic truths. First, it must note the effect and particularly the ongoing presence of such violations in the life of the victim and those who care for them. Even God does not change or undo the past. Sexual violence harms and often produces wounds that at best are slow to heal and, too frequently, reopen and fester at different points during a victim's life, as a creature created in time. In this sense, the label "victim" reminds us of our charge to lament exploitation and train our hearts to bear the ache of human suffering. If unchecked by other truths, this unblinking comprehension of the

---

[34] For explorations for how the nonviolent resist evil, see Michael J. Gorman, *Reading Revelation Responsibly: Uncivil Worship and Witness: Following the Lamb into the New Creation* (Eugene, OR: Cascade, 2010).

[35] See Mark 2:4-5. The man is healed not because of his own faith but rather because of the faith of his determined friends.

pervasiveness and lasting effects of sexual violence fosters despair of living free of its grip; we may even become like violators in their violence, set on retaliation (fantasized or enacted).

Second, Christians proclaim that, despite its braggadocio (as necessary or as victorious), violent coercion lies about its own power. It cannot alter the horizon into which all history is taken and transformed: God's good, just future. So our vision—of ourselves, of our world—must hold both these truths simultaneously. We acknowledge that the past has consequences for our present *and* that the future remains more determinative of our response to this present than our history.

Finally, living truthfully in the present means that victims are never *merely* victims: they are set free to enact the expansive if strange sensibility of the gospel rather than the small, predictable rationality of violence.[36] They are freed not only to see victimizers as they truly are but also to extend them God's mercy.

In a world ruled by victimizers, Helen's pity unmasks their ultimate impotence. In a world strewn with victims, her judgment prophesies of the inevitability of God's just peace. But the mystery of Helen's liberation cannot be cleanly excised from the present. In the present, her wounds still bleed; in the present, we glimpse the beauty and wonder of her compassion only through the filter of heart-rending lament.[37]

---

[36] A quote attributed to Flannery O'Connor puts it, "You shall know the truth, and the truth shall make you odd."

[37] For models of liturgies and suggestions about how local congregations can respond to sexual violence, see Monica Coleman, *The Dinah Project: A Handbook for Congregational Response to Sexual Violence* (Eugene, OR: Wipf and Stock, 2010). For an example of thinking about sexual trauma theologically, see Shelley Rambo, *Spirit and Trauma: A Theology of Remaining* (Louisville: Westminster John Knox, 2010). Rambo's *Resurrecting Wounds: Living in the Aftermath of Trauma* (Waco, TX: Baylor University Press, 2018) specifically addresses veterans, but some of her work here also applies to sexual violence victims. Pamela Cooper-White has written extensively on sexual violence (including abuse in the church); see her *The Cry of Tamar: Violence against Women and the Church's Response*, 2nd edn (Minneapolis: Fortress, 2012) and her recent collection of essays, *Gender, Violence, and Justice: Collected Essays on Violence against Women* (Eugene, OR: Wipf and Stock, 2019).

9

Bearing Witness to Jesus, Resurrected Survivor of Sexual Violence

Hilary Jerome Scarsella

Across the globe, the church is thoroughly embroiled in a larger social crisis about how to respond to survivors' experiences of sexual violence—both when that violence is perpetrated by figures of authority in the church and when it is perpetrated by friends, family, colleagues, public figures, and strangers beyond. At the center of this crisis are a number of ethically pressing questions: Under what conditions should we believe people who say they were sexually abused? What kind of action ought to follow from our belief? What forms of evidence are necessary to hold perpetrators and enablers of sexual violence accountable? What kind of claim does the ubiquity of sexual violence make on the theologies and politics through which we structure our communities, institutions, and relationships?

There is a pervasive sense in Western communities—secular and religious—that in order to take action with respect to sexual violence, a certain threshold of certainty must be met regarding the relevant historical facts.[1] It is generally presumed that these facts must be established through the kinds of evidence that would be authoritative and persuasive in a court of law—eyewitness testimony, forensic evidence, a paper trail. However, these forms of evidence are often not available in situations of sexual violence, and so communities are inevitably confronted with the task of determining what to do in the absence of evidence-based certainty. How ought Christian communities respond to testimonies of sexual violence when it is not possible to gain direct access to what happened behind closed doors? What ought to govern a community's politics around sexual violence when the kind of certainty Western culture demands as a premise for action is, quite literally, impossible?[2]

---

[1] While shared characteristics of the sexual violence crisis can be found in many parts of the world, there are also important differences between regions. Because my immediate context is the United States and because the United States has a Western cultural identity that is shared, for example, with Western Europe and other predominately white nations of European colonial expansion (e.g., Canada and Australia), I write this chapter with Western contexts like these in mind. I invite those from other parts of the world to read this chapter with attention not only to what resonates but also to what does not. The gaps such readers find in my thinking are likely areas in need of attention precisely from persons at their point of perspective.
[2] The threshold of certainty that I have described here is particularly reflective of Western responses to testimonies of sexual violence perpetrated by white, cis,

Using the tools of constructive theology and ethics, I seek theological ground that can support communities of faith in taking political action in solidarity with survivors of sexual violence— ground able to support that action particularly when access to a sense of certainty regarding the facts and circumstances of a given instance of sexual violence is limited. In other words, since it is often the case that clear legal, historical, and scientific forms of evidence are unavailable to prove survivors' claims, my writing is motivated by the need to cultivate alternative ground on which to build political resistance to sexual violence and solidarity with survivors.

I do not come to this project as a neutral party. I am a white woman, born in the United States. I have the social privilege that gathers around those who are in heterosexual marriages, but something of my sexuality is queer. I am a survivor of sexual violence in multiple forms, and I am a professional advocate for survivors connected to Christian contexts. I am a scholar of theology, ethics, and the wider study of religion, gender, sexuality, and trauma. Like every member of my mother's family dating back to the sixteenth century, I was raised Mennonite, and I continue to find meaning in that identity. The deeply Catholic sensibilities of my father's side have shaped me as well.

One way for theologically minded communities to begin constructing answers to the questions that shape the contemporary sexual violence crisis is to consider the sexually violent dimensions of Jesus's crucifixion. I argue that engaging in this kind of reflection, first, reveals that sexual violence is positioned at the heart of Christianity insofar as acts of sexual violence were perpetrated against Jesus during his crucifixion. Second, I propose that if it is reasonably possible that the sexual violence perpetrated against Jesus included sexual assault, then those who consider themselves followers of Jesus must bear witness to this *possibility*. Third, I make the case that bearing witness to possibility (as opposed to

---

heterosexual men. The US history of lynching is one of many examples that reveal the certainty threshold at issue in today's discourse on sexual violence as racially textured. If the argument I put forth in this chapter is to be further developed, a racial analytic will need to be centered.

certainty) can be practiced as a concrete mode of resistance to sexual violence.³

Sexual Violence and Jesus's Crucifixion

In ancient Rome, crucifixion was a form of execution reserved for those considered a political threat to the empire. It was a way for Rome to demonstrate to the empire's diverse publics that rebellion would be met with catastrophic consequences and, therefore, was not in their best interest. As David Tombs writes, "Crucifixion was intended to be more than the ending of life; prior to actual death it sought to reduce the victim to something less than human in the

---

³In this chapter, I lay the groundwork for a proposal I am developing elsewhere: that attentiveness to the poetic dimensions of Jesus's politics allows for greater solidarity with sexual violence survivors and that planting ourselves in the soil of this poetic sensibility may open an ethical way for belief and political action in the absence of certainty. Theologians who have reflected on the traumatic dimensions of Jesus's crucifixion and resurrection have drawn attention to the specular qualities of the resurrected Christ. The resurrected Jesus has a body that eats, embraces loved ones, and bears wounds. But his body also moves through walls. It appears and disappears in materially unconventional ways. He is Who He Is, but those who love him struggle to recognize him. On the road to Emmaus, close companions fail to realize they are in his company. Mary of Magdalene mistakes him for a gardener. There is a there-/not there-ness to the resurrected Jesus. What I find relevant for contemplating the politics of Jesus is that it is *this* material/immaterial, there/not there, difficult to recognize, walks-through-walls Jesus upon whom Christians are to found their knowledge, their faith, their communities, and their political commitments. It is *this* specular Jesus who gives the great commission, *this* Jesus to whom Christians are to bear witness. The warrant this Jesus offers for that which Christians are to regard as *true* is not the warrant of certainty. The warrant this Jesus gives for the life Christians are to live comes in the form of an incomprehensibility. It comes in the form of a murdered, living, material ghost. Shelly Rambo's reading of John 20:1-18 is particularly useful for reading the politics of Jesus on sexual violence through a theopoetic lens: *Spirit and Trauma: A Theology of Remaining* (Louisville: Westminster John Knox, 2010), 83–90. Similarly useful is Mayra Rivera's attention to the specular in *Poetics of the Flesh* (Durham, NC: Duke University Press, 2015); and "Thinking Bodies: The Spirit of a Latina Incarnational Imagination," in *Decolonizing Epistemologies: Latina/o Theology and Philosophy*, ed. Ada María Isasi-Díaz and Eduardo Mendieta (New York: Fordham University Press, 2011), 207–25.

eyes of society."[4] This was the root of its strength as a ritualized practice of state violence. Crucifixion was designed to ensure that the execution of a politically threatening individual or group would put an end to the wider subversive movement represented by those crucified. According to Tombs, one of the strategies Rome used to degrade and dehumanize those executed by crucifixion was sexual humiliation.

> In a patriarchal society, where men competed against each other to display virility in terms of sexual power over others, the public display of the naked victim by the "victors" in front of onlookers and passers-by carried the message of sexual domination. The cross held up the victim for display as someone who had been—at least metaphorically—emasculated. Depending on the position in which the victim was crucified, the display of the genitals could be specially emphasized. Both Josephus and the Roman historian Seneca the Younger attest the Romans' enthusiasm for experimentation with different positions of crucifixion. Furthermore, Seneca's description suggests that the sexual violence against the victim was sometimes taken to the most brutal extreme with crosses that impaled the genitals of the victim.[5]

Thus, for Tombs—and I agree with his assessment—"Crucifixion in the ancient world appears to have carried a strongly sexual element and should be understood as a form of sexual abuse that involved sexual humiliation and sometimes sexual assault."[6]

As I use the term, sexual violence is any mode of interpersonal or systemic abuse, coercion, manipulation, silencing, or overt violence

---

[4] David Tombs, "Crucifixion, State Terror, and Sexual Abuse," *Union Seminary Quarterly Review* 53 (Autumn 1999): 101.
[5] Tombs, "Crucifixion, State Terror, and Sexual Abuse," 101-2. Documentation regarding referenced descriptions of crucifixion made by Josephus and Seneca the Younger can be found, respectively, in Josephus's *The Jewish War*, trans. G. A. Williamson (New York: Penguin, 1970 [1959]), book V, section 452; and Martin Hengel, *Crucifixion: In the Ancient World and the Folly of the Message of the Cross* (Philadelphia: Fortress, 1977), 25.
[6] Tombs. "Crucifixion, State Terror, and Sexual Abuse," 101.

that has a sexual form of expression, a sexual logic, or both.⁷ The gospels tell us that as Jesus was beaten and crucified, he was forcibly stripped of his clothes three times. Though today's standard crucifix depicts Jesus on the cross with a cloth draped around his waist, both historical evidence and the biblical witness suggest that he was mocked by the crowds and nailed to that tree naked. The forced removal of his clothing, the exposure of his genitals to public view, the use of sexual humiliation as a means of torture, and the inclusion of sexual degradation in his murder—these are all characteristics of what Jesus suffered during crucifixion, and, in light of the above definition, they are, undeniably, acts of sexual violence. We can say confidently, then, that Jesus's crucifixion was sexually violent. Jesus was a victim of sexual violence.⁸

What does it do, then, for our politics of engaging sexual violence to conceive of Jesus as a murdered victim and resurrected survivor of this form of harm? What are the theological and ethical implications?⁹ Following certain strands within liberation theology, one kind of argument that could be made is that in becoming a victim of sexual violence, Jesus takes on and, in some way, redeems the suffering of the world's sexually abused. This is the kind of argument that might result from a simplistic transposition of the Christological and soteriological visions put forth by James Cone

---

⁷Definition first published in Hilary Jerome Scarsella and Stephanie Krehbiel, "Sexual Violence: Christian Theological Legacies and Responsibilities," *Religion Compass* 13, no. 9 (September 2019): 3.

⁸Given the contemporary situation of widespread hostility in the church toward LGBTQ+ sexualities, I feel compelled to state that the sexual violence perpetrated against Jesus by Roman men must not be conflated with gay sexuality. The sexual violence of Roman crucifixion was not a product of same-sex sexual orientation. It was a mechanism of domination rooted in thoroughly heterosexual sexual hierarchies. Within the Roman cultural context, women were the proper sexual objects of men, and women were marked as socially inferior in part by their vulnerability to men's sexual control. Men's sexual violence against other men, thus, signaled that the one being assaulted was *as inferior as a woman*—no longer deserving of the status of a man.

⁹Tombs explores questions like these with male survivors of sexual violence in Rocío Figueroa and David Tombs, *Recognising Jesus as a Victim of Sexual Abuse: Responses from Sodalicio Survivors in Peru* (Otago, New Zealand: Centre for Theology and Public Issues, University of Otago, 2019).

or Gustavo Gutiérrez onto the landscape of sexual violence.[10] However, womanist, *mujerista*, and feminist theologians from Delores Williams to Rita Nakashima Brock and Rebecca Ann Parker (and many in between) have argued that predicating salvation, liberation, or the possibility of survival on the necessity of the oppressive violence from which one needs relief can only, in the end, reinforce the power of that violence to continue to harm.[11] In contemporary situations of sexual and intimate partner abuse, it is common for victims to be counseled by their pastors and priests to remain in relationship with the one harming them for the sake of the victim's own redemption or that of the perpetrator. Thus, a theological response to recognizing Jesus as a crucified victim and resurrected survivor of sexual violence that makes contemporary survivors' prospects for well-being dependent on Jesus having experienced sexual atrocity as well is a response fundamentally incapable of subverting the structures of thought and practice through which systems of sexual violence are maintained.

The argument that I want to make instead is that when Christians worship the resurrected Jesus, they are worshiping a victim of sexual abuse. When Christians bear witness to the life, death, and resurrection of Jesus, they are bearing witness to sexual violence, to the death and trauma it imposes, and to the life that is possible in its aftermath. To care about the suffering of Christ is, then, to care about the suffering of those who have experienced sexual violence. To deny sexual violence or refuse to contend with it is to turn away from Jesus. At the heart of Christianity—at the heart of what it means to bear witness to the truth that Christians believe is made manifest through Jesus—*is* sexual violence. Insofar as we cannot do theology without attending to Jesus's crucifixion and resurrection or to the life Jesus lived that resulted in these, we cannot do theology

---

[10]James H. Cone, *God of the Oppressed* (Maryknoll, NY: Orbis, 1997); Gustavo Gutiérrez, *A Theology of Liberation: History, Politics, and Salvation* (Maryknoll, NY: Orbis, 1973).

[11]Delores Williams, *Sisters in the Wilderness: The Challenge of Womanist God-Talk* (Maryknoll, NY: Orbis, 1993); Rita Nakashima Brock and Rebecca Ann Parker, *Proverbs of Ashes: Violence, Redemptive Suffering, and the Search for What Saves Us* (Boston: Beacon, 2001). See also Joanne Carlson Brown and Carol R. Bohn, *Christianity, Patriarchy, and Abuse: A Feminist Critique* (Cleveland: Pilgrim, 1989); Marie M. Fortune, *Sexual Violence: The Sin Revisited* (Cleveland: Pilgrim, 2005).

without attending to sexual violence. Anabaptist theology places emphasis on what the social dimensions of Jesus's life, death, and resurrection mean for the world today. This feature of the tradition gives Anabaptists a particular responsibility to center sexual violence as a social problem that demands both sustained reflection and active intervention.

Sexual Assault and Jesus's Crucifixion

While it is clear that Jesus was a victim of sexual violence, it is an open question whether his crucifixion included sexual assault. For the purposes of this chapter, when I refer to sexual assault, I mean acts in which a person's genitals are acted on by another without their consent or acts in which a person is coerced to touch the genitals of another. This includes but is not limited to oral, vaginal, and anal rape with an object or any part of a perpetrator's body and being touched on any part of one's own body by a perpetrator's genitals without having given consent.

The accounts of Jesus's crucifixion given in the gospels do not include a description of sexual assault, but Tombs suggests there is reason to consider that it may have occurred. For one, sexual assault would be well in line with the sexual strategies of domination described in the gospel accounts of Jesus's crucifixion—namely, the repeated stripping of his clothing, the parading of his naked body before a mocking crowd, and the forced exposure of his genitals as he was fixed to the cross and killed. The possibility that outright sexual assault was perpetrated against him would not, therefore, introduce a foreign strategy of violence into the narrative. It would merely represent an intensification of the sexually violent dimensions of Jesus's crucifixion that are already articulated in the text.

There is another reason to remain open to the possibility that sexual assault could have been included in the strategies of domination and degradation used against Jesus during crucifixion. Tombs first wrote on the sexually violent dimensions of Roman crucifixion in an essay that read Jesus's execution in light of the strategies of terror used against political dissidents in 1970s and 1980s Latin America. In the contemporary Latin American context, both sexual humiliation and sexual assault were used prolifically to accomplish political ends consistent with those of Roman crucifixion—silencing dissent and quashing revolution.¹² In a recent volume on the gendered dynamics of state terror and genocide, both sexual humiliation and sexual assault were found to figure prominently in diverse programs of political domination across the globe.¹³ Scholars on gendered and sexual dynamics of political warfare have thus demonstrated that sexual assault has long been strategically operationalized "to terrorize the [targeted] population . . . demoralize the enemy, provide soldiers with the spoils of war and train them to commit hyperviolent acts . . . and reaffirm historic relations of power between [perpetrators] and [victims]."¹⁴ Admitting readily that the Latin American context of the 1970s and 1980s cannot tell us what did or did not happen in first-century Rome, Tombs connects the sexually violent dimensions of Jesus's crucifixion with the tendency for both ancient and contemporary programs of political torture to include sexual assault as an explicit strategy of domination.¹⁵ In light of this connection, Tombs argues that testimonies of sexual assault voiced by survivors of state terror in Latin America are "highly suggestive" of what Jesus may have suffered:¹⁶

> Both Matthew and Mark describe Jesus as being handed over weakened and naked—already a condemned man without any recourse to justice—to soldiers who took him inside the praetorium and assembled the other troops. Both Gospels explicitly state that it was the *whole cohort (speira)* of Roman

---

¹²Tombs, "Crucifixion, State Terror, and Sexual Abuse," 89–92, 96–100.
¹³Elissa Bemporad and Joyce W. Warren, *Women and Genocide: Survivors, Victims, Perpetrators* (Bloomington, IN: Indiana University Press, 2019).
¹⁴Victoria Sanford, Sofia Duyos Álvarez-Arenas, and Kathleen Dill, "Sexual Violence as a Weapon during the Guatemalan Genocide," in *Women and Genocide: Survivors, Victims, Perpetrators*, ed. Elissa Bemporad and Joyce W. Warren (Bloomington, IN: Indiana University Press, 2019), 218.
¹⁵One of the things that turning to Tombs's work does for the conversation sustained on sexual violence in this chapter is that it expands the concept of sexual violence beyond its usual contemporary significations in Western discourse (i.e., child abuse, intimate partner violence, workplace harassment—all of which are important to attend) to a notion of sexual violence that includes these while also recognizing that sexual violence is at play in forms of harm not usually conceptualized sexually (i.e., lynching, indigenous genocide, mass incarceration, LGBTQ+ injustice, Roman crucifixion, etc.).
¹⁶Tombs, "Crucifixion, State Terror, and Sexual Abuse," 104.

soldiers—between six hundred and one thousand men—that was assembled together to witness and participate in the "mockery." This probably included a significant number of Syrian auxiliaries who might have viewed their Jewish neighbours with particular hostility. In view of the testimonies to gang rapes that are given by victims detained by security forces in the clandestine torture centres of Latin America, this detail of overwhelming and hostile military power sounds a particularly disturbing note.[17]

What Tombs is suggesting is that our general knowledge about how sexual assault is used in programs of state terror warrants concern that Jesus may have been raped or otherwise sexually assaulted when he was alone with the Roman soldiers whose political mission was to destroy him.

The Roman historian Seneca tells us that Roman military personnel did, indeed, perpetrate sexual assault against male captives with some frequency, stating that "bad army officers and wicked tyrants are the main sources of rapes of young men."[18] Forging a connection between the fact of military rape in the ancient Mediterranean world and the suitability of this type of violence for accomplishing the political goals of crucifixion, Richard Trexler identifies forced anal or oral penetration by another man as, in Roman society, the "premier sign of male dependence," or in Tombs's terms, emasculation.[19] Thus, given (1) what we know about the general frequency with which military dominance is asserted through sexual means, (2) that soldiers apparently did sexually assault men in the ancient world to degrade, dehumanize, and humiliate, (3) that there was a period during Jesus's crucifixion in which he was behind closed doors in the company of assailants who stripped him of his clothes and forced his nakedness, it is eminently reasonable to hold open the possibility that Jesus may have been sexually assaulted in the praetorium.[20]

---

[17]Tombs, "Crucifixion, State Terror, and Sexual Abuse," 104–5.
[18]Richard C. Trexler, *Sex and Conquest: Gendered Violence, Political Order and the European Conquest of the Americas* (Cambridge, UK: Polity, 1995), 34.
[19]Trexler, *Sex and Conquest*, 20.
[20]A 2018 reissuing of Tombs's 1999 article includes an afterward written by Fernando Segovia in which Segovia affirms Tombs's method of reasoning as following the liberationist tradition of theology and biblical interpretation. Fernando F. Segovia,

Possibility and the Political Task of Bearing Witness

To hold open the possibility that Jesus was sexually assaulted is not to make the claim that we know this to be historically true. If it happened, it is likely to have happened out of view of any of Jesus's loved ones who went on to tell the story of what he was made to endure. If Jesus was sexually assaulted, in other words, it happened the way sexual assault often does—without leaving the kind of evidence that can be called on to secure knowledge of its historical circumstances for those who were not present in the moment of its occurrence. We do not and cannot have historical certainty that Jesus either was or was not sexually assaulted by the Roman soldiers who crucified him. However, it is precisely our lack of access to evidence-based certainty in one direction or the other that becomes significant for considering the relationship of sexual assault in Jesus's story to contemporary engagement with the crisis of sexual violence.

Our position of epistemological limitation regarding the sexual violence Jesus endured is not unlike the position in which we often find ourselves with respect to contemporary survivors' testimonies of sexual violence. Consider, for example, the case of an adult (let's call her Maria) who comes forward to report that twenty years prior, when she was fourteen years old, her pastor sexually abused her. At the time Maria's community is made aware of what she has suffered, no physical evidence remains. There are no eyewitnesses or written records available to consult. Her community must decide how to orient itself to her testimony without assistance from the kinds of evidence Western societies have come to regard as necessary for determining historical truth. Or consider the testimonies of Christine Blasey Ford and Deborah Ramirez against US Supreme Court Justice Brett Kavanaugh during his confirmation process. Both gave credible testimonies that Kavanaugh had sexually

---

"Jesus as a Victim of State Terror: A Critical Reflection Twenty Years Later," in *Crucifixion, State Terror, and Sexual Abuse: Text and Context*, ed. David Tombs (Dunedin, New Zealand: Centre for Theology and Public Issues, University of Otago, 2018), 22–31.

assaulted them.²¹ Yet, he was confirmed to the Supreme Court because neither Ramirez nor Blasey Ford could produce the kind of evidence that would allow confidence in their testimonies to rise to the level of certainty. Kavanaugh's supporters in congress argued that a candidate's appointment to the Supreme Court ought not be influenced by allegations of sexual violence unless those allegations could be, in a strict sense, *proved*.²²

This argument is a quintessential example of the prevailing logic by which Western communities—in and beyond the church—tend to organize their politics of response to sexual violence. Both in and outside of the courtroom, contemporary Western discourse on sexual violence makes the appropriateness of political solidarity with survivors dependent on evidence-based certainty. If the pastor who sexually abused Maria was still in a ministerial role when she came forward, the chances of him being removed from his position of access to other victims or otherwise held to account would be slim for as long as Maria is unable to "prove her case" within the context of her faith community. The contemporary problem may be summed up thusly: the legal mandate not to coercively imprison or execute the accused unless their guilt has been proved beyond reasonable doubt has been expanded into the social sphere in such a way that everyday communities (including communities of faith) are rendered

---

[21] Video footage of Ford's testimony before the Senate Judiciary Committee can be found at *C-SPAN*, "Supreme Court Nominee Brett Kavanaugh Sexual Assault Hearing, Professor Blasey Ford Testimony," 3:04:21, September 27, 2018, https://www.c-span.org/event/?451895/judge-kavanaugh-professor-blasey-ford-testify-sexual- assault-allegations. For Deborah Ramirez's account, see Robin Pogrebin and Kate Kelly, "Brett Kavanaugh Fit in with the Privileged Kids: She Did Not," *New York Times*, September 14, 2019, https://www.nytimes.com/2019/09/14/sunday-review/brett-kavanaugh-deborah-ramirez-yale.html. Also, Ronan Farrow and Jane Mayer, "Senate Democrats Investigate a New Allegation of Sexual Misconduct, From Brett Kavanaugh's College Years," *New Yorker*, September 23, 2018, https://www.newyorker.com/news/news-desk/senate-democrats-investigate-a-new-allegation-of-sexual-misconduct-from-the-supreme-court-nominee-brett-kavanaughs-college-years-deborah-ramirez.

[22] See, for example, the statement transcribed in Stavros Agorakis, "Read the Full Transcript of Sen. Collins's Speech Announcing She'll Vote to Confirm Brett Kavanaugh," *Vox*, October 5, 2018, https://www.vox.com/2018/10/5/17943276/susan-collins-speech-transcript-full-text-kavanaugh-vote.

incapable of practicing meaningful solidarity with survivors so long as openings for doubt remain.

For those who consider themselves followers of Jesus, constructing a politics for engaging sexual violence in the absence of certainty may be assisted by including reflection on the following question: If it were Jesus—if it *is* Jesus—what would we do? If it is reasonable and possible that Jesus was sexually assaulted, and if we are likely never to discover evidence that would serve as proof, how ought we—theologically, ethically, and politically speaking—orient ourselves to the limits of our knowledge?

If it is, as I have argued, reasonably possible that the sexual violence perpetrated against Jesus included sexual assault, then those who consider themselves followers of Jesus must bear witness to this *possibility*. Christians recognize four accounts of the life of Jesus and regard all four gospels as true despite their differences. The Christian tendency in narrating the life of Jesus is to synthesize the stories of the four gospels together. Rather than prioritizing fidelity to one or another of the gospel accounts, it has been the prevailing tradition of Christian spirituality to err on the side of telling the most expansive narrative one can about the life of Jesus because the risk of telling too narrow a story about God incarnate towers over the risk of the alternative. Likewise, I propose, the risk of failing to bear witness to the possibility that Jesus was sexually assaulted during crucifixion is far graver than the risk of bearing witness to a possibility that was not historically actualized. If it is plausibly possible that Jesus was sexually assaulted, not bearing witness to that possibility would constitute a Christian failure to bear witness to the suffering of Christ. Just as failing to bear witness to the ways that Jesus's life, crucifixion, and resurrection were marked by the violence of empire leads to theologically devastating incongruities between Jesus's politics and Christian practice, so too does failure to bear witness to the sexually violent dimensions of Jesus's life, crucifixion, and resurrection render Christian politics and practice theologically incoherent—and, through incoherence, dangerous.

For Anabaptists, the call to bear witness is not a call, simply, to speak with words what one knows about Jesus. It is a call to live one's life in a way that makes Jesus and the socially transformative love of God present in the here and now. Thus, bearing witness is an inherently political act. What makes one's social and political practices *Christian* is the degree to which these are conceptualized and lived in faithfulness to the life that Jesus modeled. In Anabaptist terms, then, the integrity of Christian discipleship depends on bearing as full a political witness as possible to what Jesus suffered and to the life that led him there. If it is reasonably possible that Jesus was sexually assaulted during crucifixion, Anabaptist Christians must bear political witness to this possibility.

Notice that to get here, we have had to depart from two key elements of the usual Western approach to sexual violence. First, whereas contemporary discourse makes the appropriateness of political action dependent on evidence-based certainty, the political act of witnessing does not. Orienting ourselves to the problem of sexual violence as it is manifest in the life of Jesus makes political response to sexual violence warranted and necessary on the grounds of reasonable possibility. Second, a shift occurs in our relationship to the limits of our knowledge. In the contemporary Western context, if those in a position to hold perpetrators and enablers accountable are not provided with the evidence they feel they need in order to act, the failure is not considered theirs. Rather, the survivor is the one considered ultimately responsible for producing evidence that certifies her testimony. For as long as a survivor is unable to do so, her community cannot be blamed for inaction. However, when we contemplate the possibility of sexual assault in Jesus's crucifixion, it becomes clear that those who do not have direct access to survivors' experiences of sexual violence bear responsibility for the limits of our knowledge. Instead of regarding Jesus as having failed to supply us with definitive evidence to direct the content of our witness, we discover that it is we who have failed. Insofar as we require evidence-based certainty as the premise for responding in faithful solidarity to the possibility that Jesus was sexually assaulted, we make a choice to structure our political lives in a way that renders us incapable of bearing Jesus's crucifixion as full a witness as it warrants. The limits of our knowledge do not absolve us of the responsibility to act in political solidarity with survivors. The limits of our knowledge require us to restructure our politics such that solidarity with survivors is both possible in the midst of uncertainty and constitutive of our witness.

Implications for Anabaptist Theology and Practice

If it is incumbent on Christians to bear witness to the possibility that Jesus was sexually assaulted during crucifixion, the next question is how to do so. I propose that one way Christians are constrained to bear witness to the possibility of sexual assault in Jesus's life is by holding possibility open with respect to survivors' testimonies today. Anabaptist theology and ethics have long emphasized Matt. 25:40 in which Jesus tells his followers, "Whatever you did for one of the least of these . . . you did for me" (NIV). In the context of sexual violence, the least of these are survivors, particularly those whose experiences of harm leave no concrete proof. Bearing witness to the possibility that Jesus was sexually assaulted thus means building modes of political solidarity with contemporary survivors that can be practised in the absence of certainty. It means building a politics of sexual-violence intervention based on the authority of credible possibility rather than certainty. It means taking responsibility for the limits of our knowledge rather than burdening survivors with the task of releasing us from our epistemological constraints. It means responding to survivors' testimonies of sexual violence with no less political urgency and commitment than would be called for in response to the sexual abuse and assault of Jesus, who Christians call God. The implications for Anabaptist theology and practice going forward are many. I close by emphasizing three.

First, Anabaptism must center sexual violence in its theological and ethical reflection. Because (1) Jesus was a victim of sexual violence, (2) it is possible that he was a victim of sexual assault, (3) Anabaptism takes the life of Jesus as a source of privileged authority for Christian theology and ethics, and (4) Anabaptism has thus far failed to recognize the sexually violent dimensions of Jesus's life, Anabaptist theology and practice must make sexual violence a central and sustained concern.

Second, Anabaptist theology must reconceptualize its commitment to peace in terms that resist sexual violence and create opportunities for survivors of sexual violence to flourish. Historically, Anabaptist peace theology has not taken sexual violence as a significant context of concern, and the result has been catastrophic for women and all persons vulnerable to sexual exploitation.²³ While innovative approaches to peace theology exist beyond John Howard Yoder, his serial sexual violence is indicative of the risk taken when Anabaptist peace theology is not organized around the problem of violence in its sexual form.²⁴

Third, Anabaptists must develop concrete spiritual, theological, and social practices that enable political action in solidarity with survivors when certainty regarding the facts of survivors' testimonies is not available. We need strategies. We need creativity, imagination, and innovation. We need to bring all of the tools of the tradition and all of the wisdom of our global neighbors to bear on the task of dislodging sexual violence from our homes, our communities, and our churches.

Sustaining a long-term focus on sexual violence, reorganizing the pursuit of peace to center that focus, and developing practical strategies of political solidarity with survivors are three steps necessary for Anabaptist theology and practice to hold possibility open with respect to survivors' testimonies of sexual violence today. In doing so, Anabaptist theology and practice will have the opportunity to begin to bear witness to the sexual violence perpetrated against Jesus and to the possibility that his crucifixion included sexual assault. This is only a beginning. The road ahead is long. Its paths twist through decidedly uncertain terrain. We must prepare ourselves for a demanding journey and commit ourselves to the generations-long task of seeing it through.

---

²³See, for example, Elizabeth G. Yoder, *Peace Theology and Violence against Women* (Elkhart, IN: Institute of Mennonite Studies, 1992); Susan Thistlethwaite, *Women's Bodies as Battlefield: Christian Theology and the Global War on Women* (New York: Palgrave Macmillan), 2015.

²⁴For an assessment of John Howard Yoder's sexually violent behavior and its impact, see Rachel Waltner Goossen, "'Defanging the Beast': Mennonite Responses to John Howard Yoder's Sexual Abuse," *Mennonite Quarterly Review* 89, no. 1 (January 2015): 7–80, esp. 52–80.

PART FOUR

Responding to and Learning from John Howard Yoder's Sexual Violence

10

Repairing the Moral Canopy after Institutional Betrayal

Sara Wenger Shenk

Rarely have I spoken about the institutional processes that lay behind Rachel Waltner Goossen's January 2015 *Mennonite Quarterly Review* article "'Defanging the Beast': Mennonite Responses to John Howard Yoder's Sexual Abuse."[1] Yet, on January 7, 2017, I served on a panel at the Society of Christian Ethics (SCE) in New Orleans with Stanley Hauerwas and Traci West to do just that. Moderator Karen Guth asked us to reflect on professional and institutional responses to the sordid sexual legacy of John Howard Yoder, a former professor of theology at Anabaptist Mennonite Biblical Seminary (AMBS) and renowned peace theologian who also taught at Notre Dame and in many venues around the world, sponsored by peace, education, and mission-related agencies. The overall theme of this SCE annual meeting was "Structural Evil, Individual Harm, Personal Responsibility." Yoder was a former president of the SCE and influenced the peace ethics of many participants, which prompted that year's stated intent to reflect self-critically on issues of sexual violence, professional ethics, and the problem of complicity. In my invitation to the panel, I was told, "Because of your leadership in guiding AMBS through the institutional complexities of Yoder's case . . . the SCE believes it has much to learn from your experience and insight, and we very much hope you will consider participating." Among the learnings sought from the panel was this: "What can we learn from Mennonite institutional responses to Yoder's harmful legacy?"

Although I am not a peace theologian by academic discipline, others have helped me see that the institutional work we did at AMBS and in Mennonite Church USA (MC USA) is germane to everything peace theology is about. We acted out of theologically informed convictions to walk in the nonviolent way of Jesus. These convictions emboldened us at AMBS to listen to victims of sexual violence, call for transparency and truth-telling, adjudicate wisely when discerning next steps, confess our institutional complicity in exacerbating the harm victims of Yoder experienced on AMBS's watch, and apologize. We apologized for having failed to live up to our commitment to the gospel of Jesus Christ and for having failed

---

[1] Rachel Waltner Goossen, "'Defanging the Beast': Mennonite Responses to John Howard Yoder's Sexual Abuse," *Mennonite Quarterly Review* 89, no. 1 (January 2015): 7–80.

to exercise the moral authority that was our sacred responsibility as an institution committed to teaching and modeling a theology of peace. We sought explicitly to embody how we as individuals and institutions are called to walk in the way of Jesus and make peace with each other, our neighbors, and even with those who regard us with antipathy and hate—our enemies. I hope the narrative I share here will encourage other institutions facing their own challenges and histories of abuse to imagine how they might respond in ways that liberate captives to the violence of sexual abuse—the perpetrators, the victims, and those who cover up the abuse.

With that hope in mind, I offer in this chapter gleanings from a significant collection of materials. As a practical theologian, I seek to listen intently and interdisciplinarily in order to gather up fragments of evidence, synthesize a composite picture of what I see or is revealed to me, and provide a framework of interpretation that I trust has ethical and theological resonance with our deepest commitment to the gospel's imperative to proclaim release to the captive and to set the oppressed free. I share from our AMBS institutional story (which throughout is interwoven with MC USA's processes). I speak from my perspective as a president who led AMBS through the complexities of revisiting Yoder's sexual abuse history: key decisions, guiding priorities, and performative actions spoken and taken.[2] This was a journey over several years, thankfully taken in the company of courageous, wise collaborators—including, most importantly, victims of Yoder's sexual experimentation and violence. Undergirding this narrative is my reflection on why I see wise judgment, truth-telling, and authoritative institutional action as theologically informed, moral imperatives.

Prior to 2013, the legacy of AMBS leadership relative to Yoder's sexual exploitation was mostly silence or alignment with the official narrative that Yoder had cooperated with the disciplinary process and was commended for writing and teaching again in the church. That all changed as AMBS leaders, including the two primary women leaders (president and academic dean), determined that for

---

[2] Michelle Sokol, "Mennonite Seminary Apologizes to Victims of Famed Theologian John Howard Yoder," *National Catholic Reporter*, April 9, 2015, https://www.ncronline.org/news/accountability/mennonite-seminary-apologizes-victims-famed-theologian-john-howard-yoder.

the sake of the gospel of Jesus Christ, the victims of Yoder's sexual exploitation, and AMBS's integrity as a learning community, the truth must be told. And because of Jesus, we believed that when we discover the truth and share it publicly, we are all set free.

Personal Narrative

When I came to AMBS as president in the fall of 2010, I was minimally aware of the shadow of Yoder's legacy that lingered over the institution. I had never studied at AMBS and met Yoder only once in passing, not long before his death in 1997. I remember well when his *Politics of Jesus* came out in the early 1970s and the thrill it was for me and my college peers to watch a Mennonite peace theologian articulate such a groundbreaking paradigm for peace theology—and become a rock star. Over the years, I paid cursory attention to his writings and occasionally referenced them in my own writing. I heard many colleagues in all kinds of venues reference his work with appreciation.

I largely assumed, as did many persons, that the church-based disciplinary process that extended from 1992 to 1996 had adequately dealt with the problem. I assumed that that process had succeeded in getting Yoder to acknowledge his sexual violations and that there had been worthy grounds for recommending—in the words of the 1996 press release—that "the church (again) use his gifts of writing and teaching."[3] And many persons did use his writing and teaching—not only Mennonites but also in widening interdenominational and international circles of influence. Books, articles, and doctoral dissertations seemed to multiply by the day (as most peace theologians and practitioners know better than I). There were jests about how Yoderian scholarship had become something of its own publishing industry.

After arriving at AMBS, I discovered, however, not enthusiasm about Yoder but sobriety—a circumspect, critical thoughtfulness by those who had been through the fire a couple of decades earlier and an attentiveness to unfinished work. In my second year (2011), one

---

[3]Press release, "Disciplinary Process with Yoder Concludes," *Gospel Herald*, June 18, 1996: 11.

of the senior professors, Ted Koontz, approached then academic dean Rebecca Slough and me to describe his awareness of ongoing concern among some of Yoder's victims. He wondered whether there was more work that AMBS should do. I asked about what internal work AMBS faculty had recently done and how cognizant the new faculty were, for example, of the institution's history with Yoder. We three agreed that it seemed timely, given the turnover in faculty and what appeared to be the burgeoning popularity of Yoder's scholarship in the wider scholarly world, for AMBS to do some internal work (1) to develop and review a historical timeline, (2) to hear from victims' ongoing concerns, and (3) to develop a shared understanding of how we would teach and communicate about Yoder's theology and sexual exploitation going forward.

We set up three sessions with the AMBS faculty to do this work. Following the second session, a leading advocate for sexual abuse victims, Carolyn Holderread Heggen, who was herself a victim of Yoder's abuse, honored dean Slough and me with her in-depth story of violation and the prolonged resistance a former president of AMBS, Marlin Miller, had shown in response to her impassioned pleas for him to intervene more directly in the 1980s and early 1990s. Heggen, who has been publicly identified with this story,[4] pleaded with us, out of her love for the church and AMBS, to make things right. She knew that a fuller telling of the story must happen. She also suspected the existence of AMBS files rendered inaccessible from public review since she knew of files from other church-based disciplinary processes that had been made inaccessible.

Heggen's story and plea prompted me into action. I did background work to learn what files there might be and to ascertain whether there were any legally binding reasons they could not be made accessible. I learned that, while there would be legal risks in making them accessible for research and publication, I could decide to do so, which I determined to do in March–April 2012 when I found a historian up to the task.

Within a year or so after AMBS had done the internal work referenced above, I was invited to co-chair with Ervin Stutzman, then MC USA executive director, an MC USA denominational discernment group convened to review the broader scope of Yoder's

---

[4]Goossen, "Defanging the Beast," 54.

sexual violations while working for other Mennonite agencies. For a time, I wore two hats, one for AMBS and one for the broader church. I was fortunate to collaborate with and learn from colleagues in the denominational discernment group and at AMBS as well as, most importantly, the survivors of Yoder's abuse.

Institutional Narrative

There was no guidebook that I was aware of to show the way. Over and over again, I discovered (always in consultation with others) what was needed next by first taking a step that seemed to align with my internal moral compass and then prayerfully discerning how the way opened onto the next necessary move. Reflecting back, I can identify several priorities that became guiding motifs for me in my leadership role at AMBS: (1) the need for transparency and documentation to learn what had happened; (2) the desire for victims to help guide the process, to show us what needed to be done; and (3) the need to figure out what it would mean to take institutional responsibility even when the horrible things happened on someone else's watch. Rather than emerging full-blown in an explicit way at the beginning of the process, these priorities came into focus gradually as we moved forward, step by step. I often wondered what it meant to take institutional responsibility when this happened on someone else's watch. How could I apologize on their behalf? Initially I didn't think I could do it with integrity. Yet, reflecting on how an institution is a living organism, I realized that telling the truth about what happened in an earlier stage of its life might bring release and healing for those violated and for the institution itself.

Transparency and Documentation—Truth-Telling and Breaking the Silence

I observed early on what I referred to as shadow boxing—dueling allegations about what happened based on partial information or misinformation that people latched onto as their defining narrative. My driving motivation quickly became to learn what could be known about my own institution. If there was information available that could shed light on the situation, I wanted to find it in order to better understand what had happened. How complicit had AMBS leaders been? What had they attempted in listening to victims? What had been done to hold Yoder accountable that was never reported publicly? What documents were there that hadn't been accessible and what story did they tell? I signaled my intention in a July 2013 public blog post: "As the current president of AMBS, I'm committed to a new transparency in the truth telling that must happen. We must strive to get the facts straight, to acknowledge healing work that has been done, and to shoulder the urgent healing work that must still be done."[5]

While I heard much relief and gratitude in response to this call for transparency, I also heard major objections to opening things up again, including objections from prominent church leaders. The dominant narrative, that there had been repentance on Yoder's part and reconciliation with the church, had been in place for many years. We were accused of retrying a dead man, of damaging the peace witness of the church, of scapegoating Yoder, of adding pain to the family, of looking backward vengefully instead of forgiving and allowing the disciplinary process report to stand as a reliable outcome. And there was the occasional threat that legal action would be brought against AMBS.

Stutzman and I were fortunate to find (and persuade) an eminently qualified historian, Rachel Waltner Goossen, who could work fairly, professionally, and sensitively with the AMBS documents I made available. We also were able—with others' help, including Heggen's and Goossen's—to persuade church-related agencies, church leaders, and some victims to release files, share written evidence, and participate in interviews. It took enormous effort to create the conditions under which persons felt safe and authorized to tell their part of a story that had been cloaked in silence for decades. Goossen's new, extensive, credible, and historically contextualized official story was made public through the January 2015 *Mennonite Quarterly Review* article mentioned above. This article was meant to replace what had been the official story: the brief June 1996 news

---

[5]Sara Wenger Shenk, "Revisiting the Legacy of John Howard Yoder," Practicing Reconciliation Blog, July 25, 2013, https://www.ambs.edu/publishing/blog/715800/revisiting-the-legacy-of-john-howard-yoder.

release following the conclusion of the church-based disciplinary process—a process and announced outcome that lacked credibility from the perspective of Yoder's victims.

Listening to the Voices and Perspectives of Victims

The most gratifying aspect of the journey back into this sordid, sad story was to have such good counselors and comrades on the way: women who had been victimized by Yoder or, in some cases, by others. Their generous sharing made it possible to see reality from their perspective. Repeatedly these women assured us with comments such as this: "There is much for which the church needs to repent in this sad story. But it is exciting to imagine what blessings of spiritual vitality and missional effectiveness might await us as a church and her institutions if we will confess, make amends, learn from our tragic mistakes, and bring some measure of closure to this unfinished story." And this: "Your vision promises to renew and reinvigorate our Church in ways we've never dreamed before. With sincerest gratitude." These courageous, resilient, and wise women served as consultants and editors and joined in planning aspects of worship services of lament, confession, and commitment.

Taking Institutional Responsibility

I remember well the moment when it became clear to me that we at AMBS needed to offer our own institutional acknowledgment and apology. For a while, I had thought we could simply be included in a denominationally based service of lament since AMBS was one of many church-related organizations and leaders that had failed to hold Yoder accountable. In some ways, that would have been the reasonable thing to do. Yet, given the prominence and extent of AMBS's association with Yoder, coming in under the denominational umbrella came to seem deficient to me. The recognition crystallized as I drove to work one day. I realized that we had an AMBS-specific moral obligation: to ourselves as an institution—a living-breathing learning community—and, most importantly, to those victimized at AMBS or because AMBS hadn't told the truth about Yoder's sexual exploits in a timely, decisive way. We needed to offer an AMBS-specific public acknowledgment, a public service of confession and lament that named our institutional failure and directly honored the courage of those who called us to account.

Services of Lament, Confession, and Commitment

Academic dean Slough and I led a team to plan the AMBS services of lament, confession, and commitment for March 2015. The team was composed of six women and two men: one of Yoder's victims, three AMBS professors, a student studying pastoral care, and an AMBS alumna. Slough drew on her many years of study of ritual and worship to help in developing the services. We consulted with retired faculty, administrators, and a former board chair who had served when Yoder was at AMBS. We drew up goals to guide our planning, making our intent for the services explicit on our AMBS website and to anyone who inquired, particularly victims who were considering whether it would feel safe to participate in the services:

- for AMBS to host an event that ensures physical, psychological, and spiritual safety for all who choose to attend;
- for AMBS to confess its organizational failures;
- for AMBS to express sorrow and regret and to apologize for its inadequate response to women hurt by Yoder's actions;
- for AMBS to commit to policies and practices of timely action, transparency, accountability, and preventive intervention when dealing with sexual misconduct and abuse;
- for women victimized by Yoder's behavior and AMBS's inadequate responses to feel a new sense of release and freedom;
- for AMBS to participate in a larger denominational effort to recompense in at least a small measure some of the material costs women undertook on their road to healing;
- for AMBS and all present to pray in hope for healing, commit to solidarity with all victims (direct or indirect) of

sexual and/or physical violation, renew resolve to guard the safety of everyone, and grow in moral courage as leaders for God's reconciling mission in the world.

Being transparent and as clear as we knew to be about what was expected of each service, who was invited, who would be speaking, whether the press would have access, and so on was absolutely critical for assuring victims that it would be safe to participate and that these services were designed with their needs and hopes at the center of our planning.

Our gatherings unfolded as follows. In order to allow for open fellowship and a felt need for remembering and shared consolation among alumni who had been at AMBS during Yoder's years, we planned a March 21 evening reunion event. Current faculty and administrators were present to engage with questions and perspectives. On March 22, we offered a morning service designed to "honor the women's truth." This was not open to the public. It was an intimate gathering of truth-telling, reflection, and prayer for those who were victimized by Yoder while they were at AMBS and those bearing witness to their experience. AMBS employees were present to receive the stories of those who chose to speak. Designated trauma support persons were on hand throughout the day for anyone desiring additional accompaniment. Following the morning service, AMBS faculty led a cleansing pilgrimage throughout seminary rooms and spaces where Yoder worked and some of the abuse had occurred.

The afternoon included a public service of lament, confession, and commitment. In this service, AMBS administrators and board members expressed sorrow for the harm done while Yoder was a member of the faculty, confessed and apologized for AMBS's inadequate responses, and expressed commitment to ongoing transparency and to fostering healing. This service included a psalm of lament for abused women, a statement from a former board chair who had presided over some of the deliberations related to Yoder, a statement of confession and apology by me as president, a commitment statement by the board, an employee commitment statement, evocative visual art and ritual, Scripture, songs, witness "to what we have seen and heard" by a representative for Yoder's victims, and a concluding sermon, "The Year of the Lord's Favor," again by me as president.⁶ Here is an excerpt of my public apology as president on behalf of the school:

> I am sorry. I am sorry that trusted leaders injured, disregarded, and devalued you.
>
> I am sorry that we neglected to genuinely listen to your reports of violation: and that even after hearing your warnings, we failed to raise the alarm.
>
> I am sorry that by choosing to remain silent about your violation, we isolated you, only deepening your sense of betrayal.
>
> I am sorry that in our exhaustion and desire for closure, we didn't listen to those of you who said, this is not finished; the full truth of what happened has not yet been named.
>
> Above all, I am sorry that we failed to exercise the moral authority that was our sacred responsibility.
>
> What was done to you, whether sinful acts of commission or omission, was grievously wrong. It should never have been allowed to happen. We failed you. We failed the church. We failed the Gospel of Jesus Christ.
>
> Yet we are not left without hope. We long for your restored trust; even on some distant day, for your forgiveness. Kyrie eleison.

At the conclusion of these two intense days, I heard emotional and sometimes jubilant testimonies from former and current AMBS community members about what a "catharsis" the storytelling, cleansing, and worship experiences were for AMBS. I heard from many victims of sexual abuse about their profound relief—the "release from captivity" that they had longed and labored for over many years, paid a great price for, and now welcomed with tears of gratitude. It had been a community-wide effort—drawing from the wisdom of victims of sexual abuse, those who work with victims, theologians, pastoral care specialists, family members, institutional leaders, professors, and students—to begin to repair what had been

---

⁶"AMBS Response to Victims of John H. Yoder Abuse," http://www.ambs.edu/about/ambs-response-to-victims-of-yoder-abuse.

grievously torn: the moral canopy meant to provide shelter and safety for a community to flourish.

Mending the Moral Canopy

In all of the above, I was motived by a desire to use whatever moral authority I had, and we had as an institution, to repair what I have come to describe as a "moral canopy" that had been so badly ripped.[7] The image of a moral canopy describes a shared, explicit, moral framework essential for persons to meaningfully engage in difficult communal conversations and actions with integrity, transparency, trust, and mutual respect. When leaders and those we trust abuse power and harm vulnerable persons, they badly damage the moral canopy of a faith community. No human community has survived without finding or constructing shelters from the elemental forces that threaten us all. This is true both physically and spiritually. What we need as Anabaptist communities committed to peace is a storm-worthy moral canopy under which we can stand together, even with our differences.[8]

As part of reweaving or repairing a canopy, those of us on whose watch horrendous violations occur must do what we can to provide a transparent, truthful account of what happened. We must say clearly that what happened should never have happened and that we are sorry for what we did or did not do that allowed persons to be harmed. The canopy can only begin to be painstakingly patched or restored when leaders and others involved say publicly and wholeheartedly that what happened was horribly wrong and a violation of our most cherished confessions and convictions. I offer three factors required to mend this tear in the moral canopy—for the community, for victims, and, yes, even for the perpetrator: (1) institutional betrayal, exacerbating

---

[7]Sara Wenger Shenk, "Arguing Our Way toward a Storm-worthy Moral Canopy," Practicing Reconciliation Blog, January 5, 2017, https://www.ambs.edu/publishing/blog/841477/arguing-our-way-toward-a-stormworthy-moral-canopy. Rebecca Slough uses a similar image, "a canopy of promises," to describe "a safe theological and therapeutic place for victim-survivors." Rebecca Slough, "Congregational Responses to Abuse and Trauma: The Persistent Hope of Shalom," *Mennonite Quarterly Review* 89, no. 1 (January 2015): 98.

[8]Shenk, "Arguing Our Way."

the impact of traumatic experiences on individual victims, must be acknowledged; (2) documented knowledge must be acquired, shared, and acknowledged as truthful in the community at large; (3) public apology by leaders who carry the moral authority associated with the institution must be offered. Acknowledging institutional betrayal, telling the truth, and taking responsibility in public on behalf of the institution were necessary actions to begin to repair the moral integrity of the canopy meant to provide shelter for our community of faith.

Institutional Betrayal Acknowledged

Inasmuch as harmful actions happened on the institution's watch and undermined the moral values AMBS stands for, we determined that decisive action was needed. In light of the felt betrayal by earlier leaders, we needed to offer a public confession and apology from the institution.

A graduate student from Brandeis University helped to deepen my understanding of the repercussions of institutional betrayal on victims of sexual exploitation—something I had known largely intuitively and experientially. She contacted me in October 2017 and asked for an interview. She was studying the way institutions respond to incidents of sexual violence perpetrated within or in connection to the institution. "My goal is to develop a framework," she said, "of best practices when it comes to handling these incidents at emotional and spiritual levels." She had read many of my articles and blog posts surrounding the Yoder events, particularly the blog post "But I've seen him do so much good."[9] She repeatedly expressed her gratitude for the work AMBS has done as an institution and how rare it is. She pointed me to an article describing the sense of institutional betrayal related to an incident of sexual assault at Notre Dame when the university declined to comment publicly or speak with the victim's parents after their daughter's suicide. The university's response deepened the parents' sense of betrayal. "It

---

[9]Sara Wenger Shenk, "But I've Seen Him Do So Much Good," Practicing Reconciliation Blog, September 16, 2016, https://www.ambs.edu/blog/715868/but-i-ve-seen-him-do-so-much-good.

is not our intention to take down this great institution," they said. "But it has disappointed us. That hurts, and it hurts our family."[10]

Researchers Carly Parnitzke Smith and Jennifer Freyd describe how institutions have the potential to either worsen post-traumatic outcomes or become sources of justice, support, and healing. The authors describe the impact of institutional action and inaction and the ways inaction exacerbates the impact of traumatic experiences. Calling that inaction *institutional betrayal*, they write, "Understanding the exacerbative effects of this type of betrayal can help the clinician and the client make sense of otherwise perplexing reactions to traumatic experiences."[11]

It was profoundly evident that what victims were grieving in the Yoder saga was not only that a renowned professor violated them but also that the institutions responsible to hold him accountable had egregiously failed to do so, intensifying their pain exponentially. So any public acknowledgment needed to be twofold—both to tell the truth about the scope and nature of Yoder's violations and to tell the truth about AMBS's failures to hold him publicly accountable.

Factual Knowledge and Truthful Acknowledgment in the Commons

Based on widespread feedback I have received from many faith communities where I have traveled in Canada, the United States, and beyond—and based on what I have heard directly from victims of sexual abuse by Yoder and others—I believe we achieved a more truthful, complete, and complex documentation of factual knowledge than previously existed. With the publication of the January 2015 issue of *Mennonite Quarterly Review*, we also saw how factual truth that was widely read and acknowledged in the community at large was experienced as profoundly liberating and healing.

---

[10]S. St. Clair and T. Lighty, "'It Feels Like a Betrayal': Notre Dame's Inquiry of Alleged Sex Attack Upsets Parents of Teen Who Accused Athlete, Killed Herself," *Chicago Tribune*, December 16, 2010, http://articles.chicagotribune.com/2010-12-16/news/chi-20101216-nd-story_1_mary-seeberg-campus-police-notre-dame, cited by Carly Parnitzke Smith and Jennifer J. Freyd, "Institutional Betrayal," *American Psychologist* 69, no. 6 (2014): 575, http://dx.doi.org/10.1037/a0037564.

[11]Smith and Freyd, "Institutional Betrayal," 584.

This factor in mending the moral canopy was stated most succinctly to me by Ruth Krall, retired professor of religion, nursing, and psychology at Goshen College, who has written extensively about Yoder and advocated for sexual abuse victims and prevention. Krall made the following observations after reading Stanley Cohen's *States of Denial: Knowledge about Atrocities and Suffering*.[12] She wrote,

> For healing to occur there needs to be truthful, complete, complex factual knowledge and there needs to be truthful and honest acknowledgment of that knowledge in the commons—the actual facts of what occurred revealed in the commons and acknowledged as truthful. Knowledge and acknowledgment—the two essentials for healing the wounds of sexual violation done by an elevated, therefore, elite member of a religious community. It is not only that knowledge and acknowledgment of factual truth heals survivors; it can heal perpetrators, those who protect perpetrators, and the entire community of collusion and complicity.[13]

She continued, "Victims can heal by their own emotional and spiritual work—but perpetrators need an informed community in order to heal; and communities need both factual knowledge and truthful acknowledgement in order to heal."[14] She lamented that Yoder, the perpetrator, was never able to benefit from factual knowledge that was widely shared and widely acknowledged "in the commons" as truthful.

Public Apology by Leaders with Moral Authority

The public services of lament, confession, and commitment were important in furthering the work of healing.[15] Not only did we

---

[12]Stanley Cohen, *States of Denial: Knowing about Atrocities and Suffering* (Cambridge, UK: Polity, 2001).
[13]Personal e-mail, September 18, 2016.
[14]Personal e-mail, September 18, 2016.
[15]"AMBS Response to Victims of John H. Yoder Abuse," http://www.ambs.edu/about/ambs-response-to-victims-of-yoder-abuse.

confess our institutional failures, we also directly apologized. The need for direct apology as distinct from confession and lament was brought to my attention by academic dean Slough. She mentioned the book *Sorry About That: The Language of Public Apology*, in which author Edwin Battistella points out the difference between apologies and confessions and lays out the various dimensions of apology.[16] According to Battistella, apologies, in contrast to other forms of confession, explicitly acknowledge and take responsibility for harm that was done to the victim. This counsel to speak direct words of apology shaped our approach to the public service, providing a pivotal, authoritative, and performative action that elicited tears of relief. What happened was not perfect, nor did it bring full closure, but there was an acknowledged catharsis, a genuine and deeply appreciated turning point for key participants in this sad story. Through such acts, the moral canopy begins to be repaired and, once again, to provide shelter for community flourishing.

By making our apology publicly, we were also able to begin repairing the moral canopy beyond the circle of those directly affected by Yoder's actions. In the weeks and months following our public services of lament, confession, and commitment, I heard from many women who had engaged with what was posted on the AMBS website and, possibly, in news reports about the events. A president emerita of a sister seminary who watched the service on the AMBS website wrote to me with gratitude for AMBS's boldness in "naming and accepting institutional responsibility for the failure to confront evil and sickness," which is "rarely witnessed in institutional leadership." A survivor of sexual abuse wrote to me of the "deep and profound effect" reading the text of the services on the website had on her, concluding, "AMBS has modeled for conferences, congregations, and other parts of the church how to deal with the very difficult problem of sexual abuse by leaders of the church." Likewise, after viewing the service materials on the website, homiletics professor Joni S. Sancken reached out to request an interview for a book she was writing that explores preaching in a context of trauma. In her book, she cites AMBS as a model of

---

[16]Edwin L. Battistella, *Sorry About That: The Language of Public Apology* (New York: Oxford University Press, 2014).

how public acknowledgment of institutional failures can itself be an act of repairing the moral canopy. Sancken writes, "Wenger Shenk's boldness in calling out present day leaders, empowering the witness of survivors, and seeking reconciliation and healing as a means of glorifying God serves as a testimony that can contribute to the very reconciliation, restoration, and healing that she seeks and serves as an example for other preachers."[17]

Concluding Thoughts

I have often heard people express ambivalence about the necessity of judgment in the exercise of leadership. Most of us have experienced harsh and unfair judgment at some point in our lives and usually find those who sharply judge others to be intolerant and lacking in mercy. What is often overlooked, it seems to me, is the necessity of leaders to exercise wise judgment and trustworthy authority in order to restore justice on behalf of those who are marginalized, silenced, and shamed and to extend mercy to all who have been captive to misinformation and fear.[18] I am grateful that the leadership AMBS offered was largely experienced as wise judgment and trustworthy authority that made credible again a theology of peace grounded in our tradition as a peace church, our stated convictions as a Mennonite seminary, and Jesus's life, ministry, death, and resurrection.

I offer a few words from the final sermon of our AMBS public service of lament, confession, and commitment:

> We've all seen graphic images of bombed out buildings, entire city blocks blown to smithereens, homes and lives shattered by violence. What we've been slow to see—more like, deliberately

---

[17]Joni S. Sancken, *Words That Heal: Preaching Hope to Wounded Souls* (Nashville: Abingdon, 2019), 62. For a similar assessment see Darryl W. Stephens, "A Deacon's Eye for Healing Congregations," *Currents in Theology and Mission* 42, no. 3 (July 2015): 213–19.

[18]At a formative time in my identity as a woman leader, I was inspired by Carol Lakey Hess's description of Deborah, the prophet spoken of in Judges 4–5. Carol Lakey Hess, *Caretakers of Our Common Household: Women's Development in Communities of Faith* (Nashville: Abingdon, 1997), 215–25.

avoided seeing—is the devastation of sexual violence. It's an insidious, stealthy, often invisible devastation that creeps in to dismantle lives, destroy reputations, shatter families, and poison entire communities with its ruination. But we're here today, in the good company of Isaiah, and of Jesus and the Spirit to testify with joy that ruination is not the end of the story.

Isaiah declares, "They shall build up the ancient ruins, they shall raise up the former devastations; they shall repair the ruined cities, the devastations of many generations" (Isa. 61:4). Who are these builders? Who is it that builds up the ancient ruins, that raises up the devastations, even the devastations of many generations? Well, it's not the high and mighty, the successful and powerful who come back with their big earth moving machines to set all to rights. No. It's the broken hearted. It's those who've been oppressed. It's the ones who know what it is to be held captive. Yes. This is what astonishes us. This is the dumbfounding good news of the gospel. It's those who mourn, who have been faint in spirit who will be called "oaks of righteousness." Oaks of righteousness. A "planting of the Lord, to display his glory . . ." (Isa. 61:3).

- When the truth is publicly declared and sets us free, *we give glory to God.*
- When the brokenhearted and faint spirited tell their stories and show the way to rebuild our communities, *we give glory to God.*
- When prophetic women stand as oaks of righteousness calling the rest of us toward repentance and salvation, *we give glory to God.*
- When powerful men protect, dignify, and empower vulnerable women and children, *we give glory to God.*
- When children are unafraid and no one hurts or destroys on God's holy mountain, *we give glory to God.*
- When what is good and praiseworthy endures despite our massive failures, *we give glory to God.* . . .

In the strong love of God—where nothing is wasted, nothing is lost, we use what was broken to rebuild the ancient ruins;

we become builders who repair the devastations of many generations.[19]

The above proclamations make clear the theologically informed convictions that emboldened us at AMBS to listen to victims of sexual violence, call for transparency and truth-telling, adjudicate wisely when discerning next steps, confess our institutional complicity in exacerbating the harm victims of Yoder experienced on AMBS's watch, and apologize. The renewed freedom, healing, and joy many of us experienced inspire us to walk in the nonviolent way of Jesus with a new spring in our steps, light in our spirits, integrity in our public witness, and flourishing in our life together.

---

[19]Service of Lament, Confession, and Commitment, March 22, 2015, Chapel of the Sermon on the Mount, Anabaptist Mennonite Biblical Seminary, Elkhart, Indiana, https://www.youtube.com/watch?v=Frjqi696KDc.

11

Adopting the 2015 MC USA Churchwide Statement on Sexual Abuse

Linda Gehman Peachey

In 2013, Mennonite Church USA (MC USA) initiated a new process to attend to the ongoing painful legacy of John Howard Yoder's sexual violence. Those who knew this history found it distressing that his reputation as a theologian and ethicist kept growing, as scholars continued to study his work and publish his writings even after his abuses had been made public.[1] Women especially began speaking up again and sharing their concerns with church leaders. For instance, Carolyn Holderread Heggen spoke to Sara Wenger Shenk and Rebecca Slough, then president and dean at Anabaptist Mennonite Biblical Seminary (AMBS), to request action by this seminary where Yoder had taught.[2] She also spoke with Elizabeth Soto Albrecht, moderator of MC USA, and Ervin Stutzman, MC USA executive director. Heggen and others called on the church to give a more complete accounting of Yoder's behavior and the church's failure to adequately address it or care for those he harmed.[3] MC USA and AMBS then formed a six-member discernment group to guide this process.[4]

---

[1] In 2010, for example, Gordon Houser wrote an article in *The Mennonite*, highlighting the continuing influence of Yoder's thought, with ten books to be published that year. He made no mention of Yoder's abuse but stressed the value of Yoder's insights for our churches. Gordon Houser, "Yoder Books Keep Coming," *The Mennonite* 13, no. 6 (June 2010): 59.

[2] Herself a survivor of Yoder's abuse, Heggen has been an important voice for victims and survivors in the Mennonite Church. Carolyn Holderread Heggen, *Sexual Abuse in Christian Homes and Churches* (Scottdale, PA: Herald, 1993). As the author of this influential book and someone who for many years was a speaker on sexual violence and an advocate for victims, she heard many stories and reports of Yoder's sexual abuse and knew it was a widespread problem. For more details about her conversation at AMBS, see Shenk's chapter in this volume, "Repairing the Moral Canopy after Institutional Betrayal."

[3] For a timeline of some of the activities and articles related to this process, see MC USA, "John Howard Yoder Digest," March 5, 2015, http://mennoniteusa.org/resource/john-howard-yoder-digest/.

[4] The Discernment Group included Ervin Stutzman and Sara Wenger Shenk as co-chairs, and Ted Koontz, Chuck Neufeld, Linda Gehman Peachey, and Regina Shands Stoltzfus. Carolyn Holderread Heggen also served as an adviser to the group, as a survivor and important connection to other survivors and their questions, comments, and suggestions. Daniel Miller, Conference Pastor for Indiana-Michigan Mennonite Conference, joined the group as a listener in July 2014, in order to keep the conference apprised of our work, since that conference had played such a significant role in Yoder's discipline process in 1992-6.

I write as a member of this group, one who was significantly involved in writing the statement emerging from its work. My concerns and expertise grew out of more than fifteen years of working on peace and justice issues at Mennonite Central Committee (MCC) and, most recently, as director of women's advocacy from 2004 to 2011. During those years, I wrote and collaborated on numerous resources for MCC US on abuse response and prevention, addressing child abuse, sexualized violence, and pornography. I also had the opportunity to hear women's stories of abuse and their efforts toward justice and healing.

Over its two-year existence, the discernment group took a number of important steps, including preparing a church-wide statement, the full text of which is included as an appendix. In this chapter, I outline the major events and concerns that led to drafting and passing the Churchwide Statement on Sexual Abuse and steps taken since 2015 to work on implementation.[5] I also describe some of the challenges encountered in the writing process along with ongoing issues the church still needs to address.

Work of the Discernment Group

The work of the discernment group included:

- encouraging MennoMedia (the publishing agency of MC USA and MC Canada) to include a statement in Yoder's books acknowledging his sexual violence;[6]

---

[5]This chapter, thus, functions as a continuation of the overview I provided in 2015. Linda Gehman Peachey, "Naming the Pain, Seeking the Light: The Mennonite Church's Response to Sexual Abuse," *Mennonite Quarterly Review* 89, no. 1 (January 2015): 111–28.

[6]The statement approved by the board of directors for inclusion in Yoder's books reads:

> John Howard Yoder (1927–1997) was perhaps the most well-known Mennonite theologian in the 20th century. While his work on Christian ethics helped define Anabaptism to an audience far outside the Mennonite Church, he is also remembered for his long-term sexual harassment and abuse of women. At Herald Press we recognize the complex tensions involved in presenting work by someone who called Christians to reconciliation and yet used his position of power to

- authorizing historian Rachel Waltner Goossen to document accurately the nature and scope of Yoder's abuse and the church's efforts to address his behavior;[7]
- assembling resources on responding to and preventing sexual abuse;[8]
- creating a "Care and Prevention Fund" to provide some compensation to sexual abuse survivors;
- organizing workshops and a Service of Lament and Hope at the 2015 biennial convention;
- writing the 2015 Churchwide Statement on Sexual Abuse, passed by the MC USA delegate body on July 3, 2015.[9]

A major purpose of the statement was to commit the church to a deeper understanding of the roots of sexual abuse and to more prevention, training, and accountability across the denomination. The discernment group therefore tried to articulate some of the life-giving truths from our faith that we need to embody more faithfully along with the distorted strands within Christian history and theology that need to be rejected. We also listed specific actions and commitments for both congregations and church institutions.

Following standard practice, church leaders presented the statement to the 2015 MC USA delegate body for discussion and

---

abuse others. We believe that Yoder and those who write about his work deserve to be heard; we also believe readers should know that Yoder engaged in abusive behavior. This book is published with the hope that those studying Yoder's writings will not dismiss the complexity of these issues and will instead wrestle with, evaluate and learn from Yoder's work in the full context of his personal, scholarly and churchly legacy.

See MennoMedia, "Yoder Books to Include Publisher's Statement," *Mennonite World Review*, December 23, 2013, http://www.mennoworld.org/archived/2013/12/23/yoder-books-include-publishers-statement/.

[7]Goossen published her findings in January 2015. Rachel Waltner Goossen, "'Defanging the Beast': Mennonite Responses to John Howard Yoder's Sexual Abuse," *Mennonite Quarterly Review* 89, no. 1 (January 2015): 7–80.

[8]MC USA, "Resources on Sexual Abuse Response and Prevention," http://mennonitusa.org/resources-on-sexual-abuse-response-and-prevention/.

[9]MC USA, "Churchwide Statement on Sexual Abuse," July 3, 2015, http://mennonitusa.org/wp-content/uploads/2015/07/Churchwide_Statement_On_Sexual_Abuse_2015July03.pdf.

feedback. Elizabeth Soto Albrecht, moderator of MC USA at that time, later described her strong feelings about this statement to me in an e-mail: "I had to pray with all my strength to lead an objective process regarding something that was totally subjective in my soul." As she elaborated, of the seven statements passed that year, "this one was especially close to my heart, and I selfishly needed this Statement to pass on the delegate floor when they voted. I understood that what was at stake was my own woundedness and that of many women in the church who were victims of sexual abuse." To her surprise, "there were not really any strong opposing voices when the floor mic opened, other than that the statement could be stronger and it should include men."[10] When the vote took place, it passed overwhelmingly.

Many feared, however, that the statement would remain just an aspiration, with little energy or resources devoted to carrying it out. Especially concerned was the steering committee of the Women in Leadership Project, who wrote to the MC USA executive director that summer, urging that a group be designated to oversee the implementation of the statement. The executive board staff cabinet then partnered with Mennonite Education Agency to form a six-member Panel on Sexual Abuse Prevention to guide the denomination's work for a limited time. This group served from January 2016 to January 2018 and, among other tasks, created a resource for responding to sexual abuse by noncredentialed individuals in the church.[11]

Also during those years, MC USA's Leadership Development office worked to improve and clarify the policy and procedures for responding to sexual misconduct by credentialed leaders. MC USA also contracted with FaithTrust Institute to provide healthy boundary training for conference leaders, who could then train pastors throughout the country. This training is now required for everyone seeking ministerial credentials in MC USA.

---

[10] Private e-mail correspondence, September 23, 2019. Soto Albrecht discloses some of her own story in Elizabeth Soto Albrecht, *Family Violence: Reclaiming a Theology of Nonviolence* (Maryknoll, NY: Orbis, 2008), 2.

[11] MC USA, "Prevention and Response: Sexual Abuse and Non-Credentialed Individuals," April 17, 2018, http://mennoniteusa.org/resource/prevention-and-response-sexual-abuse-and-non-credentialed-individuals/.

Conferences have also set up better processes for responding to misconduct disclosures, including training people who can help investigate when allegations are made. All of these actions assist in implementing the commitments made in the statement and are changing our congregations and church structures in tangible ways.

Reflections on Writing the Statement

While the statement came from the entire group, Regina Shands Stoltzfus and I wrote the initial drafts. In 2014, Dan Miller joined the discernment group as a listener and played a major role in the editing process. The statement also received input and feedback from Elizabeth Soto Albrecht (MC USA moderator), Carolyn Holderread Heggen (survivor and advocate adviser to the discernment group), the MC USA Constituency Leaders Council, and the executive board. This process took eight months and many drafts and was sometimes fraught with significant disagreement in the discernment group.

The areas we found to be most challenging in writing the statement reflect the theological and cultural shifts that still challenge and require attention in the church. Prior to the adoption of the statement, I wrote about five areas in need of work: (1) men's active and visible involvement in addressing sexual violence, (2) understanding power dynamics, (3) examining our theology and worship practices, (4) attending to the structural nature of sexualized violence, and (5) understanding how sexualized violence intersects with other forms of domination and exploitation.[12] These challenges have not gone away. There remains the need for men to engage more fully and helpfully in the work of abuse prevention and to learn more about power dynamics—and how to share power—in our families, congregations, and institutions. The above list is not comprehensive but touches on the major points of tension and challenge. Here, I discuss three continuing challenges.

---

[12] Peachey, "Naming the Pain, Seeking the Light," 126–8.

Sexuality and Systemic Violence

The church still tends to understand sexual violence as an individual problem and struggles to see how it connects with and supports other kinds of oppression, such as racism, colonialism, and economic inequality. When Regina and I wanted to highlight these connections, others feared this would dilute attention to sexual violence. Unfortunately, this narrow focus has meant that the church has responded primarily to the experiences of white people, with less attention to larger systems of exploitation and violence. Although Appendix B to the statement mentions these realities, the statement itself does not reference them. Thus, people who read only the main text of the statement would not be prompted to consider how our belief systems and practices contribute not only to sexual violence in our families and communities but also to the conquest, rape, and violation of other people and their land.

For example, Andrea Smith explains, "The project of colonial sexual violence establishes the ideology that Native bodies are inherently violable—and by extension, that Native lands are also inherently violable."[13] Since Western, platonic theology considers certain bodies as inferior and sexually dangerous, these bodies can then be demonized and treated as less than human.[14]

This logic dictates that certain bodies can be regulated, violated, or used for the benefit of those considered superior. Similarly, Musa Dube argues that imperializing narratives often conflate women and land. For instance, when the Israelites were about to enter Canaan, they met Rahab, who, tellingly, is described as a prostitute, a label that "denotes her inadequacy, her wildness, and her need to be tamed by those with superior morals, those who must save

---

[13]Andrea Smith, *Conquest: Sexual Violence and American Indian Genocide* (Cambridge, MA: South End, 2005), 12.
[14]In her book *What's Faith Got to Do with It? Black Bodies/Christian Souls*, Kelly Brown Douglas describes how platonic dualism negatively influenced Western Christian theology by emphasizing the spirit and denigrating the body. This was heightened under Augustine who argued that the body and especially sexuality need to be controlled by reason and the mind. Sexuality thus became a means for maintaining unjust power, by distinguishing between groups of people in terms of their bodies.

her."[15] By portraying her as welcoming the enemy and submitting to Israel's supposed superiority, the text reveals much about how dominating peoples have sought to justify their actions against others and the earth itself.

Such understanding is essential if we are to grasp the ways in which sexuality and sexual violence are woven into the fabric of our social, economic, religious, and political life. Only such an accounting will help us start to address the full scope of the problem. We can do this best when we start with those who are most vulnerable in our society. Indeed, Smith proposes that we should center women of color in our work, for when we do this, "it becomes clear that we must develop approaches that address interpersonal, state (e.g., colonization, police brutality, prisons), and structural (e.g., racism, poverty) violence simultaneously."[16] In this way, we may "build a movement that more effectively ends violence not just for women of color but for all people."[17] Unfortunately, our process and resulting statement failed to give priority to the voices and perspectives of women of color. This means we have not incorporated their wisdom and needs into our work of responding to and preventing sexualized violence. Now more than ever, this remains an urgent task.

Sexuality and Hierarchical Dualism

Another area of contention in the group was the extent to which the statement and the Service of Lament and Hope could address the rejection and hurt felt by those in the LGBTQ community because of their sexual orientation or gender identity. This rejection, too, is sexualized violence. Unfortunately, disagreement about LGBTQ inclusion showed up throughout the convention, generating intense debate and even confrontation during delegate sessions. Indeed, the church was so conflicted that delegates passed two incompatible resolutions: one to urge forbearance with one another on differences over inclusion and another reaffirming earlier membership

---

[15]Musa W. Dube, *Postcolonial Feminist Interpretation of the Bible* (St. Louis: Chalice, 2000), 77.
[16]Smith, *Conquest*, 160.
[17]Smith, *Conquest*, 160.

guidelines prohibiting same same-sex marriage relationships.[18] This conflict within the church itself made it difficult to navigate how to address sexualized violence against LGBTQ persons in the statement. Although Appendix B to the statement acknowledges in section 2 that those who are LGBTQ are often vulnerable to abuse, it does not address how the church itself has so often excluded and condemned them. Nor did the Service of Lament and Hope mention this. This failure became painfully evident as members of the LGBTQ community wept bitterly during the lament service, realizing that the harm done to them and to their friends by the church would not be acknowledged in any way.

While questions about sexual orientation and gender identity have tended to center around biblical interpretation, there is an undercurrent of assumptions tied to the platonic theology mentioned above and in the statement's Appendix B.2. As noted there, platonic thought has emphasized the spirit and disparaged the body. This created a hierarchy in which spirit, reason, maleness, whiteness, and transcendence were identified with God, while the earth and bodies—especially female and nonwhite bodies—were viewed as inferior, sexually promiscuous, and therefore dangerous. This binary worldview then justified the exploitation of the earth as well as the violation and misuse of the bodies of those who were considered second-class.

Our society's patriarchal and imperialistic systems depend so much on these dualistic hierarchies that they could not function without them. Many, therefore, feel threatened by the prospect of a world in which these binaries are blurred or no longer matter. This is especially disconcerting as women seek more equality and an end to domination and violence. Unfortunately, rather than engaging more deeply in fruitful discussion about the qualities that should characterize our intimate and sexual relationships, the church has tended to focus its anxieties and energy on those who deviate from the traditional sexual binaries. Thus, for example, the 1995

---

[18] MC USA, "On the Status of the Membership Guidelines," resolution, July 2, 2015, http://mennoniteusa.org/wp-content/uploads/2015/07/ResolutionOnStatusofMembershipGuidelines_2015Jul02.pdf; MC USA, "Forbearance in the Midst of Differences," resolution, July 2, 2015, http://mennoniteusa.org/wp-content/uploads/2015/07/ForbearanceResolution_2015Jul02.pdf.

Confession of Faith in a Mennonite Perspective is explicit about who can marry and engage in sexual union. Yet, it says almost nothing about the nature of that relationship; nowhere does it say that married people should love, respect, and care for one another. Perhaps this is assumed. However, since it does mention the realities of divorce, abuse, and sexual misconduct, it would be important to emphasize the qualities that make for strong and healthy marriages.[19] Here the statement is helpful as it clearly affirms that all people are created in God's image and deserve relationships that are committed, mutual, and deeply respectful.

Theology and Worship Practices

A third area of work concerns how we speak of suffering, sacrifice, obedience, forgiveness, and reconciliation. This was not an area of disagreement in the discernment group, but we could have given it more attention. As Mennonite and Anabaptist Christians, we have sought to uphold the values of nonviolence and peacemaking. We have therefore stressed the values of meekness, sacrificial service, and love of enemies. Too often, however, we have insisted on forgiveness and reconciliation without balancing these values with truth-telling, repentance, and accountability.[20] Too often, we have failed to recognize that Jesus also sought justice and liberation for himself and people in his community.

One statement cannot do everything, and this statement does urge that church leaders pay careful attention to what they communicate to victims and survivors through their sermons, teaching, and worship. Yet it would have been helpful to lay out some specific steps for how the church would mobilize its institutions to continue this theological work. Who will examine our hymns and our worship liturgies to make sure they speak good news to survivors? Who will educate and encourage our pastors to seek justice and healing for those who have been sexually violated? Who will examine our

---

[19]Article 19, "Family, Singleness, and Marriage," *Confession of Faith in a Mennonite Perspective* (Scottdale, PA: Herald, 1995), 72–4.
[20]For a discussion of the elements of justice-making, see Marie M. Fortune, *Is Nothing Sacred? When Sex Invades the Pastoral Relationship* (San Francisco: Harper and Row, 1989), 114–18.

educational materials to ensure they offer liberation and hope to those who are suffering exploitation and violence? Who will keep asking these questions and challenge us when necessary?

Conclusion

The convening and work of the discernment group was an important step for the Mennonite Church in dealing with the difficult challenge of sexualized violence in our homes and churches. This group accomplished much in naming and addressing the harmful legacy of John Howard Yoder. It assisted the church in repenting for its failure to address his violence and facilitated attention to the needs of victims and survivors. With the 2015 Statement on Sexual Abuse, we were able to name our aspirations and our weaknesses and to commit the church to substantive change in the years ahead.

This work is not complete. We must still wrestle with how our systems depend on and continue to promote false binaries that privilege some people over others. We must still work to undo the ways these systems violate people and resist accountability. We must still learn to listen to the wisdom of those who suffer most from these systems, the very people who can provide new insights into our theological understandings. All of this work will assist us in growing into more faithful and just "communities of grace, joy and peace." [21]

---

[21] "God calls us to be followers of Jesus Christ and, by the power of the Holy Spirit, to grow as communities of grace, joy and peace, so that God's healing and hope flow through us to the world." MC USA, "Vision for Healing and Hope," http://mennonit eusa.org/what-we-believe/.

12

Lessons from Anabaptist Women's Responses to John Howard Yoder's Sexual Violence

Karen V. Guth

Rachel Waltner Goossen's history of Mennonite responses to John Howard Yoder's sexual violence appeared in the January 2015 issue of *Mennonite Quarterly Review*.[1] Since that time, there has been much opportunity for persons, organizations, and institutions associated with Yoder to reflect on the gravity of his violence, the courage of the women who resisted it, and the complex ethical questions this case raises for Anabaptists and non-Anabaptists alike. As an outsider to the Anabaptist tradition, I have learned much from Anabaptist women's responses to Yoder's violence and have tried to grapple with the implications of their responses for my work as a Christian ethicist.

This chapter is my attempt—as a Christian ethicist trained in Protestant and secular educational institutions who now teaches at a Jesuit undergraduate college—to reflect on what scholars and teachers of theology and religion might learn from Anabaptist women's responses to the harms Yoder perpetrated. After providing some background on how I have tried to address Yoder's violence in my scholarship and professional guild, I identify six lessons from Anabaptist women for the broader field: the importance of (1) women's experience, (2) connecting theory and practice, (3) reconceptualizing what constitutes violence, (4) paying attention to institutional power, (5) challenging traditional conceptions of authority, and (6) enacting moral repair. Addressing sexualized violence is one of the most pressing moral problems of our time; we would do well to learn from the moral wisdom of these women.

Christian Ethics and Yoder's Violence

My own constructive work as a scholar of Yoder's theology addresses his sexual violence in several ways. I have called for transparency about his abuse, shown how Yoder's violence should make a

---

[1] Rachel Waltner Goossen, "'Defanging the Beast': Mennonite Responses to John Howard Yoder's Sexual Abuse," *Mennonite Quarterly Review* 89, no. 1 (January 2015): 7–80. See also Rachel Waltner Goossen, "Mennonite Bodies, Sexual Ethics: Women Challenge John Howard Yoder," *Journal of Mennonite Studies* 34 (2016): 247–59.

difference for scholarship in Christian ethics, and challenged my scholarly guild to take responsibility for its complicity in his abuse.

The first imperative for scholars in Christian ethics is to be transparent about Yoder's violence. Protestant social ethics was deeply impacted by Yoder's scholarly contributions. His work was a mainstay in graduate and undergraduate courses in my field. Anyone trained in my discipline would have been required to read his work and that of scholars, like Stanley Hauerwas, who were deeply influenced by Yoder. Yet, even now, over half a decade after Goossen's article, Yoder's work is frequently cited in the Christian ethics literature. Although some of these citations now include footnotes acknowledging his violence, it is rare for the fact of Yoder's violence to figure into the substantive analysis of this work. Even more unfortunate still, some scholars continue to cite Yoder's work without acknowledging his violence. In a paper presentation at the 2015 Society of Christian Ethics (SCE) annual meeting, I noted the silence around Yoder's violence in both my graduate training and the secondary literature of my field, raising this lack of transparency as a justice issue in and of itself and as a problem for peace church theology in the field.[2]

In my book *Christian Ethics at the Boundary: Feminism and Theologies of Public Life*, I argue that theologians working out of the peace church tradition need to develop a "feminist pacifist politics." Doing so requires them to move beyond a narrow conception of violence as military violence. It calls for more substantive engagement with feminist and womanist theologies to learn from their sustained attention to systemic forms of violence, like sexism, racism, classism, and traumatic forms of violence, including sexualized violence.

Unfortunately, the very theologians most dedicated to Yoder's pacifist project are the least likely to engage feminist theology. Consequently, part of my work in the book is to make a strategic appeal to these theologians about the importance of incorporating feminist analysis. I detail Yoder's claims about feminist theology,

---

[2] Karen V. Guth, "Doing Justice to the Complex Legacy of John Howard Yoder: Restorative Justice Resources in Witness and Feminist Ethics," *Journal of the Society of Christian Ethics* 35, no. 2 (Fall/Winter 2015): 119–39, http://dx.doi.org/10.1353/sce.2015.0037.

highlighting his characterization of feminism as a culture created by Christians, his description of Jesus as a feminist, and his contention that feminism is part and parcel of the pacifist politics of Jesus. Contrary to several misinterpretations of my position, this is not an effort to "redeem" Yoder's thought or to hold up feminist themes in his work as some kind of response to his victims.[3] It is rather to argue that Yoder's pervasive sexual violence renders it that much more incumbent on those he influenced to study the work of feminists, womanists, and others who attend to sexual violence and analyze systemic forms of violence. In my view, the indispensability of feminist theologies to peace church theology should be obvious. But if theologians who have championed Yoder's theology need a warrant from their own predecessor to include feminist analysis in their pacifist visions, they have it. Yoder knew in theory but not in practice that feminist theologies matter for doing peace church theology well. Peace church theologians have an opportunity to develop a feminist pacifist politics and to correct Yoder's egregious failures to embody it.

I also sought to address Yoder's violence on an institutional level. I have tried to challenge my main scholarly guild, the SCE—of which Yoder was the president from 1987 to 1989—to grapple with its complicity in Yoder's violence. One of these efforts was the 2015 paper presentation, which sparked discussion of how the society ought to respond. At the 2017 meeting, many of the ideas generated during the discussion came to fruition thanks to the leadership of then SCE president Cristina Traina, who supported several efforts to address the SCE's complicity in Yoder's violence. Here again, we looked to Anabaptist women—particularly Anabaptist Mennonite Biblical Seminary (AMBS) president Sara Wenger Shenk and others at the seminary—for models. With the help of Gerald Schlabach, I organized a panel titled "Structural Evil, Individual Harm, and Personal Responsibility: The John Howard Yoder Case as Opportunity for Self-Critical Reflection." I extended invitations

---

[3]Stanley Hauerwas, "In Defense of 'Our Respectable Culture': Trying to Make Sense of John Howard Yoder's Sexual Abuse," *ABC Religion and Ethics*, October 18, 2017; Julie Hanlon Rubio, Review of *Christian Ethics at the Boundary: Feminism and Theologies of Public Life* by Karen V. Guth, *Journal of the Society of Christian Ethics* 38, no. 2 (Fall/Winter 2018): 196–7, http://dx.doi.org/10.1353/sce.2018.0045.

to Sara Wenger Shenk in a desire to learn from her leadership in the AMBS process, Stanley Hauerwas for his relationship with Yoder and role in promoting Yoder's work, and Traci West for her work on sexualized violence. My goal was to create a panel that would foster intradisciplinary dialogue between peace church theologians and feminists (broadly construed) in thinking through what the society might learn from Yoder's case. Following the panel, the SCE also held a liturgy of lament for victims of sexualized violence, which was organized by members of our subcommittee, including Janna Hunter-Bowman, Kate Ott, Kim Penner, Karen Peterson-Iyer, Gerald Schlabach, and Todd Whitmore. The liturgy was powerful and unprecedented. One member spoke of the service as the only time the SCE had been "church" to her.[4] And, while not a direct response to Yoder's case, I think it is fair to view the work that Darryl Stephens and others have done on the SCE's Professional Conduct Committee as another example of the kind of work the SCE is doing to address sexual violence.

Lessons for Theology and Religion

With their responses to Yoder's violence, Anabaptist women have put sexual violence front and center for Christian ethics. In what follows, I aim to identify a few of the lessons I believe Anabaptist women's and institutional responses to Yoder's violence might offer the study of theology and religion more broadly.

The Importance of Women's Experiences

The first lesson is the continued importance of women's and other marginalized persons' experiences for theology and ethics. In the midst of the #MeToo movement, we might see Yoder's case as part of a larger cultural shift in which women's voices, experiences, and insights finally have begun to be taken more seriously. This

---

[4]Grace Kao, "A Time of Reckoning: The SCE and John Howard Yoder," *Feminism and Religion*, January 13, 2017, https://feminismandreligion.com/2017/01/13/a-time-of-reckoning-the-sce-and-john-howard-yoder-by-grace-yia-hei-kao/.

movement has raised many of the questions of prominent cultural figures like Bill Cosby, Harvey Weinstein, and R. Kelly that might also be asked about Yoder's case. It is striking to me how structurally similar the coverage of these disparate cases is to Yoder's: each time someone raises the question of what to do with the work of these figures; each time others point out that this question is the least important one on the table—that we need, rather, to focus on the women harmed by these predators; and each time questions about the larger cultural and institutional structures and practices that enable this violence are neglected. I view these similarities both as signs of hope that women's experiences are beginning to be acknowledged and as indications of how much further we need to go in terms of recognizing women not merely as victims but also as courageous moral agents and in making the kinds of systemic reforms needed to promote women's flourishing.

The Politics—Not Only the Theory—of Jesus

The second lesson is the importance of connecting theory and practice. It seems to me that Yoder's case is in some respects different from the others raised by the #MeToo movement. And it is so because of the politics of Jesus. For Mennonites, beliefs do not mean much unless they are embodied in a person's life. If one believes Jesus is the embodiment of God's will, then one embodies that belief in one's way of life. Consequently, many of the typical responses to cases of great thinkers, artists, performers, or celebrities behaving badly—like separating their work from their life—do not work in Yoder's case. There is an added irony to Yoder's case: a man whose main contribution to the field of Christian ethics was a renewed emphasis on the importance of Jesus as the revelation of God's will seems not to have understood his own point. Another way of putting this is to say that a valuable lesson we can take from Yoder's case is the mistake of separating theory from practice. This is one reason the work of so many women contributing to this book is critical to the study of theology and Christian ethics. It is important not just in the sense of correcting flaws in Yoder's and others' peace church theologies (although, as I discuss below, this kind of work is a major contribution to the field) but also with respect to work unrelated to Yoder's theology.

What Constitutes Violence?

Anabaptist women's responses to Yoder's violence reveal a third lesson: the need to conceive of violence more widely than Yoder and others in the peace church tradition who tend to construe violence narrowly in military terms. In resisting Yoder's violence, Anabaptist women simultaneously modeled peacemaking practices and pointed to sexual abuse as a form of violence. In my own work, I have focused on the need for scholars like Hauerwas to pay attention to violence beyond that of the military or the state—to attend to the expansive forms violence takes in the everyday lives of those on the margins: the systemic violence of sexism, racism, classism as well as the violence of other traumas like sexualized violence.

I have also turned to the literature on moral injury to provide a fuller sense of the harms involved. The harm is not merely the perpetration of sexualized violence but also the facts that (1) these violations were committed by someone who was regarded as a legitimate religious and academic authority and (2) Mennonite institutions failed for so long to prevent it. This means that the harm of sexual violence is compounded by what psychiatrists call moral injury and institutional betrayal. According to Jonathan Shay, moral injury results when there is "a betrayal of what's right, by someone with legitimate authority, in a situation with high stakes."[5] Psychologists Carly Parnitzke Smith and Jennifer F. Freyd define institutional betrayal as "common trusted and powerful institutions (schools, churches, military, government) acting in ways that visit harm upon those dependent on them for safety and well-being."[6] Both violations constitute distinct traumas in and of themselves.

Institutional Power

A fourth lesson of Mennonite women's responses is the importance of paying attention to the misuse of power, not only by respected

---

[5] Jonathan Shay, "Casualties," *Daedalus* 140, no. 3 (Summer 2011): 179–88, http://www.jstor.org/stable/23047357.
[6] Carly Parnitzke Smith and Jennifer J. Freyd, "Institutional Betrayal," *American Psychologist* 69, no. 6 (September 2014): 575–87, http://dx.doi.org/10.1037/a0037564.

authorities but also by others in institutional power. This is one reason why the work of Kim Penner, Malinda Berry, and others who assess the lack of attention to power in peace church theology is so important. Just as Mennonite women's responses highlight the need to take seriously various forms of violence neglected in peace church theology, their work draws attention to the need for robust analyses of power.

Moreover, the harm Yoder caused cannot be fully understood without attending to the damage it caused to women's theological leadership in Mennonite institutions. Many women's lives and careers as theologians and pastors were ruined by the devastations of Yoder's and others' sexual violence. This volume is especially important in this regard because it draws directly on Mennonite women's expertise and insight to articulate the politics of Jesus. In doing so, perhaps it provides a witness not only to the future of Mennonite theology but also to those who were silenced or whose careers were unjustly ended or prevented.

Moral Authority and Models of Peacemaking

Finally, Mennonite women's responses challenge traditional conceptions of authority. For years, Yoder was considered the foremost authority in peace church theology. Indeed, his status as an authority both enabled his violence and rendered it difficult for many to process. If Yoder did not embody the politics of Jesus in his own life—and indeed violated it in the most heinous of ways—can we still consider him an authority in Christian ethics? Mennonite women's responses to Yoder's violence raise the question of what constitutes a "legitimate authority" and the sources of legitimacy in an especially focused way.

When I disclose Yoder's violence to my students in class, it usually gives rise to discussion of his status as a theological authority. My students inevitably voice a range of potential standpoints on this question. Some students insist that because of his violations, Yoder should no longer be considered an authority on pacifism. Others argue that his theology is one thing and his life another. Some argue that his violations reveal an inherent problem with his pacifism and therefore the superiority of Reinhold Niebuhr's realism. Others argue that Yoder's violations are especially egregious because of his stance as a pacifist and his position of power as a religious authority. Still others contend that his authority depends not on his faithfulness to his theology but the faithfulness of his theology to Jesus's teachings. Some wonder if his violations shed light on problems in his theology not heretofore noticed. Still others inquire as to what was done about Yoder's violations, opening discussions about the women who mobilized to end Yoder's violence and about various institutional efforts at moral repair.

Rarely, however, do I have a student voice a response like that of my colleague, Marvin Ellison, who suggests that the question we need to be asking is less about what impact Yoder's violence has on his status as an authority in the field and more about who the "new authorities" are and what they can teach us. He argues that we need only look to the Mennonite women who resisted Yoder's violence and who lobbied Mennonite institutions for decades to end Yoder's violence and to take responsibility for it if we want authorities on peace making. As he writes,

> The truly exemplary theologian-activists of Christian nonviolence are the women survivors of Yoder's abuse. Against the odds, they courageously stepped forward, demanded justice not retribution, and called both Yoder and the wider Mennonite community to account. . . . We should honor the collective power and wisdom of such communities of resistance and alternative consciousness as sources of fresh theological vision and truth telling, not only about violence/violation but also about the requirements of authentic peacemaking and relational justice.[7]

In short, Mennonite women's responses to Yoder's violence represent a relocation of authority on peacemaking in the field of Christian ethics. Those who actually practice the politics of Jesus are the authorities on the politics of Jesus.

---

[7] Marvin M. Ellison, "Christian Sex, Christian Ethics: Marvin M. Ellison on Jung and Stephens' *Professional Sexual Ethics*," *Marginalia: A Los Angeles Review of Books*, October 27, 2015, http://marginalia.lareviewofbooks.org/christian-sex-christian-ethics-by-marvin-m-ellison/.

Authority and Moral Harm in the Classroom

Seeing Anabaptist women as the new authorities has challenged me to think about my own role as an authority in the classroom and what that means for whether and how I teach Yoder's work.[8] As the legitimate authority in the classroom, I need to wield authority responsibly.[9] Reflecting on my role as a legitimate authority has helped me understand why I feel compelled to continue teaching Yoder and why I disclose his sexual violence. To teach Yoder without acknowledging his sexual violence is to risk inflicting moral injury by holding up a perpetrator of sexual violence as an authority on pacifism (thus betraying what is right). Not teaching Yoder seems an unsatisfying solution for the same reason. Not to teach Yoder's theology in a course that examines Christian pacifism neglects my duty to introduce students to the tradition's most significant thinkers on this topic and, perhaps more importantly, denies students the opportunity to grapple with and learn from the ethical problems his case presents. As Malinda Berry notes in her explanation for why she continues to teach Yoder's work in her courses at AMBS, "I agreed to assign *Body Politics* because I would have felt academically irresponsible to exclude Yoder's voice and perspective from our course where Anabaptist perspectives on the church are central. And it is this same work that afforded me the opportunity to speak about the crisis our denomination has experienced because of Yoder's actions. . . . Collectively, we failed over and over to enact justice *and* we can learn from our mistakes."[10] While refusing to teach Yoder's work has merit, Berry

---

[8] I discuss these lessons at length in Karen V. Guth, "Moral Injury and the Ethics of Teaching Tainted Legacies," *Teaching Theology and Religion* 21, no. 3 (July 2018): 197–209, https://doi.org/10.1111/teth.12441.

[9] For a discussion of power and authority in the classroom, see Stephanie M. Crumpton, "Trauma-Sensitive Pedagogy," in *Teaching Sexuality and Religion in Higher Education: Embodied Learning, Trauma Sensitive Pedagogy, and Perspective Transformation*, ed. Darryl W. Stephens and Kate Ott, chapter 2. Routledge Research in Religion and Education (New York: Routledge, 2020).

[10] Malinda E. Berry, "Avoiding Avoidance: Why I Assigned *Body Politics* This Spring," *Mennonite Life* 68 (2014), https://web.archive.org/web/20150924061157/http://

articulates her decision in ways that resonate with my own sense that both Yoder's work and his violence must be discussed. Doing so avoids the problem of betraying what is right as the legitimate authority in the classroom while offering students the opportunity to learn from mistakes of the past.

Teaching Yoder's case has also alerted me to the role of stakes in moral harm. What it means to teach Yoder's legacy in my context versus, for example, a Mennonite institution—or what it might mean to teach Yoder's legacy to the women he violated, as compared with other survivors of sexual violence or compared with students who have not experienced such traumas—makes all the difference. Whether Yoder's legacy—or any material—has the potential to cause harm depends on how high the stakes are for students based on their particular identities, histories, experience, and commitments.

Considering the impact of teaching Yoder's tainted legacy on my students at Holy Cross provides a case in point. On the one hand, most of my students are unlikely to suffer clinical moral injury from engaging his work. My students recognize that Yoder betrayed what was right. But because they were not themselves violated by Yoder and because they are not Mennonite, being required to engage his work is unlikely to cause harm. The stakes are simply not high enough. For students who have experienced sexual violence or perpetrated it, the stakes may be higher. The stakes may again be raised if those who have suffered sexual violence were violated by a religious authority. Recognizing how stakes vary for students depending on their particularities has helped me see the importance of inviting students to consider what is at stake for them in engaging any of the material on my syllabus.

Importance of Moral Repair

Perhaps the most important lesson from Mennonite women's response to Yoder's violence is the importance of moral repair—action that redresses the structural, cultural, and institutional scope

---

ml.bethelks.edu/issue/vol-68/article/avoiding-avoidance-why-i-assigned-body-politics-th/.

of the problem. By studying Yoder's case, professors and students can draw attention to a culture that allows for violence against women and highlight the widespread relevance of the problem. This approach spotlights academic and ecclesial institutions that fail to hold the powerful accountable when they abuse their power. In Yoder's case, it invites analysis of how the Mennonite Church and academic institutions both initially failed to hold Yoder to account and later sought institutional forms of moral repair.

In teaching about Yoder's sexual violence, I find that it is easy for my students to get caught up in the question of how to reconcile Yoder's actions with his theology. Mennonite women's responses expand our conception of the relevant issues, particularly the structural and institutional aspects of sexual violence. Teaching both aspects allows me to discuss the ways Mennonite institutions placed Yoder's and their reputations ahead of concern for those who were harmed and to highlight the agency of the women Yoder violated. It allows me to introduce these women into the story—not as victims but as powerful moral agents who held Yoder and Mennonite institutions responsible. And, as mentioned earlier, it also allows me to invite discussion of how these women's responses invite a reassessment of who constitutes the "legitimate authority." This approach remedies the problem of treating sexual violence survivors as passive victims while also pointing to the need to interrogate the ways sexual violence is built into the structure of the course and academic disciplines, especially around authority.[11]

Teaching Mennonite women's responses allows me to guide students in interrogating these very issues. It allows me to problematize the limited conception of violence in peace church theology and the lack of attention to structural forms of violence in many academic discussions of violence. It allows me to identify ways structural violence is embedded in the course, particularly in our understanding of what constitute issues of peace and violence. And it allows me to discuss feminist and womanist analyses of structural violence that need to be incorporated by peace church theologians.

---

[11]Meredith Minister, "Leading a Faculty Workshop on Teaching about Sexual Violence," in "Forum: Sexual Violence in and around the Classroom," *Teaching Theology and Religion* 20, no. 1 (2017): 75–9, https://doi.org/10.1111/teth.12369.

This focus on concrete efforts at moral repair also alleviates a common problem with teaching traumatic material: a tendency to focus on narratives that provide "redemptive closure."[12] As Sara Wenger Shenk can tell us, the work of moral repair is difficult. An exclusive focus on redemption and transformation is not true to reality. Focusing on the women's work resists this move, as it emphasizes the work and struggle involved in the reparations that contribute to moral repair. But my hope is that in studying these reparation efforts, I can encourage my students to claim their own moral agency in protesting injustice and enacting reform. In this way, Mennonite women's responses to Yoder's violence become a model not only for addressing sexualized violence but also for addressing myriad injustices in contemporary public life.

Conclusion

Although Yoder's case may seem like an isolated Mennonite issue, it is far from it. The lessons of Yoder's case are relevant not only to contemporary #MeToo debate about what to do with the work of artists exposed as sexual abusers but also more broadly to countless cases that I call "tainted legacies"[13]—from Martin Heidegger's Nazism to Confederate monuments in the United States—all of which raise the question of how to respond to legacies implicated in traumatic pasts. Separating the work from the person who produced it or refusing to engage it—whether that means omitting Yoder from one's syllabus or destroying controversial monuments—may provide easy solutions to complex problems, but such responses eliminate opportunities for profound learning. The lessons of Anabaptist women's responses to Yoder's violence move beyond the simple question of how Yoder's violations affect the status of his work or his role as an authority in Christian ethics. They point

---

[12]Liora Gubkin, "From Empathetic Understanding to Engaged Witnessing: Encountering Trauma in the Holocaust Classroom," *Teaching Theology and Religion* 18, no. 2 (April 2015): 103–20, https://doi.org/10.1111/teth.12273.

[13]See Karen V. Guth, "Moral Injury, Feminist and Womanist Ethics, and Tainted Legacies," *Journal of the Society of Christian Ethics* 38, no. 1 (Spring/Summer 2018): 167–86, http://dx.doi.org/10.1353/sce.2018.0010.

to the importance of women's experience for theology and religion and the need to connect theory and practice. They reveal deficiencies in conceptions of violence that are limited to state-wielded forms and spotlight misuses of power by authority figures and others in institutional power. They suggest the need to reconceive of who constitutes a legitimate authority and raise the question of what we might learn if we attend to the powerful actions of those we often relegate to the status of victims. In short, Anabaptist women's responses to Yoder's violence model the kind of moral repair of structural injustices needed in cases across contemporary public life.

APPENDIX

Churchwide Statement on Sexual Abuse*

Passed by the Mennonite Church USA Delegate Assembly at Kansas City, Missouri, July 3, 2015

---

*Editors' note: This appendix reproduces the statement in its entirety with permission from the Mennonite Church USA. For the original statement, see http://mennoniteusa.org/wp-content/uploads/2015/07/Churchwide_Statement_On_Sexual_Abuse_2015July03.pdf

Mennonite Church USA's vision statement calls us ". . . to grow as communities of grace, joy and peace." The 10-year Purposeful Plan (developed in 2011) defines seven priorities of a missional church, dedicated to following Jesus' way of love and nonviolence toward all.[1]

These commitments call us to give attention to the tragedy of sexual abuse in our families, churches and communities. According to data collected from the *2006 Church Member Profile,* 21 percent of women in Mennonite Church USA congregations and 5.6 percent of men reported having experienced sexual abuse or violation. We lament that sexual abuse exists not only in our society but also within our own homes, congregations and institutions.

This is not what God intended. God created human beings in God's image and declared this very good. God's incarnation in Jesus also affirms that human bodies are good. Our sexuality is part of this good order, created to enable us to enjoy companionship and intimacy and to form families and build community. Our spirituality and our sexuality are not disconnected or competing aspects of our lives but express our longing for intimacy with God and with others.

When people violate others sexually, the church is called to be a place of healing. Yet we confess that we have often responded with denial, fear and self-preservation. We have tended to listen to voices who have positional power, rather than to those who have been violated and those who are most vulnerable. In this way, we have enabled sexual abuse to continue while silencing and disregarding the testimony of victims. We lament that our inaction permits abuse to continue and the ways we obstruct God's healing.

Abuse wounds the body of Christ. Whenever sexual boundaries are crossed, the wounds extend beyond the direct victims. Abuse also harms the friends and families of both victims and perpetrators, those called upon to bind up the wounds, and the church itself. We join our anguished cries with all who have been traumatized in this way.

---

[1] The 2011 Purposeful Plan identifies these priorities: Christian Formation, Christian Community, Holistic Christian Witness, Stewardship, Leadership Development, Undoing Racism and Advancing Intercultural Transformation, and Church-to-Church Relationships.

We confess we are uncomfortable with the pain and anger of survivors as well as the behavior of perpetrators. In our discipline processes we struggle to find ways to support survivors as they reclaim their lives. We have often failed to focus first on their needs; we lament our tendency to give more attention to the perpetrator than to victims and survivors.

Finally, we have failed to focus on teaching and supporting healthy sexuality. We have failed to promote relationships that are truly committed, mutual and deeply respectful. In doing so, we have minimized and neglected the needs of those who suffer from sexual violence and abuse.

For all of this, we repent and seek to change our ways.

We resolve to tell the truth about sexual abuse; hold abusers accountable; acknowledge the seriousness of their sin; listen with care to those who have been wounded; protect vulnerable persons from injury; work restoratively for justice; and hold out hope that wounds will be healed, forgiveness offered, and relationships established or reestablished in healthy ways.

What we will do

(See *Appendix A: Actions and commitments* for more information on each action.)

As congregations:

1. Develop and teach healthy, wholesome sexuality.
2. Make sure that child protection policies and procedures are in place and followed, including compliance with state-mandated regulations or laws requiring training for volunteers and child care workers and the reporting of any violations.
3. Teach members the realities of sexualized violence, especially by church leaders or other trusted individuals.
4. Ensure that worship services and sermons are sensitive to the needs of victims/survivors.
5. Give attention to systems that create and sustain institutionalized sexual violence (ranging from the

mainstream entertainment industry to pornography and prostitution) by feeding a climate that condones or excuses violence against women and children.
6. Make sure pastors' job descriptions are manageable and leaders are practicing self-care.

As church institutions:

1. Require training in sexuality and professional ethics as part of the credentialing process as well as in continuing education for all ministers.
2. Require all agencies to develop and implement clear, accessible and public policies on sexual harassment and abuse.
3. Provide consultation and adequate supervision for all church leaders. Make sure job descriptions are manageable and employees are practicing self-care.
4. Give attention to systems that create and sustain institutionalized sexual violence (ranging from the mainstream entertainment industry to pornography and prostitution) by feeding a climate that condones or excuses violence against women and children.
5. Examine religious teachings that make it difficult for victims to protect themselves or speak up when they have been violated and hurt.
6. Teach and model mutuality between men and women and challenge the ongoing legacy of patriarchy in the church.

Appendix A: Actions and Commitments

For congregations:

1. Develop and teach healthy, wholesome sexuality. Create space for conversation and education and remove the secrecy and shame attached to sexuality. Work to dispel the idea that sexuality is "private," and teach that it is part of our life together as followers of Jesus.

a. Offer Sunday school or other classes for all ages. Use resources such as the *Circle of Grace* curriculum (available from DovesNest.net) and *Body and Soul: Healthy Sexuality and the People of God* (Faith & Life Resources, 2010).
   b. Teach sexual literacy. For example, teach children correct names for body parts and their right to say "No!" when something feels wrong or uncomfortable.
   c. Place written resources in the church library and equip parents for teaching and modeling healthy sexuality at home.
2. Make sure child protection policies and procedures are in place and followed. These should include:
   a. Safe meeting places with windows in all interior doors.
   b. Two adults present when meeting with children and youth.
   c. Screening for all staff and volunteers.
   d. Regular training for parents, teachers and youth workers about sexual harassment and abuse.
   e. Procedures for reporting disclosures or allegations of abuse. These should include clear guidance about when police and/or child protection offices should be notified.
   f. Compliance with all state-mandated laws/regulations for reporting and training.
   g. Guidelines for relating to a known sex offender in the congregation.
3. Teach members the realities of sexualized violence, especially by church leaders or other trusted individuals.
   a. Teach everyone about consent and who can ethically/legally consent to sexual activity. Identify power dynamics that render consent impossible (underage, student and/or employee, disabled, etc.)
   b. Use correct language to speak about sexual abuse; it is not adultery or an affair but a misuse of power, and when committed by a pastor or church leader, a serious violation of one's professional role.
   c. Make available in public places (such as restrooms) information about how to report sexual abuse or pastoral sexual misconduct.

4. Ensure that worship services and sermons are sensitive to the needs of victims/survivors.
    a. Name the sin of abuse in public prayers and laments.
    b. In teaching about anger, forgiveness, loving enemies and obedience, be aware of how abuse victims and survivors may hear these instructions. Make sure they will hear good news and an invitation to healing and wholeness.
5. Give attention to systems that create and sustain institutionalized sexual violence (ranging from the mainstream entertainment industry to pornography and prostitution) by feeding a climate that condones or excuses violence against women and children.
6. Make sure pastors' job descriptions are manageable and leaders are practicing self-care.
    a. Create clear job descriptions and regular performance evaluations. Ensure that workload and stress are manageable.
    b. Provide generous leave policies, including opportunities for education and sabbaticals, as well as supports such as accountability, consultation and supervision.
    c. Share leadership between pastors and lay members and cultivate relationships that are healthy and transparent. Support pastors in tending their family relationships.

For church institutions:

1. Require training in sexuality and professional ethics as part of the credentialing process, as well as in continuing education, for all ministers. Training should include an understanding of ethical guidelines regarding boundaries, power and authority, and sexual conduct, so that ministers are able to:
    a. Understand healthy interpersonal boundaries as essential to establishing and maintaining trust.
    b. Recognize the issues of power in our sexual ethics.
    c. Understand the importance of professional ethics, including the denomination's policies and expectations.
    d. Be knowledgeable about human sexuality, one's own sexual self and how to deal with sexual feelings that may arise for congregants and vice versa.

e. Be familiar with resources for sexual abuse prevention and the denomination's policies for reporting and responding to sexual violation.
   f. Appreciate the connection between sexual integrity and spiritual wholeness.
   g. Be conversant with scriptural and theological resources for all of the above.[2]
2. Require agencies to develop and implement clear, accessible and public guidelines and policies on sexual harassment and abuse.
   a. Provide training and assistance on prevention as well as procedures for responding to sexual violation.
   b. Maintain a list of trusted professionals who have experience in dealing with sexual violation by church leaders and require agencies to use their expertise when responding to allegations of abuse.
   c. Develop ways to hold agencies accountable for implementing these policies.
3. Provide consultation and adequate supervision for all church leaders. Provide ongoing training on best practices of ministry in areas such as cyber safety, healthy communication, clergy self-care, life-long sexuality education, and ministry with sex offenders.[3]
4. Seek to undo systems that create and sustain institutionalized sexual violence (ranging from the mainstream entertainment industry to pornography and prostitution) by feeding a climate that condones or excuses violence against women and children. Provide training and resources for congregations to use in addressing issues such as date rape, pornography, prostitution and sexual slavery.

---

[2]Adapted from The United Methodist Church, "Sexual Ethics as Integral Part of Formation for Ministerial Leadership," in *The Book of Resolutions of The United Methodist Church 2012* (Nashville, TN: The United Methodist Publishing House, 2012), 149.

[3]Adapted from The United Methodist Church, "Sexual Ethics as Integral Part of Formation for Ministerial Leadership," in *The Book of Resolutions of The United Methodist Church 2012* (Nashville, TN: The United Methodist Publishing House, 2012), 150.

5. Examine religious teachings that make it difficult for victims to protect themselves or speak up when they have been violated and hurt.
    a. Be especially alert to teachings that advocate:
        i. Physical punishment of children.
        ii. Unquestioning obedience to those in authority or leadership.
        iii. Suffering and bearing the cross as signs of discipleship.
        iv. Submission of women to their husbands.
        v. Forgiveness and reconciliation without sufficient attention to justice.
    b. Provide alternative teachings that are nonviolent and life-giving to all, such as:
        i. Promoting restorative discipline practices.
        ii. Encouraging questions and the ability to trust one's instincts and speak up when something feels wrong.
        iii. Stressing God's concern for life, healing and wholeness and that Jesus' death resulted from his care for those who were suffering and willingness to challenge the forces that excluded and oppressed people.
        iv. Promoting deep respect and mutuality (mutual submission) between marriage partners.
        v. Practicing restorative justice as part of the movement toward forgiveness and reconciliation.
6. Teach and model mutuality between men and women and challenge the ongoing legacy of patriarchy in the church. This should include:
    a. Attention to complementary teams of male and female leadership.
    b. Respectful language in all relationships.
    c. Listening to all voices in making decisions.
    d. Using healthy conflict resolution skills.
    e. Recognizing that those in authority need to earn their trust and that their positions are not divinely ordained.
    f. Stressing God's concern for life, healing and wholeness, especially for those being oppressed or victimized.[4]

---

[4] Adapted from *Abuse: Response and Prevention*, Mennonite Central Committee booklet, at https://mcc.org/sites/mcc.org/files/media/common/documents/abuseprevention booklet2016engweb.pdf.

Appendix B: Lenses for Understanding Sexual Abuse

1. **Viewing sexual abuse through a biblical lens**
   Christians affirm that God created the world and declared it good. This includes human beings and their bodies. The *Confession of Faith in a Mennonite Perspective* declares:

   > We believe that human beings were created good, in the image of God (Genesis 1:26-27, Romans 8:29).... Because both Adam and Eve were equally and wonderfully made in the divine image, God's will from the beginning has been for women and men to live in loving and mutually helpful relationships with each other.[5]

   In addition, human sexuality is one of the good ways in which people express and receive love. The Song of Solomon provides a wonderful example of sexual desire expressed in a joyfully mutual, respectful and committed relationship. Both individuals share their delight in and yearning to please the other without any need to control, misuse or dominate.

   Yet the Bible is also painfully honest and shares heartbreaking accounts of people violating others and using them for their own sexual gratification. 2 Samuel 13 details how David's son Amnon plotted to rape his half-sister, Tamar. Remarkably, there is no suggestion that she is to blame. Rather, responsibility lies with the men: Amnon, of course; but also his friend Jonadab, who encouraged Amnon to get what he wanted; and King David, who participated in the scheme. Although David became angry when he learned what happened, he did nothing to support his daughter or hold his son accountable.

   Why was David so oblivious to this tragedy and so unable to confront his son? Tellingly, just two chapters

---

[5]*Confession of Faith in a Mennonite Perspective*, Article 6, "The Creation and Calling of Human Beings," Herald Press, 1995, 28.

earlier, David had done something similar with Bathsheba. He had used his power as king to demand that she be brought to him and then arranged to have her husband killed. Sadly, we know nothing of what Bathsheba felt or what life was like for her in David's house.

Indeed, Bathsheba is often blamed for David's sin, as if she had provoked or invited his attention. Unfortunately, blaming women for introducing immorality is as old as our oldest religious traditions, including the biblical narratives. Particular interpretations of the creation of humans as well as the "fall" of humanity designate the woman as a poor imitation of the first human creature—and therefore subjected to him—and as the conduit through which human sin entered the world. Woman's nature, according to many interpretations of the "fall" narrative, is duplicitous, ignorant, willful, evil and seductive.

As Phyllis Trible has noted in *God and the Rhetoric of Sexuality*, conversations between the Bible and American ideology illuminate narratives that influence both the concept of manifest destiny and the liberation motif of those who champion human and civil rights. Trible notes that traditional interpretations of the narrative in Genesis 2:7–3:24 proclaim male superiority and female inferiority as the will of God. Woman is the temptress and troublemaker, dependent upon and dominated by her husband. The biblical creation narrative, Trible asserts, is a love story gone awry. Yet it is not the only word in Scripture. As such, there is room within the biblical narrative to craft a foundation for liberation. Trible reads Song of Songs as a liberating text, where the voices of the lovers "extol and enhance" the creation of sexuality in Genesis 2.

A constant thread running through all of Scripture is the directive for God's people to care for the most marginalized: the widows, the fatherless (or children in general), the strangers and the poor. The community is to care for and protect these vulnerable populations.

The narratives of Jesus' encounters with women, including foreign women and women who were estranged from their communities because of illness or allegations of immoral behavior, indicate a reframing of notions that render women as secondary humans. In the gospels, women are persons in their own right with agency and gifts. Jesus holds persons accountable for their actions, including actions that violate the body integrity of another person. Marie Fortune notes that Jesus' teaching on lust (Matthew 5:28) can be interpreted to mean that men are responsible not to violate women through any thoughts or actions and that for a man to desire to possess and dominate a woman is an offense against her. Applied to the experience of sexual violence, the passage does not emphasize promiscuity— it cautions against the potential for sexual coercion in thought, word and deed (Fortune, *Sexual Violence: The Sin Revisited*, 103).

Leaders in the early church continued to emphasize respect and mutual submission, and to reject self-indulgence or selfishness.[6] Indeed, Paul urged believers not to use their "... freedom as an opportunity for self- indulgence. ... For the whole law is summed up in a single commandment, 'You shall love your neighbor as yourself'" (Galatians 5:13-14).

Today, all baptized disciples of Jesus—men and women— are responsible to pull back the veils of silence, secrecy and shame that hide the sin of sexual exploitation and male privilege in our communities. With this document, we renew our resolve to walk in the light, "until all of us come ... to maturity, to the measure of the full stature of Christ" (Ephesians 4:13).

2. **Viewing sexual abuse through a cultural lens**

   For centuries, western Christians have lived in a context where sexual abuse, including abuse by priests, pastors and other church leaders, has been largely ignored, and the wounds of those who have suffered abuse have been largely unattended. We as Mennonite congregations have participated in this sin, at least minimizing the abuse and blaming or discrediting the victims. Recognizing and dealing openly with this sin is painful. Nevertheless, we are grateful to God and the leading of the Spirit that we live in a time

---

[6]Ephesians 5:21, 25–33.

and place in which the injury caused by sexualized violence is becoming widely known and condemned. We believe this opens the door to the possibility of healthier and more genuinely Christian relationships between women and men.

We also acknowledge that some teaching about sexuality contribute to sexualized violence, including a distorted notion that our bodies are shameful and bad. Other distortions include beliefs, endorsed and supported throughout history, that some bodies are more valued—the primary example or standard for humanity—while others are less valued. Violence toward the latter is often overlooked or even condoned. We see this demonstrated in the violence (e.g., lynching, sexual assault, murder) experienced by people of color throughout our history. These patterns are also evident in the disparities between the ways in which people of different racial/ethnic backgrounds are charged and sentenced for crimes. White men who are charged and convicted of sexualized violence against women of color routinely receive less harsh sentencing than men of color who are convicted of sexualized violence against white women.

According to ethicist Kelly Brown Douglas, Christianity that is deeply influenced by platonic thought has emphasized the spirit and disparaged the body, thereby giving rise to Christian participation in attacks against Black bodies. This teaching lays the false foundation for belief that certain bodies may be easily disregarded and allows for the dehumanization—or even demonization—of those who are defined only by their sexuality. This foundation has allowed for the participation of Christian people in the lynching and sexual abuse of the bodies of both Black men and women.

Additionally, some persons have used Scripture to uphold the belief/practice that women and children are the property of men for their service and pleasure. These distortions of Scripture add fuel to the economic and cultural conditions that feed the sex trade, prostitution, pornography, advertising, the fashion industry, etc. This distortion also leads to shaming girls and women for their sexuality while at the same time ignoring or excusing boys and men who engage in abusive sexual behavior.

These distorted notions also create conditions for some who have institutional power to create rules and regulations that benefit them and to disregard or ignore rules and regulations that might hold them accountable and protect those who are vulnerable. This enables those with power to overlook and abuse less valued persons, such as those who are poor, LGBTQ (lesbian, gay, bisexual, transgender, queer), disabled or female.

3. **Viewing sexual abuse through a justice lens**
"Justice" has a variety of meanings in our context and English language. In American society, "justice" often means following legally prescribed procedures (e.g., "justice has been done" when courts make a decision where the rules have been followed properly) or retribution (e.g., one who has stolen from another should "pay" for that injustice by spending time in prison). There are also other meanings.

As Mennonite Christians, we understand "justice" to mean "restorative justice."[7] This understanding of justice is intimately connected to the biblical term *shalom*, which refers to the well-being of the community.[8] When there is *shalom*, things are the way they should be, and relationships are right. When anyone in the community impoverishes, injures, or abuses another, they sin. Things are not OK. Restorative justice refers to processes through which we work to restore relationships and well-being. Restorative justice is especially attentive to the poor, weak and oppressed since they are typically the main victims when *shalom* is absent.

A number of elements are needed for right relationships to be restored. We list some of them here, noting especially how they apply when we seek to restore *shalom* when it has been broken by sexual abuse.[9] In tending to these elements,

---

[7]See *Changing Lenses: A New Focus for Crime and Justice* by Howard Zehr and *Beyond Retribution: A New Testament Vision for Justice, Crime and Punishment* by Christopher Marshall.
[8]Perry Yoder, *Shalom: The Bible's Word for Salvation, Justice and Peace*. Evangel Publishing House, 1998.
[9]Points a–g are adapted from Marie Fortune, *Is Nothing Sacred?* Cleveland, OH: United Church Press, 1999.

congregations can be part of a network of support for individuals and families.

a. **Truth-telling.** The sin of sexual abuse must not remain hidden or minimized if relationships are to be righted within the community that is affected by it. This does not mean demonizing offenders, but it does mean naming abuse as sin that disrupts *shalom*. This may include working with those who have been violated to contact the appropriate local governing authorities to report the abuse, which is required by law in cases involving children. Congregations can still provide support and resources for a restorative justice process when the legal system is involved.
b. **Acknowledgement.** Giving the victims space to tell their story and stating clearly that what was done to them was wrong.
c. **Compassion.** Listening with loving care to those who have been wounded, taking seriously their accounts of their experiences and being willing to suffer with them. This has often been lacking in our dealings with sexual abuse in the past. It also means treating the one accused of abuse with care and fairness in the midst of the difficult process of confronting him or her with evidence of abuse.
d. **Protecting vulnerable ones from further injury.** We should surround those who have been abused with support and seek to make sure that they and other potential victims are safe from any further abuse.
e. **Accountability.** Holding abusers accountable for their actions, refusing to blame victims and refusing to accept excuses or minimize abusive behavior.
f. **Restitution.** In order to make things right, efforts must be made to find ways of making restitution to the victims; restoring to them what has been taken, insofar as and in whatever ways are possible.
g. **Validation of the victims/survivors.** Stating clearly that they were wronged, setting them free from shame and restoring them to the community.
h. **Repentance.** For right relationships to be fully restored,

abusers need to own up to their guilt. They need to confess, take responsibility for the abuse, make long-term changes in beliefs and behavior and make restitution. According to Ezekiel 18:30-32, ". . . repentance involves getting a 'new heart.'"[10]

i. **Forgiveness.** This, like other elements listed here, cannot be forced, demanded or rushed. In fact, if the victim forgives too quickly, forgiveness can seem to make things right before there is a chance to understand the serious harm done and what repentance and restoration really entail. Yet the vision of *shalom*, the Christian gospel, holds out the hope that, over time, forgiveness can lead to further well-being.

Survivors may choose forgiveness as a gift to themselves so they can move on and live their lives with joy and peace. Ultimately, forgiveness is a process she or he ". . . experiences by the grace of God, so that the abuse does not dominate her or his life anymore. It is a process of letting go and moving on in healthy ways."[11] For the offender, receiving forgiveness can mean gaining freedom from debilitating guilt and accepting his or her need for accountability. Seeking forgiveness means acknowledging the seriousness of the sin and releasing any anger or bitterness toward those who reported the abuse and are holding him or her accountable. It also means doing the hard psychological, emotional and spiritual work of making sure he or she will not abuse again.

For all, including the whole community affected by the abuse, forgiveness can mean naming both the grievous sin with its impact on others and the unmerited grace that cannot be earned but only received.

j. **Restoration of *shalom*: reconciliation.** The ultimate hope of restorative justice is to establish or reestablish right relations in the community. In situations of sexual

---

[10] *Understanding sexual abuse by a church leader or caregiver*, 2nd edition. Mennonite Central Committee, 2011, 20.
[11] Ibid., 20.

violence, reestablishing personal relationships between victims and their offenders may not be possible or wise. At the same time, the larger community can promote healing and safety for those who have been harmed; protect those who are vulnerable; and insist on learning, accountability and support for those who have violated others. In this way, all can move toward the vision of God's *shalom* for all.

4. **Definitions**

    Sexual abuse refers to sexualized behavior that occurs in a relationship where one party has more power than the other and meaningful consent is difficult, if not impossible. Sexual abuse takes advantage of another in order to use, control or intimidate him or her for one's own purposes. It is violence that has been sexualized.[12] It can include actual physical contact of a sexual nature, such as hugs, kisses, touching, assault and intercourse. Sexual abuse can also involve more covert acts such as using sexual innuendo or pornography in the relationship, emotional and spiritual manipulation, or inappropriate disclosures of a personal nature regarding sexual matters.

    Sexual harassment is any unwanted and unwelcome behavior of a sexual or gender-specific nature. It can interfere with a person's ability to work, get an education or engage in ministry, among other things. It often takes two forms:

    - *Quid pro quo* harassment occurs when someone is pressured to trade sexual favors in return for a job, promotion or grade.

    - Environmental harassment refers to unwelcome sexual behavior that creates a hostile environment. It can include sexually suggestive remarks, jokes or gestures, displaying degrading pictures or objects, unwelcome propositions and unwanted physical contact such as touching, hugging, pinching, patting or other sexual demands.

---

[12]Some use the term "sexualized violence" to address the fact that great violence has been done to the person.

Sexual Immorality: While all sexual abuse is immoral and sinful, not all sexual immorality is abusive. Sexually immoral behavior can occur when individuals of relatively equal power voluntarily engage in intimate, sexual acts outside of a committed, monogamous relationship and/or violate their marriage covenant by engaging in such acts with someone other than their spouse.

Professional power and responsibility: It is important for all professionals to recognize the power they hold by virtue of their training and position in the community. This includes pastors, teachers, counselors, administrators or anyone in a position of trust or leadership. Even when they may not feel powerful, it is important for leaders to recognize that others see them as strong and authoritative and often defer to them.

Understanding this dynamic helps guard against misusing power or overstepping appropriate boundaries. Because they have greater power, leaders always bear primary responsibility to protect the boundaries of the relationship. It is also their responsibility to act in the best interests of the person with lesser power, rather than to use the person or exploit any of his or her vulnerabilities.

Appendix C: Resources

Sermons

- Untold Stories (2 Samuel 13:1-21)—Meghan Larissa Good, Albany (Ore.) Mennonite Church. http://mennoniteusa.org/wp-content/uploads/2015/03/2Samuel_-13.pdf

Books and pamphlets

- *Body and Soul, Healthy Sexuality and the People of God.* Faith & Life Resources, 2010.
- Cooper-White, Pamela. *The Cry of Tamar, Violence against Women and the Church's Response,* 2nd edition. Fortress Press, 2012.

- Fortune, Marie M. *Sexual Violence, The Sin Revisited.* The Pilgrim Press, 2005.
- Gaede, Beth Ann, editor. *When a Congregation is Betrayed: Responding to Clergy Misconduct.* The Alban Institute, 2006.
- Heggen, Carolyn Holderread. *Sexual Abuse in Christian Homes and Churches.* Herald Press, 1993. Reprinted Wipf & Stock, 2006.
- Jung, Patricia Beattie and Darryl W. Stephens, eds. *Professional Sexual Ethics: A Holistic Ministry Approach.* Minneapolis: Fortress Press, 2013.
- McClintock, Karen A. *Preventing sexual abuse in congregations: A resource for leaders.* The Alban Institute, 2004.
- Melton, Joy Thornburg. *Safe Sanctuaries for Ministers: Reducing the Risk of Abuse in the Church.* Discipleship Resources, 2009.
- Melton, Joy Thornburg. *Safe Sanctuaries: Reducing the risk of abuse in the church for children and youth.* Discipleship Resources, 2008.
- *Mennonite Quarterly Review*, January 2015.
- Smith, Andrea. *Conquest: Sexual Violence and American Indian Genocide.* South End Press, 2005.
- *Understanding sexual abuse by a church leader or caregiver*, 2nd edition. Mennonite Central Committee, 2011: https://mcc.org/sites/mcc.org/files/media/common/documents/understandingsexualabuseeng.pdf
- West, Traci C. *Disruptive Christian Ethics: When Racism and Women's Lives Matter.* Westminster John Knox Press, 2006.
- Yoder, Carolyn. *The Little Book of Trauma Healing: When Violence Strikes and Community Security is Threatened.* Good Books, 2005.

Websites

- Clergy Sexual Misconduct Awareness and Prevention, Baylor University: http://www.baylor.edu/clergysexualmisconduct

- Dove's Nest, Faith Communities Keeping Children and Youth Safe: http://DovesNest.net/
- Godly Response to Abuse in the Christian Environment (GRACE): http://netgrace.org/
- The Hope of Survivors: http://www.thehopeofsurvivors.com/
- Safe Church Project, Samaritan Counseling Center: http://scclanc.org/clergy-congregation-care/safe-church/
- Our Stories Untold: http://www.ourstoriesuntold.com
- Survivors Network of Persons Abused by Priests: http://www.snapnetwork.org
- Andrea Smith blog: https://andrea366.wordpress.com
- United Methodist Sexual Ethics: http://umsexualethics.org

BIBLIOGRAPHY

Agencia Presidencial para la Acción Social y la Cooperación Internacional, *Ley de Víctimas y Restitución de Tierras* (Bogotá: 2011), articles 114–118. http://www.centrodememoriahistorica.gov.co/descargas/ley_victimas/ley_victimas_completa_web.pdf.

Agorakis, Stavros. "Read the Full Transcript of Sen. Collins's Speech Announcing She'll Vote to Confirm Brett Kavanaugh." *Vox*, October 5, 2018. https://www.vox.com/2018/10/5/17943276/susan-collins-speech-transcript-full-text-kavanaugh-vote.

Alcoff, Linda Martín. "Anti-Latino Racism." In *Decolonizing Epistemologies: Latina/o Theology and Philosophy*, edited by Ada María Isasi-Díaz, and Eduardo Mendieta, 107–26. New York: Fordham University Press, 2012.

"AMBS Response to Victims of John H. Yoder Abuse." http://www.ambs.edu/about/ambs-response-to-victims-of-yoder-abuse.

Anonymous. "My Story." n.d. Mennonite Central Committee (MCC) website: Abuse: Response and Prevention, http://abuse.mcc.org/abuse/en/domestic/stories/change.html (accessed June 30, 2010).

Armster, Michelle E. "Who Is It?" *Report* 156 (July–August 2001): 8–9.

Battistella, Edwin L. *Sorry about That: The Language of Public Apology.* New York: Oxford University Press, 2014.

Bechler, Le Roy. *The Black Mennonite Church in North America 1886–1986.* Scottdale, PA: Herald, 1986.

Becker, Palmer. *Anabaptist Essentials: Ten Signs of a Unique Christian Faith.* Harrisonburg, VA: Herald, 2017.

Bedford, Nancy. "Theology, Violence and White Spaces." In *Envisioning the Good Life: Essays on God, Christ, and Human Flourishing in Honor of Miroslav Volf*, edited by Matthew Croasmun, Zoran Grozdanov, and Ryan McAnnally-Linz, 149–62. Eugene, OR: Cascade, 2017.

Bell, Melissa, and Nichole Bayliss. "The Tough Guise: Teaching Violent Masculinity as the Only Way to Be a Man." *Sex Roles* 72, no. 11–12 (2015): 566–8. https://doi.org/10.1007/s11199-015-0479-8.

Bemporad, Elissa, and Joyce W. Warren. *Women and Genocide: Survivors, Victims, Perpetrators.* Bloomington, IN: Indiana University Press, 2019.

Bender, Harold S. "The Anabaptist Vision." *Church History* 13 (March 1944): 3–24.

Benjumea Rua, Adriana y Natalia Poveda Rodríguez. "El derecho a la tierra para las mujeres: una mirada a la ley de víctimas y restitución de tierras." *Corporación Humanas,* n.d. https://www.humanas.org.co/alfa/dat_particular/ar/Articulo_Tierras_AB_y_NP.pdf.

Berry, Malinda E. "Avoiding Avoidance: Why I Assigned *Body Politics* This Spring." *Mennonite Life* 68 (2014). https://web.archive.org/web/20150924061157/http://ml.bethelks.edu/issue/vol-68/article/avoiding-avoidance-why-i-assigned-body-politics-th/.

Berry, Malinda E. "'This Mark of a Standing Human Figure Poised to Embrace': A Constructive Theology of Social Responsibility, Nonviolence, and Nonconformity." Ph.D. dissertation, Union Theological Seminary, 2013.

Bloom, Linda. "Mennonites Reconnect with UMC Founder." *UMNS,* June 27, 2016. https://www.umnews.org/en/news/mennonites-reconnect-with-umc-founder.

Boff, Leonardo. "Fe y Política." *Koinonía,* Agenda Latinoamericana 2008. http://servicioskoinonia.org/agenda/archivo/obra.php?ncodigo=613.

Borrero, Cindy. "Betsabé Espinal, Mujer Valiente y Luchadora: Pionera en la Defensa de los Derechos Laborales en Colombia." CEDESIP: Centro de Estudios Sindicales y Políticos. March 7, 2019. http://www.cedesip.org/betsabe-espinal-mujer-valiente-y-luchadora-pionera-en-la-defensa-de-los-derechos-laborales-en-colombia/.

Bradbury, Shelly, and Peter Smith. "In the Shadow of Forgiveness." *Pittsburgh-Post-Gazette,* June 1, 2019, https://www.apnews.com/3000fa23351b4d28b1e49c439d0063e9.

Brandt, Di. "Pornography Silences Women." *Report* 64 (January–February 1986): 6–7.

Brock, Rita Nakashima, and Rebecca Ann Parker. *Proverbs of Ashes: Violence, Redemptive Suffering, and the Search for What Saves Us.* Boston: Beacon, 2001.

Brock, Rita Nakashima, and Rebecca Ann Parker. *Saving Paradise: How Christianity Traded Love of This World for Crucifixion and Empire.* Boston: Beacon, 2008.

Brown, Joanne Carlson, and Carol R. Bohn. *Christianity, Patriarchy, and Abuse: A Feminist Critique.* Cleveland: Pilgrim, 1989.

Bucher, Christina. "Servanthood in Isaiah." *Report* 89 (March–April 1990): 5–7.
Camará, Helder. *Spiral of Violence*. London: Sheed and Ward, 1971. http://www.alastairmcintosh.com/general/spiral-of-violence-camara.pdf.
A Canadian Reader, Letters. *Report* 64 (January–February 1986): 12.
Cannon, Katie Geneva. *Black Womanist Ethics*. Atlanta: Scholars Press, 1988.
Cannon, Katie Geneva. "Christian Imperialism and the Slave Trade." *Journal of Feminist Studies in Religion* 24, no. 1 (Spring 2008): 127–34. https://www.jstor.org/stable/20487919.
Cardenal, Ernesto. *The Gospel in Solentiname*. Maryknoll, NY: Orbis, 1992.
Carter, Warren. *Households and Discipleship: A Study of Matthew 19–20*. Sheffield, UK: Sheffield Academic, 1994.
Carter, Warren. *Matthew and the Margins, a Socio-political and Religious Reading*. Sheffield, UK: Sheffield Academic, 2000.
Castro, Jennifer, ed. *All You Need Is Love: Honoring the Diversity of Women's Voices in Theology*. Elkhart, IN: Women in Leadership Project, Mennonite Church USA, 2016.
Cavanaugh, William. "Don't Change the World." *The Table*, July 13, 2017. Biola University Center for Christian Thought. https://cct.biola.edu/dont-change-world/.
Cavanaugh, William. *Torture and the Eucharist: Theology, Politics, and the Body of Christ*. Oxford: Blackwell, 1998.
Chabal, Patrick. *Africa: The Politics of Suffering and Smiling*. World Political Theories. London: Zed, 2009.
Chopp, Rebecca S. "Praxis." In *Dictionary of Feminist Theologies*, edited by Letty M. Russell and J. Shannon Clarkson, 221–2. Louisville: Westminster John Knox, 1996.
Coakley, Sarah. *Powers and Submissions: Spirituality, Philosophy, and Gender*. Oxford: Blackwell, 2002.
Cohen, Stanley. *States of Denial: Knowing about Atrocities and Suffering*. Cambridge, UK: Polity, 2001.
Coleman, Monica. *The Dinah Project: A Handbook for Congregational Response to Sexual Violence*. Eugene, OR: Wipf and Stock, 2010.
Cone, James H. *The Cross and the Lynching Tree*. Maryknoll, NY: Orbis, 2011.
Cone, James. H. *God of the Oppressed*. Maryknoll, NY: Orbis, 1997.
Cooper-White, Pamela. *The Cry of Tamar: Violence against Women and the Church's Response*, 2nd ed. Minneapolis: Fortress, 2012.
Cooper-White, Pamela. *Gender, Violence, and Justice: Collected Essays on Violence against Women*. Eugene, OR: Wipf and Stock, 2019.

Copeland, M. Shawn. "Wading through Many Sorrows: Toward a Theology of Suffering in Womanist Perspective." In *A Troubling in My Soul: Womanist Perspectives on Evil and Suffering*, edited by Emilie M. Townes, 109–29. Maryknoll, NY: Orbis, 1993.

Crary, David. "Evangelicals Confront Sex Abuse Problems in #MeToo Era." *Associated Press*, August 17, 2018. https://www.apnews.com/b7 68d035ed8443ad97d193a5c36e240c

Crumpton, Stephanie M. "Trauma-Sensitive Pedagogy." In *Teaching Sexuality and Religion in Higher Education: Embodied Learning, Trauma Sensitive Pedagogy, and Perspective Transformation*, edited by Darryl W. Stephens and Kate Ott, chapter 2. Routledge Research in Religion and Education. New York: Routledge, 2020.

C-SPAN. "Supreme Court Nominee Brett Kavanaugh Sexual Assault Hearing, Professor Blasey Ford Testimony." 3:04:21, September 27, 2018. https://www.c-span.org/event/?451895/judge-kavanaugh-profess or-blasey-ford-testify-sexual- assault-allegations.

Dary Fuentes, Claudia. "Las iglesias ante las violencias en Latinoamérica: Modelos y experiencias De Paz en contextos de conflicto y violencia (Churches in the Face of Violence in Latin America: Models and Experiences of Peace in Contexts of Conflict and Violence)." CLALS Working Paper Series No. 3, rev. August 6, 2014. Washington, DC: Center for Latin American & Latino Studies, American University. http://ssrn.com/abstract=2412771.

De Farrari, Teresa M. "The Politics of Jesus: Vicit Agnus Noster." *Catholic Biblical Quarterly* 36, no. 1 (1974): 149–50.

De La Torre, Miguel A. *The Politics of Jesús: A Hispanic Political Theology*. Lanham, MD: Rowman & Littlefield, 2015.

"Después de medio siglo, Colombia y las FARC concluyen un acuerdo de paz." *20minutos*, August 25, 2016.

Diálogo Democrático-Un Manual para Practicantes. Manual preparado por ACDI, IDEA, OEA, PNUD. Facilitado por Instituto de Paz de los Estados Unidos en Colombia en 2010. https://www.oas.org/es/sap/dsd me/pubs/DIAL_%20DEMO_s.pdf.

Douglas, Kelly Brown. *Stand Your Ground: Black Bodies and the Justice of God*. Maryknoll, NY: Orbis, 2015.

Douglas, Kelly Brown. *What's Faith Got to Do with It? Black Bodies / Christian Souls*. Maryknoll, NY: Orbis, 2005.

Driedger, Diane. "Disabled Women and the Church." *Report* 80 (September–October 1988): 12–13.

Driedger, Leo, and Donald B. Kraybill. *Mennonite Peacemaking: From Quietism to Activism*. Scottdale: Herald, 1994.

Du Bois, W. E. B. *The Souls of Black Folk*. Edited by Brent Hayes Edwards. New York: Oxford University Press, 2007.

Dube, Musa W. *Postcolonial Feminist Interpretation of the Bible.* St. Louis, MO: Chalice, 2000.

Dyck, Carol. "Capturing God's Mystery in Song." *Report* 76 (January–February 1988): 12–14.

Ellison, Marvin M. "Christian Sex, Christian Ethics: Marvin M. Ellison on Jung and Stephens' *Professional Sexual Ethics*." *Marginalia: A Los Angeles Review of Books*, October 27, 2015. http://marginalia.larevie wofbooks.org/christian-sex-christian-ethics-by-marvin-m-ellison/.

Epp-Tiessen, Esther. *Mennonite Central Committee in Canada: A History.* Winnipeg: CMU Press, 2013.

Estupiñán, Miguel. "Creer en la Reconciliación: Un Proyecto de los Menonitas y la Iglesia Protestante de Holanda." *Vida Nueva Digital*, September 6, 2017. https://www.vidanuevadigital.com/2017/06/09/c reer-la-reconciliacion.

Farrow, Ronan, and Jane Mayer. "Senate Democrats Investigate a New Allegation of Sexual Misconduct, From Brett Kavanaugh's College Years." *New Yorker*, September 23, 2018. https://www.newyorker.com /news/news-desk/senate-democrats-investigate-a-new-allegation-of-sexual-misconduct-from-the-supreme-court-nominee-brett-kavanaughs -college-years-deborah-ramirez.

Figueroa, Rocío, and David Tombs. *Recognising Jesus as a Victim of Sexual Abuse: Responses from Sodalicio Survivors in Peru.* Ortago, New Zealand: Centre for Theology and Public Issues, University of Otago, 2019. http://hdl.handle.net/10523/8976.

Finger, Reta Halteman. "Community and Individual in the New Testament." *Report* 121 (July–August 1995): 7–8.

Finger, Thomas N. *A Contemporary Anabaptist Theology: Biblical, Historical, Constructive.* Downers Grove, IL: Intervarsity, 2004.

Fiorenza, Elisabeth Schüssler. *In Memory of Her: A Feminist Theological Reconstruction of Christian Origins.* 10th ed. New York: Crossroad, 1994.

Fiorenza, Elisabeth Schüssler. *Jesus: Miriam's Child, Sophia's Prophet: Critical Issues in Feminist Christology.* New York: Continuum, 1994.

Fortune, Marie M. *Is Nothing Sacred? When Sex Invades the Pastoral Relationship.* San Francisco: Harper and Row, 1989.

Fortune, Marie M. *Sexual Violence: The Sin Revisited.* Cleveland: Pilgrim, 2005.

Gabiam, Nell. *The Politics of Suffering: Syria's Palestinian Refugee Camps.* Public Cultures of the Middle East and North Africa. Bloomington, IN: Indiana University Press, 2016.

Garner, Steve. "Surfing the Third Wave of Whiteness Studies: Reflections on Twine and Gallagher." *Ethnic and Racial Studies* 40, no. 9 (2017): 1582–97. https://doi.org/10.1080/01419870.2017.1300301.

GemPaz. "Encuentro Nacional de GEMPAZ 2016." http://www.gemp az.org/index.php/noticias-gempaz/encuentro-nacional-de-gempaz-2016.

GemPaz. "Manifesto of the VIII GemPaz National." June 6, 2019. https://www.facebook.com/notes/gempaz/manifesto-of-the-viii-gempaz-national-encounter-peace-is-a-matter-of-humanity-an/27298221204 24823/.

General Conference Mennonite Church, and Mennonite Church. *Confession of Faith in a Mennonite Perspective*. Scottdale, PA: Herald, 1995.

Gingerich, Debra. "Compiler's Comments." *Report* 163 (September–October 2002): 2–3.

Glick, Rhoda S. "Inspiration for the Church." *Report* 171 (January–February 2004): 8–10.

González, Justo L. *The Story Luke Tells: Luke's Unique Witness to the Gospel*. Grand Rapids, MI: Eerdmans, 2015.

Goodkind, Nicole. "Georgia Mayor Reportedly Won't Hire Black Administrator Because 'City Isn't Ready.'" *Newsweek*, May 6, 2019. https://www.newsweek.com/georgia-mayor-atlanta-race-relations-141 6577 (accessed May 31, 2019).

Goossen, Rachel Waltner. "'Defanging the Beast': Mennonite Responses to John Howard Yoder's Sexual Abuse." *Mennonite Quarterly Review* 89, no. 1 (January 2015): 7–80.

Goossen, Rachel Waltner. "Historical Justice in an Era of #MeToo: Legacies of John Howard Yoder." The Martin Marty Center for the Public Understanding of Religion. December 7, 2017. https://divinit y.uchicago.edu/sightings/historical-justice-era-metoo-legacies-john-ho ward-yoder.

Goossen, Rachel Waltner. "Mennonite Bodies, Sexual Ethics: Women Challenge John Howard Yoder." *Journal of Mennonite Studies* 34 (2016): 247–59.

Gorman, Michael J. *Reading Revelation Responsibly: Uncivil Worship and Witness: Following the Lamb into the New Creation*. Eugene, OR: Cascade, 2010.

Grandin, Greg. *The End of the Myth: From the Frontier to the Border Wall in the Mind of America*. New York: Metropolitan, 2019.

Grant, Jacquelyn. "The Sin of Servanthood." In *A Troubling in My Soul: Womanist Perspectives on Evil and Suffering*, edited by Emilie M. Townes, 199–218. Maryknoll, NY: Orbis, 1993.

Grant, Jacquelyn. *White Women's Christ and Black Women's Jesus*. Atlanta: Scholars Press, 1989.

Graybill, Beth. "Toward a New Theology: Pacifism and Women's Resistance." *Report* 164 (November–December 2002): 3–5.

Gregory of Nazianzus. *To Cledonius the Priest against Apollinarius* (Epistle 101). http://www.newadvent.org/fathers/3103a.htm.

Grimsrud, Ted. *Instead of Atonement: The Bible's Salvation Story and Our Hope for Wholeness*. Eugene, OR: Cascade, 2013.

Groff, Gwen. "Looking Back: Women's Concerns Directors Reflect." *Report* 165 (January–February 2003): 1–2.

Groff, Gwen, and Emily Will, "Sharing Our Stories." *Report* 70 (January–February 1987): 1.

Gubkin, Liora. "From Empathetic Understanding to Engaged Witnessing: Encountering Trauma in the Holocaust Classroom." *Teaching Theology and Religion* 18, no. 2 (April 2015): 103–20. https://doi.org/10.1111/teth.12273.

Gupta, Nijay K. *Colossians*. Macon, GA: Smyth & Helwys, 2013.

Guth, Karen V. "Doing Justice to the Complex Legacy of John Howard Yoder: Restorative Justice Resources in Witness and Feminist Ethics." *Journal of the Society of Christian Ethics* 35, no. 2 (Fall/Winter 2015): 119–39. http://dx.doi.org/10.1353/sce.2015.0037.

Guth, Karen V. "Moral Injury and the Ethics of Teaching Tainted Legacies." *Teaching Theology and Religion* 21, no. 3 (July 2018): 197–209. https://doi.org/10.1111/teth.12441.

Guth, Karen V. "Moral Injury, Feminist and Womanist Ethics, and Tainted Legacies." *Journal of the Society of Christian Ethics* 38, no. 1 (Spring/Summer 2018): 167–86. http://dx.doi.org/10.1353/sce.2018.0010.

Gutiérrez, Gustavo. *A Theology of Liberation: History, Politics, and Salvation*. Maryknoll, NY: Orbis, 1973.

Habegger, Luann. "Note to Readers." *Report from the Peace Section Task Force on Women in Church and Society* 1 (August 1973): 1.

Halpern, Cynthia. *Suffering, Politics, Power: A Genealogy in Modern Political Theory*. Albany: SUNY Press, 2002.

Haney-Lopez, Ian. *White by Law: The Legal Construction of Race*. New York: New York University Press, 1996.

Harder, Lydia Neufeld. *The Challenge Is in the Naming: A Theological Journey*. Eugene, OR: Wipf and Stock, 2018.

Hauerwas, Stanley. "In Defense of 'Our Respectable Culture': Trying to Make Sense of John Howard Yoder." *ABC Religion and Ethics*, October 18, 2017. https://www.abc.net.au/religion/in-defence-of-our--culture-trying-to-make-sense-of-jo/10095302.

Haverstick, Patricia. "Looking Forward: Compiler's Comments." *Report* 170 (November–December 2003): 1–3.

Heggen, Carolyn Holderread. "Sexual Abuse by Church Leaders and Healing for Victims." *Mennonite Quarterly Review* 89, no. 1 (January 2015): 81–93.

Heggen, Carolyn Holderread. *Sexual Abuse in Christian Homes and Churches*. Scottdale, PA: Herald, 1993. Reprint, Eugene, OR: Wipf and Stock, 2006.

Hendricks, Obery M., Jr. *The Politics of Jesus: Rediscovering the True Revolutionary Nature of the Teachings of Jesus and How They Have Been Corrupted*. New York: Doubleday, 2006.

Hengel, Martin. *Crucifixion: In the Ancient World and the Folly of the Message of the Cross*. Philadelphia: Fortress, 1977.

Hershberger, Guy Franklin. *War, Peace, and Nonresistance*. Scottdale, PA: Herald. 1944.

Hershberger, Michelle. *A Christian View of Hospitality: Expecting Surprises*. Scottdale, PA: Herald, 1999.

Hess, Carol Lakey. *Caretakers of Our Common Household: Women's Development in Communities of Faith*. Nashville: Abingdon, 1997.

Horsley, Richard A. *Jesus and Empire: The Kingdom of God and the New World Disorder*. Minneapolis: Fortress, 2003.

Horsley, Richard A. *Jesus in Context: Power, People, and Performance*. Minneapolis: Fortress, 2008.

Horsley, Richard A., and Tom Thatcher. *John, Jesus and the Renewal of Israel*. Grand Rapids, MI: William B. Eerdmans, 2013.

Houser, Gordon. "Yoder Books Keep Coming." *The Mennonite* 13, no. 6 (June 2010): 59.

Huesbe Llanos, Marco A. "Reforma Política Luterana en el siglo XVII de Martín Lutero a Henning Arnisaeus." Revista de Estudios Histórico-Jurídicos, 1999. Ediciones Universitarias de Valparaiso.

Hughes, Langston. *The Panther and the Lash: Poems of Our Times*. New York: Alfred Knopf, 1969.

Immerwahr, Daniel. *How to Hide an Empire: A Short History of the Greater United States*. New York: Farrar, Straus and Giroux, 2019.

"Inclusión de medidas para garantizar los derechos de las mujeres en el Acuerdo de Paz es innovadora, aunque presenta retrasos en su implementación, revela informe," https://kroc.nd.edu/assets/294959/d efinitivo_comunicado_de_prensa_31102018.pdf.

Isasi-Díaz, Ada María. *En La Lucha / In the Struggle: Elaborating a Mujerista Theology*, 10th Anniversary Edition. Minneapolis: Fortress, 2004.

Isasi-Díaz, Ada María. *Mujerista Theology: A Theology for the Twenty-First Century*. Maryknoll, NY: Orbis, 1996.

Jacobson, Matthew Frye. *Whiteness of a Different Color: European Immigrants and the Alchemy of Race*. Cambridge, MA: Harvard University Press, 1998.

Joh, Wonhee Anne. *Heart of the Cross: A Postcolonial Christology*. Louisville: Westminster John Knox, 2006.

Jones, Nicholas R. "Sor Juana's Black Atlantic: Colonial Blackness and the Poetic Subversions of *Habla de Negros*." *Hispanic Review* 86, no. 3 (Summer 2018): 265–85. doi:10.1353/hir.2018.0022.

Josephus, Flavius. *The Jewish War*. Translated by G.A. Williamson. New York, NY: Penguin, 1970 [1959].

Juana Inés de la Cruz, Sor. *Obras Completas*. México: Editorial Porrúa, 2002.

Kao, Grace. "A Time of Reckoning: The SCE and John Howard Yoder." *Feminism and Religion*, January 13, 2017. https://feminismandreligion.com/2017/01/13/a-time-of-reckoning-the-sce-and-john-howard-yoder-by-grace-yia-hei-kao/.

Kauffmann-Kennel, Mary. "The Church: A Roadblock for Battered Women." *Report* 74 (September–October 1987): 5–7.

Keller, Timothy. *Generous Justice: How God's Grace Makes Us Just*. New York: Riverhead, 2012.

Koontz, Gayle Gerber. "Focus on Women in Ministry." *Report* 19 (April–May 1978): 1–2.

Koontz, Gayle Gerber. "Seventy Times Seven: Abuse and the Frustratingly Extravagant Call to Forgive." *Mennonite Quarterly Review* 89, no. 1 (January 2015): 129–52.

Krall, Ruth. "Development of Sexual Ethics." *Report* 44 (July–August 1982): 2–4.

Kraybill, Donald B. *Simply Amish: An Essential Guide from the Foremost Expert on Amish Life*. Herald, 2018.

Landman, Inge. *Creer en la Reconciliación. Herramientas Prácticas para la Lectura Contextual de la Biblia*. Bogotá: Alen Impresores, 2017.

Lederach, John Paul. *The Moral Imagination: The Art and Soul of Building Peace*. Bogotá: Norma Editions, 2009.

Lederach, John Paul. Presentation at the Peace Summit at Javeriana University, Bogotá, Colombia, July 2017.

Levine, Amy-Jill. *The Misunderstood Jew: The Church and the Scandal of the Jewish Jesus*. New York: HarperOne, 2006.

Lincoln, C. Eric. "Foreword." In *Is God a White Racist? A Preamble to Black Theology*, edited by William R. Jones, vii–viii. Garden City, NY: Anchor, 1973.

Lincoln, C. Eric, and Lawrence H. Mamiya. *The Black Church in the African American Experience*. Durham, NC: Duke University Press, 1990.

Loewen, Margreta Susanne Guenther. "Making Peace with the Cross: A Mennonite-Feminist Exploration of Dorothee Sölle and J. Denny Weaver on Nonviolence, Atonement, and Redemption." PhD dissertation, University of St. Michael's College, University of Toronto, 2016.

Loewen, Susanne Guenther. "Can the Cross Be 'Good News' for Women? Mennonite Peace Theology and the Suffering of Women." *Anabaptist Witness* 3, no. 2 (December 2016): 109–21. http://www.anabaptistwitness.org/wp-content/uploads/2016/12/Loewen-Can-the-Cross-Be-Good-News-for-Women.pdf.

Longacre, Doris Janzen. *Living More with Less*. Scottdale, PA: Herald, 1980.

Lovett, Joy. "Black Women: A State of the Union." *Report* 59 (January–February 1985): 1–9.

Lozano, Alix. "Being a Peach Church in the Colombian Context," trans. By Rebecca Yoder-Neufeld. In *Seeking Cultures of Peace: A Peace Church Conversation*, edited by Fernando Enns, Scott Holland, and Ann Riggs, 147–54. Geneva: World Council of Churches, 2004.

Manda, Charles. "Re-Authoring Life Narratives of Trauma Survivors: Spiritual Perspective." *Hervormde Teologiese Studies; Pretoria* 71, no. 2 (2015): 1–8.

Martell-Otero, Loida I., Zaida Maldonado Pérez, and Elizabeth Conde-Frazier. *Latina Evangélicas: A Theological Survey from the Margins*. Eugene, OR: Cascade, 2013.

Marti, Gerardo. "The Religious Racial Integration of African Americans into Diverse Churches." *Journal for the Scientific Study of Religion*, 49, no. 2 (June 2010): 201–17. https://doi.org/10.1111/j.1468-5906.2010.01503.x

Martínez García, Carlos. "Las Mujeres en el Movimiento Anabautista del Siglo XVI (I)." Protestante Digital.com, May 15, 2016.

Massey, Mary. "*Imago Dei:* The Importance of the Revised Standard Version." *Report* 152 (September–October 2000): 3–4.

Masthead. *Report* 155 (May–June 2001): 19.

"MCC Acts on Task Force Recommendation." *Report* 8 (May 1975): 1–2.

McClintock, Karen A. *When Trauma Wounds: Pathways to Healing and Hope*. Minneapolis: Fortress, 2019.

MennoMedia, "Yoder Books to Include Publisher's Statement." *Mennonite World Review*, December 23, 2013, http://www.mennoworld.org/archived/2013/12/23/yoder-books-include-publishers-statement/.

Mennonite Central Committee (MCC), homepage, https://mcc.org.

Mennonite Central Committee Women's Concerns Report. 1–171 (1974–2003).

Mennonite Church (MC USA). "Churchwide Statement on Sexual Abuse," July 3, 2015. http://mennoniteusa.org/wp-content/uploads/2015/07/Churchwide_Statement_On_Sexual_Abuse_2015July03.pdf (accessed October 8, 2019).

Mennonite Church (MC USA). "Forbearance in the Midst of Differences," resolution, July 2, 2015, http://mennoniteusa.org/wp-content/uploads/2015/07/ForbearanceResolution_2015Jul02.pdf.

Mennonite Church (MC USA). "John Howard Yoder Digest," March 5, 2015, http://mennoniteusa.org/resource/john-howard-yoder-digest/.

Mennonite Church (MC USA). "John Howard Yoder Digest: Recent Articles about Sexual Abuse and Discernment." Menno Snapshots. http://mennoniteusa.org/menno-snapshots/john-howard-yoder-digest-recent-articles-about-sexual-abuse-and-discernment-2/.

Mennonite Church (MC USA). "On the Status of the Membership Guidelines," resolution, July 2, 2015, http://mennoniteusa.org/wp-content/uploads/2015/07/ResolutionOnStatusofMembershipGuidelines_2015Jul02.pdf.

Mennonite Church (MC USA). "Prevention and Response: Sexual Abuse and Non-Credentialed Individuals," April 17, 2018, http://mennoniteusa.org/resource/prevention-and-response-sexual-abuse-and-non-credentialed-individuals/.

Mennonite Church (MC USA). "Resources on Sexual Abuse Response and Prevention," http://mennoniteusa.org/resources-on-sexual-abuse-response-and-prevention/ (accessed October 3, 2019).

Mennonite Church (MC USA). "Vision for Healing and Hope," http://mennoniteusa.org/what-we-believe/ (accessed October 6, 2019).

The Mennonite Quarterly Review 68 (April 1994). Special issue featuring papers presented at the Women Doing Theology Conference, sponsored by Mennonite Central Committee, June 23–25, 1994 in Bluffton, Ohio. https://www.goshen.edu/mqr/1997/03/the-mennonite-quarterly-review-contents-april-1994/.

Metzler, Ethel Yake. "Asian Women Doing Theology." *Report* 72 (May–June 1987): 1.

Meyer, Stephen Grant. *As Long as They Don't Move Next Door: Segregation and Racial Conflict in American Neighborhoods*. Lanham, MD: Rowman & Littlefield, 1999.

Michalski, Joseph H. "Status Hierarchies and Hegemonic Masculinity: A General Theory of Prison Violence." *British Journal of Criminology* 57, no. 1 (2017): 40–60. https://doi.org/10.1093/bjc/azv098.

Minister, Meredith. "Leading a Faculty Workshop on Teaching about Sexual Violence." *Teaching Theology and Religion* 20, no. 1 (2017): 75–9. https://doi.org/10.1111/teth.12369.

Mitchell, Rhoda. "Domestic Violence Prevention through the Constructing Violence-Free Masculinities Programme: An Experience from Perú." *Gender and Development* 21, no. 1 (2013): 97–109. https://doi.org/10.1080/13552074.2013.767516.

National Sexual Violence Resource Center. "Statistics about Sexual Violence." 2015. https://www.nsvrc.org/sites/default/files/publications_nsvrc_factsheet_media-packet_statistics-about-sexual-violence_0.pdf.

Neilsen, Rhiannon S. "'Toxification' as a More Precise Early Warning Sign for Genocide than Dehumanization? An Emerging Research Agenda." *Genocide Studies and Prevention: An International Journal* 9, no. 1 (2015): 83–95. http://dx.doi.org/10.5038/1911-9933.9.1.1277.

Neudorf, Kate. Letters, *Report* 65 (March–April 1986): 13.

Ngong, David T. "Protesting the Cross: African Pentecostal Soteriology and Pastoral Care." *Journal of Theology for Southern Africa* 150 (November 2014): 5–19.

Nolt, Steven M. *The Amish: A Concise Introduction*. Baltimore: Johns Hopkins University Press, 2016.

Nyce, Dorothy Yoder. "Childbearing and the Bible: A Dictionary Approach." *Report* 55 (May–June 1984): 1–3.

Nyce, Dorothy Yoder. "Genesis 1–3: A Place to Begin." *Report* 49 (May–June 1983): 1–3.

Nyce, Dorothy Yoder. "Leadership and Ordination Intertwined." *Report* 43 (May–June 1982): 3–5.

Nyce, Dorothy Yoder. "Ten Years Later." *Report* 50 (July–August 1983): 3–4.

Omi, Michael, and Howard Winant. "Racial Formations." In *Race, Class, and Gender in the United States: An Integrated Study*, 10th ed., edited by Paula S. Rothenberg with Kelly S. Mayhew, 13–19. New York: Worth, 2014.

"Open Letter in Response to Donald Trump on his Chosen Language to Speak of Immigrants," June 1, 2018, https://www.garrett.edu/news/open-letter-president-donald-trump-his-chosen-language-speak-immigrants.

Paris, Peter J. *The Social Teaching of the Black Churches*. Philadelphia: Fortress, 1985.

Peachey, Linda Gehman. "Naming the Pain, Seeking the Light: The Mennonite Church's Response to Sexual Abuse." *Mennonite Quarterly Review* 89, no. 1 (January 2015): 111–28.

Penner, Carol. "An Anabaptist Theology Opposing Violence against Women." *Report* 164 (November–December 2002): 1–2.

Penner, Carol. "Mennonite Silences and Feminist Voices: Peace Theology and Violence against Women." Ph.D. Dissertation, University of St. Michael's College, 1999.

Penner, Carol. "Women Moving into Ministry: A Canadian Mennonite Press Survey." *Journal of Mennonite Studies* 37 (2019): 161–80.

Pogrebin, Robin, and Kate Kelly. "Brett Kavanaugh Fit In With the Privileged Kids: She Did Not." *New York Times*, September 14, 2019.

https://www.nytimes.com/2019/09/14/sunday-review/brett-kavanaugh-deborah-ramirez-yale.html.

Pohl, Christine D. *Making Room: Recovering Hospitality as a Christian Tradition*. Grand Rapids, MI: Eerdmans, 1999.

Poling, James Newton. *Rethinking Faith: A Constructive Practical Theology*. Minneapolis: Fortress, 2011.

Power, Garrett. "Apartheid Baltimore Style: The Residential Segregation Ordinances of 1910–1913." *Maryland Law Review* 42, no. 2 (1983): 289–329.

Press release, "Disciplinary Process with Yoder Concludes," *Gospel Herald*, June 18, 1996: 11.

Pressley, Jana, and Joseph Spinazzola. "Beyond Survival: Application of a Complex Trauma Treatment Model in the Christian Context." In *Treating Trauma in Christian Counseling*, edited by Heather Davediuk Gingrich and Fred C. Gingrich, 211–31. Downers Grove, IL: IVP Academic, 2017.

Pruitt, Bettye, and Philip Thomas. *Diálogo Democrático: Un Manual para Practicantes*. ACDI, IDEA, OEA, PNUD, 2008. https://www.oas.org/es/sap/dsdme/pubs/DIAL_%20DEMO_s.pdf

Rambo, Shelly. *Resurrecting Wounds: Living in the Aftermath of Trauma*. Waco, TX: Baylor University Press, 2018.

Rambo, Shelly. *Spirit and Trauma: A Theology of Remaining*. Louisville: Westminster John Knox, 2010.

Rambo, Shelly. "Trauma and Faith: Reading the Narrative of the Hemorrhaging Woman." *International Journal of Practical Theology* 13, no. 2 (2009): 233–57. DOI: https://doi.org/10.1515/ijpt.2009.15.

"Reader Feedback." *Report* 73 (July–August 1987): 14–15.

Reba Place Church Membership Questions. Adopted November 16, 2006. https://docs.wixstatic.com/ugd/c640b0_a44fb643feb4471389d255f830b57bc1.pdf.

Reedy, Janet Umble. "Reflections." *Report* 74 (September–October 1987): 9–10.

Reimer, Margaret Loewen. "The Task Force Report." *MCC Women's Concerns Committee Report* 50 (July–August 1983): 9.

Richards, Emma. "What Do Participants Say: Emma Richards." *Report* 63 (September–October 1985): 13.

Rivera, Mayra. *Poetics of the Flesh*. Durham, NC: Duke University Press, 2015.

Rivera, Mayra. "Thinking Bodies: The Spirit of a Latina Incarnational Imagination." In *Decolonizing Epistemologies: Latina/o Theology and Philosophy*, edited by Ada María Isasi Díaz, and Eduardo Mendieta, 207–25. New York: Fordham University Press, 2011.

Rodriguez, Amardo. "The Performative Nature of Knowledge." In *Liminal Traces: Storying, Performing, and Embodying Postcoloniality*, edited by Devika Chawla and Amardo Rodriguez, 65–73. Boston: Sense, 2011.

Roithmayr, Daria. *Reproducing Racism: How Everyday Choices Lock in White Advantage*. New York: New York University Press, 2014.

Ross, Rosetta E. *Witnessing and Testifying: Black Women, Religion, and Civil Rights*. Minneapolis: Fortress, 2003.

Ross, Sam, and Morag Ross. *Memoirs of Sam and Morag Ross*. Pietermaritzburg, South Africa: printed by the author, 2000.

Rubio, Julie Hanlon. "Review of *Christian Ethics at the Boundary: Feminism and Theologies of Public Life* by Karen V. Guth." *Journal of the Society of Christian Ethics* 38, no. 2 (Fall/Winter 2018): 196–7. http://dx.doi.org/10.1353/sce.2018.0045.

Sabar, Ariel. "The Unbelievable Tale of Jesus's Wife." *The Atlantic*, July/August 2016. https://www.theatlantic.com/magazine/archive/2016/07/the-unbelievable-tale-of-jesus-wife/485573/.

Salazar, Fabián. "Desafío a los teólogos en Colombia." *El Tiempo*, September 4, 2007. http://blogs.eltiempo.com/confesiones/2007/09/04/desafio-a-los-teologos-en-colombia/.

Sancken, Joni S. *Words That Heal: Preaching Hope to Wounded Souls, Artistry of Preaching Series*. Nashville: Abingdon, 2019.

Sanford, Victoria, Sofía Duyos Álvarez-Arenas, and Kathleen Dill. "Sexual Violence as a Weapon during the Guatemalan Genocide." In *Women and Genocide: Survivors, Victims, Perpetrators*, edited by Elissa Bemporad, and Joyce W. Warren, 207–22. Bloomington, IN: Indiana University Press, 2019.

Scarry, Elaine. *The Body in Pain: The Making and Unmaking of the World*. Oxford: Oxford University Press, 1985.

Scarsella, Hilary Jerome, and Stephanie Krehbiel. "Sexual Violence: Christian Theological Legacies and Responsibilities." *Religion Compass* 13, no. 9 (September 2019): 1–13. https://doi.org/10.1111/rec3.12337.

Schertz, Mary H. "God's Cross and Women's Questions: A Biblical Perspective on the Atonement." *The Mennonite Quarterly Review* 68, no. 2 (April 1994): 194–208.

Segovia, Fernando F. "Jesus as Victim of State Terror: A Critical Reflection Twenty Years Later." In *Crucifixion, State Terror, and Sexual Abuse: Text and Context*, edited by David Tombs, 22–31. Dunedin, New Zealand: Centre for Theology and Public Issues, University of Otago, 2018. http://hdl.handle.net/10523/8558.

Segovia, Fernando F. "Toward a Hermeneutics of the Diaspora: A Hermeneutics of Otherness and Engagement." In *Reading from This Place: Volume I; Social Location and Biblical Interpretation in the United States*, edited by Fernando F. Segovia, and Mary Ann Tolbert, 57–74. Minneapolis: Fortress, 1995.

Shay, Jonathan. "Casualties." *Daedalus* 140, no. 3 (Summer 2011): 179–88. http://www.jstor.org/stable/23047357.

Shenk, Sara Wenger. "Arguing Our Way Toward a Storm-worthy Moral Canopy." Practicing Reconciliation Blog, January 5, 2017. https://www.ambs.edu/publishing/blog/841477/arguing-our-way-toward-a-stormworthy-moral-canopy.

Shenk, Sara Wenger. "But I've Seen Him Do so Much Good." Practicing Reconciliation Blog, September 16, 2016. https://www.ambs.edu/blog/715868/but-i-ve-seen-him-do-so-much-good.

Shenk, Sara Wenger. "Revisiting the Legacy of John Howard Yoder." Practicing Reconciliation Blog, July 25, 2013. https://www.ambs.edu/publishing/blog/715800/revisiting-the-legacy-of-john-howard-yoder.

Slough, Rebecca. "Congregational Responses to Abuse and Trauma: The Persistent Hope of Shalom." *The Mennonite Quarterly Review* 89, no. 1 (January 2015): 95–110.

Smith, Andrea. *Conquest: Sexual Violence and American Indian Genocide*. Cambridge, MA: South End, 2005.

Smith, Carly Parnitzke, and Jennifer J. Freyd. "Institutional Betrayal." *American Psychologist* 69, no. 6 (September 2014): 575–87. http://dx.doi.org/10.1037/a0037564.

Snowden, Judith. "Who Will Listen? Who Will Hear?" *Report* 150 (May–June 2000): 3–5.

Snyder, C. Arnold, and Linda A. Huebert Hecht, eds. *Profiles of Anabaptist Women: Sixteenth-Century Reforming Pioneers*, Studies in Women and Religion 3. Waterloo, ON: Wilfrid Laurier University Press, 1996.

Sokol, Michelle. "Mennonite Seminary Apologizes to Victims of Famed Theologian John Howard Yoder." *National Catholic Reporter*, April 9, 2015. https://www.ncronline.org/news/accountability/mennonite-seminary-apologizes-victims-famed-theologian-john-howard-yoder.

Sölle, Dorothee. *Political Theology*. Translated by John Shelley. Philadelphia: Fortress, 1974.

Sölle, Dorothee. *Suffering*. Translated by Everett R. Kalin. Philadelphia: Fortress, 1975.

Soto Albrecht, Elizabeth. "Compilers' Comments." *Report* 157 (September–October 2001): 1–4.

Soto Albrecht, Elizabeth. *Family Violence: Reclaiming a Theology of Nonviolence*. Maryknoll, NY: Orbis, 2008.

Soto, Elizabeth. "The Syrophoenician Woman." *Report* 164 (November–December 2002): 10–11.

Stackley, Muriel Thiessen. "The *Report*: Helping us 'Rethink.'" *Report* 109 (July–August 1993): 10.

Stephens, Darryl W. "A Deacon's Eye for Healing Congregations." *Currents in Theology and Mission* 42, no. 3 (July 2015): 213–19.

Stephens, Darryl W. "Fiduciary Duty and Sacred Trust." In *Professional Sexual Ethics: A Holistic Ministry Approach*, edited by Patricia Beattie Jung and Darryl W. Stephens, 23–33. Minneapolis: Fortress, 2013.

Stewart, Eric C. "Masculinity in the New Testament and in Early Christianity." *Biblical Theology Bulletin* 46, no. 2 (2016): 91–102. https://doi.org/10.1177/0146107916639211.

Stoltzfus, Ruth Brunk. "Women in the Bible." *Report* 153 (January–February 2001): 4–6.

Stucky, Leona. *The Fog of Faith: Surviving My Impotent God*. Santa Fe, NM: Prairie World, 2017.

Sugrue, Thomas J. *Sweet Land of Liberty: The Forgotten Struggle for Civil Rights in the North*. New York: Random House, 2008.

"Thanks to All the Subscribers." *Report* 154 (March–April 2001): 15.

Thiessen, Vange. "Serving with a Feminist Perspective." *Report* 89 (March–April 1990): 3.

Thistlethwaite, Susan. *Women's Bodies as Battlefield: Christian Theology and the Global War on Women*. New York, NY: Palgrave Macmillan, 2015.

Tombs, David. "Crucifixion, State Terror, and Sexual Abuse." *Union Seminary Quarterly Review* 53 (Autumn 1999): 89–109. Reprinted in *Crucifixion, State Terror, and Sexual Abuse: Text and Context*, edited by David Tombs, 5–21. Dunedin, New Zealand: Centre for Theology and Public Issues, University of Otago, 2018. http://hdl.handle.net/10523/8558.

Tombs, David. "Crucifixión, terrorismo de Estado y abuso sexual: Texto y Contexto" (Project Report in the Centre for Theology and Public Issues Project Series "When Did We See You Naked?" No. 2), edited by Rocío Figueroa and David Tombs. Centre for Theology and Public Issues, University of Otago. http://hdl.handle.net/10523/8988.

Townes, Emilie M. "Living in the New Jerusalem: The Rhetoric and Movement of Liberation in the House of Evil." In *A Troubling in My Soul: Womanist Perspectives on Evil and Suffering*, edited by Emilie M. Townes, 78–91. Maryknoll, NY: Orbis, 1993.

Trexler, Richard C. *Sex and Conquest: Gendered Violence, Political Order and the European Conquest of the Americas*. Cambridge, UK: Polity, 1995.

Unceta, Koldo. *Desarrollo, Postcrecimiento y Buen Vivir: Debates e Interrogantes*, edited by Alberto Acosta and Esperanza Martínez. Quito, Ecuador: Ediciones Abya-Yala, 2014. http://filosofiadelbuenvivir.com/wp-content/uploads/2015/02/Desarrollo-postcrecimiento-y-Buen-Vivir-2014.pdf.

Unidad para la Atención y la Reparación Integral a las Víctimas, "Planes de acción para mujeres," 2018. http://www.unidadvictimas.gov.co/es/la-paz-tiene-nombre-de-mujer/9027.

van der Kolk, Bessel. *The Body Keeps Score: Brain, Mind, and Body in the Healing of Trauma.* New York: Penguin, 2014.

van der Kolk, Bessel. "In Terror's Grip: Healing the Ravages of Trauma." http://www.traumacenter.org/products/pdf_files/terrors_grip.pdf.

Volf, Miroslav. *The End of Memory: Remembering Rightly in a Violent World.* Grand Rapids: Eerdmans, 2006.

Volf, Miroslav. *Exclusion and Embrace, Revised and Updated: A Theological Exploration of Identity, Otherness, and Reconciliation.* Nashville: Abingdon, 2019.

Volf, Miroslav. *Free of Charge: Giving and Forgiving in a Culture Stripped of Grace* Grand Rapids: Zondervan, 2006.

Weaver, J. Denny. *The Nonviolent Atonement.* 2nd ed. Grand Rapids, MI: Eerdmans, 2011.

Weaver-Zercher, David L. *Martyrs Mirror: A Social History.* Baltimore: Johns Hopkins University Press, 2016.

Wells, Samuel. *Improvisation: The Drama of Christian Ethics.* Grand Rapids: Baker, 2004.

West, Traci. *Disruptive Christian Ethics: When Racism and Women's Lives Matter.* Louisville: Westminster John Knox, 2006.

Will, Emily. "Remembering." *Report* 109 (July–August 1993): 5–6.

Williams, Delores. *Sisters in the Wilderness: The Challenge of Womanist God-Talk.* Maryknoll, NY: Orbis, 1993.

Williams, Rowan. "Insubstantial Evil." In *Augustine and His Critics*, edited by Robert Dodaro and George Lawless, 105–23. Oxfordshire, UK: Routledge, 2000.

Wink, Walter. *Jesus and Nonviolence: A Third Way.* Minneapolis: Fortress, 2003.

Wink, Walter. *Naming the Powers: The Language of Power in the New Testament.* Philadelphia: Fortress, 1984.

Wink, Walter. *Unmasking the Powers: The Invisible Forces That Determine Human Existence.* Philadelphia: Fortress, 1986.

Yamasaki, April. "In Search of Wholeness." *Report* 105 (November–December 1992): 4–5.

Yoder, Elizabeth. "The Christian and the Cult of Masculinity." *Report* 13 (February 1977): 1–3.

Yoder, Elizabeth G. *Peace Theology and Violence against Women.* Elkhart, IN: Institute of Mennonite Studies, 1992.

Yoder, John Howard. *The Politics of Jesus.* Grand Rapids, MI: Eerdmans, 1972.

Yoder, John Howard. *The Politics of Jesus: Vicit Agnus Noster.* 2nd ed. Grand Rapids, MI: Eerdmans, 1994.

Yoder, Marilyn Troyer. "Toward a Curriculum for Free People." *Report* 5 (April 1974): 3–4.

CONTRIBUTORS

Nancy E. Bedford is Georgia Harkness Professor of Applied Theology at Garrett-Evangelical Theological Seminary, Evanston, Illinois.

Erin Dufault-Hunter is Assistant Professor of Christian Ethics at Fuller Theological Seminary in Pasadena, California.

Karen V. Guth is Assistant Professor of Religious Studies at the College of the Holy Cross in Worcester, Massachusetts.

Alix Lozano is Director (retired) of the Seminario Bíblico Menonita de Colombia (Mennonite Seminary of Colombia) in Bogotá, Colombia.

Linda Gehman Peachey is former Director of Women's Advocacy (formerly Women's Concerns) for the Mennonite Central Committee US and a freelance writer and teacher in Lancaster, Pennsylvania.

Carol Penner is Assistant Professor of Theological Studies at Conrad Grebel University College in Waterloo, Ontario.

Hilary Jerome Scarsella is Director of Theological Integrity for Into Account and Assistant Professor of Ethics and Director of Women and Gender Studies in Church and Society at Colgate Rochester Crozer Divinity School in Rochester, New York.

Sara Wenger Shenk is President (retired) of Anabaptist Mennonite Biblical Seminary in Elkhart, Indiana.

Elizabeth Soto Albrecht is Adjunct Instructor and former Adviser for Global Theological Education at Lancaster Theological Seminary, Lancaster, Pennsylvania.

Darryl W. Stephens is Director of United Methodist Studies and Director of the Pennsylvania Academy of Ministry at Lancaster Theological Seminary in Lancaster, Pennsylvania.

Regina Shands Stoltzfus is Professor of Peace, Justice and Conflict Studies at Goshen College in Goshen, Indiana.

Karen Suderman is Director of the Intensive English Program at Eastern Mennonite University in Harrisonburg, Virginia.

AUTHOR INDEX

The following list includes names of authors whose work is substantively engaged in this book. Some names also appear in the Subject Index.

Alcoff, Linda Martín   20 n.4
Armster, Michelle E.   x, 44
Augustine   148 n.33, 194 n.14

Bailey, Wilma   ix, 41
Battistella, Edwin L.   184
Becker, Palmer   117
Berry, Malinda E.   125–7, 206, 208
Brandt, Di   38
Brock, Rita Nakashima   61 n.21, 157
Bucher, Christina   46–7

Camará, Helder   63
Cannon, Katie Geneva   98 nn.2–3, 102 n.11
Cardenal, Ernesto   39 n.14
Carter, Warren   121
Castro, Jennifer   124 n.33
Cavanaugh, William   144 n.25
Chabal, Patrick   56
Chopp, Rebecca S.   58
Coakley, Sarah   139 n.13
Cohen, Stanley   183
Coleman, Monica   150 n.37
Cone, James H.   100, 156
Cooper-White, Pamela   150 n.37
Copeland, M. Shawn   59

De La Torre, Miguel A.   54 n.1
Douglas, Kelly Brown   62 n.24, 194 n.14, 49 n.59

Driedger, Diane   44
Dube, Musa W.   57, 64, 194
Du Bois, W. E. B.   57
Dyck, Carol   38

Ellison, Marvin M.   207
Estupiñán, Miguel   92 n.22

Finger, Reta Halteman   44 n.39
Finger, Thomas N.   31–2
Fiorenza, Elisabeth Schüssler   120 n.16
Fortune, Marie M.   3, 65 n.34, 66 n.35, 157 n.11, 197 n.20
Freyd, Jennifer J.   182, 205

Garner, Steve   19 n.2
Gingerich, Debra   48 n.57
Glick, Rhoda S.   40
González, Justo L.   123
Goossen, Rachel Waltner   ix, xi n.12, 3 n.9, 60 n.18, 140 n.14, 166 n.24, 170, 173 n.4, 175, 191, 200
Grant, Jacquelyn   57, 99 n.4
Graybill, Beth   46–7
Gregory of Nazianzus   24 n.14, 26 n.19
Grimsrud, Ted   117
Groff, Gwen   38 n.13, 40
Gupta, Nijay K.   121 n.22
Gutiérrez, Gustavo   157

AUTHOR INDEX

Habegger, Luann   35 n.2
Halpern, Cynthia   59
Hamer, Fannie Lou   110–11
Hauerwas, Stanley   201, 202 n.3, 205
Haverstick, Patricia   44 n.37
Hecht, Linda A. Huebert   89
Heggen, Carolyn Holderread   125–6, 140 n.14, 189
Hendricks, Obery M., Jr.   54 n.1
Hershberger, Michelle   81
Horsley, Richard A.   120 n.16
Hughes, Langston   22

Isasi-Díaz, Ada María   5, 58, 65 n.33

Joh, Wonhee Anne   128
Juana Inés de la Cruz, Sor   24–5

Kauffmann-Kennel, Mary   44 n.34
Koontz, Gayle Gerber   ix, x n.10, 38, 140 nn.14–15
Krall, Ruth   xi n.12, 38, 49, 183

Landman, Inge   92 n.22
Lederach, John Paul   83, 84 n.5
Lincoln, C. Eric   101–2
Loewen, Margreta Susanne Guenther   ix, 62, 125, 127–8
Longacre, Doris Janzen   viii, 127
Lovett, Joy   41

Mamiya, Lawrence H.   101
Manda, Charles   135 nn.4–5
Marti, Gerardo   109–10
Massey, Mary   44 n.38
Metzler, Ethel Yake   42–3
Meyer, Stephen Grant   103 n.16, 104 nn.17–18
Mitchell, Rhoda   29 n.26

Neudorf, Kate   37 n.7
Ngong, David T.   61
Nyce, Dorothy Yoder   xi n.13, 42 n.29, 43 n.33, 44 n.40, 46, 49 n.59, 52

Omi, Michael   106 n.21

Parker, Rebecca Ann   61 n.21, 129–30, 157
Peachey, Linda Gehman   35 n.1, 140 n.14, 189 n.4, 190 n.5, 193 n.12
Penner, Carol   ix, x n.7, 37 n.5, 40 n.20, 125–6
Pohl, Christine D.   78
Poling, James Newton   49 n.60, 124 n.32

Rambo, Shelly   135–6, 150 n.37, 154 n.3
Reedy, Janet Umble   44 n.41
Reimer, Margaret Loewen   36 n.3
Richards, Emma Sommers   46
Rodriguez, Amardo   30

Salazar, Fabián   94
Sancken, Joni S.   184–5
Schertz, Mary H.   ix, 125–6
Segovia, Fernando F.   57 n.6, 160 n.20
Shay, Jonathan   205
Shenk, Sara Wenger   175 n.5, 180 nn.7–8, 181 n.9
Slough, Rebecca   140 nn.14–15, 180 n.7
Smith, Andrea   194–5
Smith, Carly Parnitzke   182, 205
Snowden, Judith   45
Snyder, C. Arnold   89
Sölle, Dorothee   58–9, 127
Soto Albrecht, Elizabeth   39 n.17, 42, 45–6, 125–6, 192

AUTHOR INDEX

Stackley, Muriel Thiessen   39, 46 n.49
Stephens, Darryl W.   137 n.9, 185 n.17
Stewart, Eric C.   26 n.20, 27 n.21, 28
Stoltzfus, Ruth Brunk   46 n.49
Stucky, Leona   122, 130

Thiessen, Vange   46 n.52
Tombs, David   154–5, 156 n.9, 158–60
Townes, Emilie M.   61 n.20, 62, 64 n.31
Trexler, Richard C.   160

van der Kolk, Bessel   135 n.4, 137 n.10
Volf, Miroslav   138 n.11–12, 145 n.27

Weaver, J. Denny   117–19, 127
Wells, Samuel   145 n.28
Wiebe, Katie Funk   37 n.5, 49
Will, Emily   37, 38 n.13
Williams, Delores   61–2, 157
Williams, Rowan   148 n.31 and n.33
Winant, Howard   106 n.21
Wink, Walter   49 n.60, 80 n.14, 133 n.2

Yamasaki, April   42 n.28
Yoder, Elizabeth G.   44 n.35, 166 n.23
Yoder, John Howard   23–4, 49 n.60, 59–60, 71–3, 145
Yoder, Marilyn Troyer   44 n.36

SUBJECT INDEX

#MeToo   xv, 2, 142, 203–4, 211

abuse   3, 34–5, 50, 59–60, 155, 171, 196–7, 210–11. *See also* perpetrator; survivor; Yoder, John Howard, abuse by
  of Jesus   45, 145, 153, 155–7
  logic of   146–9
  by persons in authority   2, 65, 152, 161–2, 177, 180, 184, 205–6, 209–10, 212
  sexual   2, 122, 133, 136–44, 161–2, 165–6, 190–3, 205 (*see also* violence, sexualized)
  teaching acceptance of   46, 56, 60, 126, 138, 144–6, 157
  as trauma   34, 135–9, 142, 144, 149–50, 157, 209
  uncertainty of   152–3, 161–6
accountability. *See also* perpetrator, accountability for
  for abuse and violence   55, 66, 130–1, 142–3, 152, 162, 164, 197
  within Christian community   6, 88, 111, 207
  institutional   2, 177–87, 189–91, 207, 210–11
  of John Howard Yoder   175–6, 182, 189, 207, 210
  lack of   3, 198, 210
  to the state   88
African American. *See* Black
African National Congress   70, 75
Allen, Richard   101
Anabaptist Mennonite Biblical Seminary (AMBS)   x, xiv–xvi, 170–82, 184–5, 187, 189, 202–3, 208
Anabaptist Network in South Africa   70
apartheid   70–1, 74–81
apology   138, 170, 174, 176–9, 181, 184, 187
atonement   117, 119
authority. *See also* abuse, by persons in authority
  divine   28, 87, 165
  legitimate   205–6, 208–12
  moral   171, 179–81, 184–5, 206–12
  structures of   28, 78, 87–9, 200, 206
  of women   4, 65, 144

bearing witness   108–9, 153, 157, 161, 163–6, 178
Bible. *See* scripture
binaries   111, 196, 198
Black   21–6, 36, 41, 57, 62, 70, 74–5, 79, 97–111. *See also* Jesus, as Black; race

SUBJECT INDEX

Black bodies 62, 97, 99–100, 103, 105, 108, 111
Black Church 98, 100–2
Blasey Ford, Christine 142 n.20, 161–2
bodily integrity. *See also* trauma
   cultural conditions for 26
   embodiment 30, 32, 58, 66, 109, 148
   violence to 32, 119, 133, 135–7, 144, 158, 194, 196
bondage 118, 120, 123, 148
Bosch, David and Annemie 76–8, 81

Christ 6, 54, 61, 64, 72, 119, 134, 141, 145–7. *See also* Christology; freedom, in Christ; Jesus
   body of, as community xvi, 30, 65, 110, 117, 147
   body of, crucified and resurrected 24, 99, 139–41, 145, 147, 149, 153–4, 158
   good news of (*see* gospel)
   imitation of 30, 46, 63, 81, 140, 145–7 (*see also* discipleship)
   incarnation 18 n.1, 24, 26, 30, 44, 89, 99–100, 154 n.3, 157, 163
   sacrifice of 55, 100, 134 n.3, 140, 145–6, 157, 163
Christology 18, 25, 29–32, 54, 65, 128, 134, 139, 141, 145, 149, 154 n.3
civil rights 97, 101, 103–4, 109–10
Colombia 55, 83–7, 90–3. *See also* peace, peace process in Colombia

colonization 19, 57, 64, 70, 90, 94, 194–5
Committee on Women's Concerns xiv, 35, 39, 43, 48
confession 51, 119, 122, 125, 130–1, 170, 176–9, 181, 183–5, 187
Confession of Faith in a Mennonite Perspective 118–19, 123 n.31, 197
conflict transformation 92
consciousness 57, 99, 101, 106, 110, 207
contextual reading of the Bible 92–3
creation 5–6, 18, 20, 51–2, 116, 123–4, 127, 131, 149, 195–6. *See also* scripture, creation
CristoSofia xv, 65
cross 61–3, 119, 125–8, 146–7, 155–6, 158
crucifixion 22, 24, 28, 62, 125, 128, 131, 139–40, 146, 153–61, 163–6. *See also* cross

discipleship. *See also* scripture, disciples
   Anabaptist ethos of 6, 31–2, 44, 95, 107, 117, 134, 140, 187, 198 n.21
   demands of 20, 27–9, 89, 164
   obstacles to 22, 29–31
   as servanthood 46–7, 56, 72–3, 80
   work of 35, 44–5, 90, 131, 149, 153, 163–4, 170–2, 204
docetism 18, 29–31
domination
   racial 97–8, 106, 109
   relationships of 43, 73, 80, 118, 131, 155–6

systems of 20–4, 26–9, 32, 40, 55, 57, 64, 90, 100, 118, 124, 128 (*see also* oppression, systems of; principalities)
through sexual violence 155, 158–60, 193–6

earth. *See* creation
Ecumenical Group of Women Builders of Peace (GemPaz) 84, 91–5
emancipation 58, 71, 73, 147
empowerment
  divine 47, 52, 62, 66, 120, 128–9, 131, 144–7
  within oppressive systems 70, 73–4, 78–80, 212
  as power sharing 28, 42–3, 51, 63–4, 193
  of women 13, 48–9, 85, 185–6, 207, 210, 212
enemy 61, 66, 76, 145, 147–8, 159, 171, 195
  forgiveness of 119, 140
  love of 22, 66, 95, 117–18, 134, 138, 141, 145, 197
enslavement, of Africans 25, 98, 100–2, 105, 108–9
equality. *See also* inequality
  Christian teaching of 5, 32, 43, 46, 102, 108
  social 57, 63, 71, 83, 130
  of women 37, 40, 46, 50, 196
Espinal, Betsabé 90
evil
  deliverance from 47
  effects of 137–9
  power 20, 55, 61, 118, 125, 134, 139, 147
  repentance for 133, 184
  resistance to 24, 110, 127
  structures of 90

facilitated dialogue 91
feminism 34–7, 40–2, 49 n.59, 58, 90, 201–3, 210
feminist theology
  Anabaptist and Mennonite ix–xi, 36–7, 40–3, 46, 127
  critique of subordination 23, 59–61, 63, 71
  influence of 34–7, 40–3, 52, 54, 118, 139 n.13, 201–3
  interpretation of Jesus 27, 45, 157, 202
  methodology 18, 40, 42–3, 48, 57–8, 64, 201–2
forgiveness
  commitment to 2–3, 117, 197
  of enemy 119, 140
  need for 147–8
  of perpetrator 65, 122, 131, 137–8, 140, 175
  seeking 123, 130–1, 179
  unconditional 109, 121–2, 197
freedom. *See also* liberation
  from abuse 149, 177, 187
  in Christ 5, 47, 60, 123, 133, 139, 141, 146–50, 171–2, 186

gospel
  as good news 2, 4, 18, 28, 46–8, 52, 63, 107, 126, 186, 197
  message of Jesus Christ 2–4, 50, 83, 126, 170–2, 179
  proclamation 60, 118, 139, 141, 146–7, 149–50
Guth, Karen V. 170

Hauerwas, Stanley 170, 203
haustafeln 71–3
healing
  church as place of 13, 108

SUBJECT INDEX

by Jesus   62–3, 118, 120, 123, 126, 131, 149
journey of   62–6, 128, 130–1, 144, 174–5, 177–8, 182–3, 185, 187
from violence   62, 136, 149, 190, 197
of women   13, 45, 54, 56, 60, 92–3, 116
Heggen, Carolyn Holderread   173, 175, 189, 193
heterosexism   20, 111
hierarchy   25, 38, 58, 103–6, 111, 121, 195–6
Holy Spirit   20, 22, 28–32, 62, 88, 111, 147, 186
home. *See also haustafeln*
   as domain of women   34, 38, 79, 121
   as location for discipleship   4, 27–8, 70–1, 75–7, 79, 88, 120–1
   as site of violence   12, 35, 39, 65, 122, 130, 137, 166, 198
hospitality   70–1, 74–81
human rights   63, 83 n.3, 84, 87, 90, 93. *See also* civil rights

image of God   20, 23, 32, 43, 65, 99, 108, 123, 140, 145–6, 197. *See also* Jesus, images of
immigrant   21, 57, 87, 103–4
imperialism. *See* domination, systems of
incarceration   62, 75–6, 162, 195
incarnation. *See* Christ, incarnation
inequality   48, 60, 86, 93, 194
injustice
   experience of   124, 206
   protesting   58, 211

systems of   20, 29, 60, 80–1, 87, 102, 108, 130–1, 212
transformation of   93, 128
institutional betrayal   179–82, 205, 210
insubordination   70–1, 74, 76–7
interreligious dialogue   93

Jesus   20, 30–2, 34–5, 43–9, 52, 54–57, 59–63, 65, 100, 118–21, 126, 149, 156–66, 204. *See also* Christ; politics of Jesus
   as Black   22–3, 25, 44
   coded as white   22–3, 25, 29, 31, 44
   images of   22–3, 26–8, 31–2, 43–7, 65
   on the margins   27, 44–5, 52, 100, 119–20, 126, 145–7
   masculinity of   26–8
   message of (*see* gospel)
   as servant   31–2, 46, 72–3, 80
   suffering of   46, 55–6, 59, 62, 99–100, 119, 125–6, 128, 140, 153, 156–7, 159, 163–4 (*see also* crucifixion)
   teachings of   20, 32, 43–6, 60, 88, 100, 108, 122, 126, 165, 207 (*see also* scripture)
Josephus, Flavius   155
justice. *See also* injustice; JustPraxis
   gender   4, 12
   of God   56, 63, 66, 120, 123–4, 127, 131, 140, 148–50
   justice-making   3–4
   racial justice   97, 102
   restorative   117, 185
   as a virtue   27

work of   28, 58, 63–6, 71, 81,
    89–91, 110, 119, 126–7,
    134, 139, 197, 201,
    207–8
JustPraxis   54–5, 63–6. *See also*
    healing; justice; liberation

Kavanaugh, Brett   142, 143 n.23,
    161–2
Kingdom of God. *See* reign of God
Koontz, Ted   173, 189 n.4

lament   62, 138, 149–50, 176–8,
    183–7, 191, 195–6,
    203
Lark, James and Rowena   107
Latina   x, 18, 24–5, 36, 39,
    41–2, 45, 54–8, 61, 65,
    126
Latin America x, 25, 55, 158–60.
    See also Colombia;
    Puerto Rico
LGBTQ   48, 156 n.8, 195–6
liberation. *See also* liberation
    theology
  within the church   45–6, 72,
    107, 116, 182, 198
  concept of   5, 58, 66, 94–5,
    123, 133–4, 139,
    147–9
  Jesus as liberator   44, 54, 56,
    60, 62, 83, 91–2, 99,
    120, 141, 146, 157,
    197
  of Jesus's politics   xv–xvi, 3–6,
    12–13, 18, 23–4, 54, 63
  movements   75, 101
  of women   27, 58, 64, 116,
    150
liberation theology   39, 54, 94–5,
    98, 101–2, 116, 126,
    156–7, 160 n.20. *See also*
    liberation, concept of
Luther, Martin   87

Mamas (in South Africa)   75–6,
    78, 81
marginalized
  bodies   24, 62, 85, 97, 99,
    143, 194, 196 (*see also*
    Black bodies)
  persons   13, 36–7, 45, 47–8,
    50–2, 55, 64, 98–100,
    107, 118, 146, 185, 203
    (*see also* the oppressed)
margins of society   42, 44–5, 47,
    57, 99, 106, 128, 205
martyrdom   56, 147
Mary, representations of   23–5
masculinity   18, 26–9, 31–2, 155,
    160
Mennonite Central Committee
    (MCC)   xiv, 2, 12, 35,
    48, 190
  Churchwide Statement on
    Sexual Abuse   11,
    189–98, 213–31
  discernment group   173–4
  Women's Concerns
    Committee   xiv, 36, 39,
    43, 190
  Women's Concerns Report   ix,
    34–50, 52
Mennonite Church USA   11–12,
    105, 107, 170–1, 173,
    189–93, 195–6, 198,
    210. *See also* Mennonite
    Central Committee;
    Yoder, John Howard,
    responses to Yoder's
    abuse by, Mennonite
    Church USA
  moderator   xiv, 12, 189, 192–3
  Women in Leadership Project
    124 n.33, 192
Mennonite urban missions   98,
    104–8
military   108, 160, 201, 205
militarism   20, 22, 24, 36

service   34, 117
soldier   159–61
Miller, Daniel   189 n.4, 193
Miller, Marlin   173
mission   6, 52, 92, 94, 98, 104–6, 110, 126, 170, 176, 178
moral canopy   180–1, 184–5
moral injury   205, 208–9
moral repair   179–81, 184–7, 207, 209–12
moral responsibility   52, 59, 102, 171, 176, 179, 181, 183
Morrison, Toni   126–7
mujerista theology   5, 42–3, 48, 52, 55–8, 62–6, 157

Neufeld, Chuck   189 n.4
nonviolence   31–2, 62, 83, 90, 100–2, 111, 127, 137, 140, 170, 187, 197, 207. *See also* pacifism; peace, peacemaking

obedience   55, 87–8, 119, 149, 197
offender. *See* perpetrator
oppressed, the   59–60, 62, 70, 98, 100–1, 107, 111, 117–19, 126–8, 131, 147, 171, 186. *See also* marginalized, persons
oppression   118
　context of   28, 43, 61, 80, 95
　experience of   57–8, 60, 63, 107, 116, 127–8, 134
　racial   57, 59, 70, 80, 102, 107, 109
　systems of   57–60, 62, 64, 71, 93, 98, 110–11, 116, 120, 124, 139 n.13, 142, 144, 157, 194 (*see also* domination, systems of; principalities)

pacifism   59, 65, 90, 127, 138–9, 201–3, 206–8. *See also* nonviolence; peace, peacemaking
Pankratz, Teresa   39 n.15
patriarchy   xv, 3, 5, 13, 35, 44, 47, 55–8, 62, 64, 93–4, 121, 155, 196
peace   63, 66, 78, 83, 90–1, 95, 100, 117, 123, 126, 144, 149–50, 198, 210. *See also* nonviolence; pacifism
　peace church   13, 52, 98–9, 104, 108, 175, 180, 185, 190, 201–3, 205–6
　peacemaking   3–4, 34, 78–81, 83–5, 91, 110–11, 121, 131, 140, 166, 171, 197, 205–7
　peace process in Colombia   83–86, 91
　peace theology   viii–x, 3–4, 6, 34, 60, 98, 117, 165–6, 170–2, 185, 202–4, 206, 210
Penner, Kim   203, 206
perpetrator   138, 146–50, 152–3, 157–9, 164, 171, 180, 208–9. *See also* abuse, by persons in authority
　accountability for   66, 142–3, 152, 162, 164, 211 (*see also* accountability, of John Howard Yoder)
　needs of   117–19, 140–1, 180, 183
　pity for   133–4, 144, 146–8, 150
　protection of   122, 126
politics of Jesus. *See also* liberation, of Jesus's politics
　in Colombia   89, 91–2

constructive development of 24–9, 43–7, 59–60, 66, 145–7, 154 n.3, 163–6, 197
and creation 51–2
embodiment of 202, 204, 206–7
in Mississippi 111
as resistance 119–21, 125–8
in South Africa 80
and suffering 54, 63, 131
The Politics of Jesus xi, xiv, 23, 59–60, 71–3, 145, 172
post-traumatic stress disorder (PTSD) 135, 137
poverty 20, 42, 44–5, 55, 59, 63, 86, 91, 118, 120, 126, 128, 195
power
abuse of 43, 60, 137, 147, 155, 157, 159, 180, 207, 210, 212 (*see also* Yoder, John Howard, abuse by)
analysis of 6, 28, 40, 42–3, 48, 51–2, 59–60, 63–4, 70–1, 78, 98, 111, 118, 121, 144, 150 n.37, 154 n.3, 157, 181–2, 184, 205–6, 208 n.9, 212
as cooperation 64 (*see also* empowerment)
spiritual 20, 61, 98–9, 118, 120, 125, 129, 134, 138, 141, 144–7, 149
worldly 3, 5, 19, 24–6, 31–2, 40, 47–9, 52, 59, 61, 63–5, 70–1, 74, 76–81, 100–1, 118–19, 121, 128, 149–50, 160, 205–6, 212 (*see also* principalities)
powerful, the xv, 2, 24, 26, 44, 51, 59, 63–4, 72, 88, 111, 118, 127–8, 133, 146, 186, 210
powerlessness 34, 44–5, 59, 133, 136, 144–5. *See also* submission
practical theology 39, 54, 83, 91, 93–4, 171
practice. *See also* praxis
aligning with theory 18, 30–2, 38–9, 94, 98, 102–3, 110, 121, 138–9, 163–4, 207
Anabaptist theology and 4, 6, 95, 98, 117–21, 165–6, 193–4, 197, 205, 207
in relation to theory 3, 58, 157, 171, 200–4, 212
praxis 5, 54–8, 91, 94–5. *See also* JustPraxis
prayer 56, 97, 174, 178
principalities 5, 23, 77, 81. *See also* domination, systems of
prophetic role viii, 90, 92, 95, 111, 120, 150, 185–6
Puerto Rico 55–6, 61

race 24, 32, 41–2, 58, 74, 76, 78–9, 95, 97–111, 195. *See also* Black; whiteness
American racial history 97–111
anti-racism 22, 32, 97–9, 105, 107, 111
inter-racial relationships 97, 101, 105–7, 109
multiracial churches 109–10
racial reconciliation model 97, 108
racism x, 6, 18–24, 32, 41–2, 55, 59, 62, 71, 75–6, 81, 97–9, 101–6, 109–11, 194–5, 201, 205

Ramírez, Deborah 161–2
rebellion 20, 101, 118, 122, 128, 154
reconciliation 2–3, 63, 83, 86, 92–3, 97, 108, 117, 175, 178, 185, 197
redemption 118, 122, 125, 128, 134, 139, 147–9, 156–7, 202, 211
redemptive closure 211
reign of God 5, 22, 37 n.8, 43, 63, 72, 80, 110, 118–19, 126
release (from) 116, 118, 120, 138–9, 141, 144–6, 148–9, 171, 174, 177, 179. See also freedom, healing, liberation
repentance 118, 133, 143, 175–6, 179, 186, 197–8
resistance
  to accountability 173, 198, 211
  to evil 110, 125–6, 128, 148
  to feminism 37
  nonresistance 46, 59
  nonviolent 62, 101, 127
  political 64, 66, 78, 87, 92–3, 97–8, 101, 104–5, 119–20, 127, 153–4, 207
  to suffering 46, 63, 136, 146, 165, 200, 205, 207
restitution 63, 66, 85
restoration 63, 85, 94, 117–18, 123, 138, 148, 179, 185
Revolutionary Armed Forces of Colombia–People's Army (FARC–EP) 83, 87
revolutionary in subordination 73–4, 78, 80–1. See also insubordination
revolutionary subordination 23–4, 59–60, 71–3

Richards, Emma Sommers x
righteous living 90, 95. See also discipleship
rights. See human rights and civil rights
Roman Empire 26–8, 61, 100, 128, 155, 158–61
Ross, Sam and Morag 77–8, 81

sacrifice 56, 109, 143, 197. See also Christ, sacrifice of
salvation 46, 55, 60, 89, 95, 116–17, 119, 122–6, 129, 131, 145, 157, 186
scripture. See also haustafeln
  Bible study 76, 79, 92–3, 97
  creation story 99, 108, 134 n.2
  disciples 27–8, 31, 44, 60, 119
  Good Samaritan 110–11
  interpretation of 27–31, 39 n.14, 44–5, 47, 56–7, 83–4, 87–8, 92–4, 99, 156–61, 163, 196
  Jesus in 20, 26–31, 43–7, 100, 146 n.29, 159–60, 163 (see also Jesus, teachings of)
  Magnificat 64
  Mary and Martha 45, 121
  Rahab 194
  Samaritan woman (at the well) 27, 44 n.36, 45
  Sermon on the Mount 45, 63, 92, 100, 148 n.31
  woman who touched Jesus's clothes 27, 46
  women at the empty tomb 45, 154 n.3
segregation 70, 80, 93, 97–8, 103–5, 109. See also apartheid
Seneca the Younger 155, 160

servanthood. *See* discipleship, as servanthood
sexism x, 20, 24, 55, 59, 111, 201, 205
sexual diversity 93. *See also* LGBTQ
sexual orientation 32, 95, 156 n.8, 195. *See also* LGBTQ
shalom 31, 99, 127, 140
shame 116, 120, 123, 125, 137, 139, 147–8, 185
Shenk, Sara Wenger xiv, 185, 189, 189 n.4, 202–3, 211
silencing 37–8, 48, 50–1, 54, 116, 121, 138, 142, 149, 155, 158, 175, 179, 185, 206
sin 20, 23, 29, 102, 108, 116, 118, 122–4, 128, 131, 133, 138–41, 179
Slough, Rebecca 173, 177, 184, 189
Society of Christian Ethics 170, 201–3
Sofia xv, 57, 62, 65
solidarity
   God's 125–8, 131 (*see also* Jesus, suffering of)
   Jesus's 44–5, 52, 62, 100, 119
   with survivors of sexual violence 153–4, 162–6, 177
Soto Albrecht, Elizabeth xi, 12, 189, 192–3
South Africa 70–1, 74–5, 78–81
sovereignty of God 134, 148 n.31
spirituality 32, 55, 64–6, 79, 83, 91–4, 98, 130–1, 163, 166, 176, 181, 183
Stephens, Darryl W. xiv, 203
Stoltzfus, Regina Shands 189 n.4, 193

Stutzman, Ervin 173, 175, 189
submission 38, 46, 56, 59, 71–2, 118, 121, 139, 145, 147, 149, 195
subordinate role 24, 56, 59–60, 62, 72–81
suffering 70, 127, 149, 161. *See also* abuse; violence
   Jesus identification with the suffering 44, 62, 100, 131 (*see also* Jesus, suffering of; solidarity, Jesus's)
   politics of 54, 56–7, 59–60, 120, 131
   as supposedly redemptive 4, 46–7, 54–6, 60–1, 66, 99, 116, 119, 121–6, 156–7
   theology of 54–6, 59, 197–8
   transformation of 46–7, 62–6, 125, 128–9, 145, 156–7
   voluntary 46, 54–6, 59–60 (*see also* revolutionary subordination)
survivor 34, 39, 139, 146, 159, 183–5. *See also* victim
   of abuse 34, 174
   of sexual violence 146, 153, 156–7, 161–6, 184, 189 nn.2, 4, 191, 197–8, 207, 209–10
Syro-Phoenician woman 27, 45–6

tainted legacies, teaching of 208–9, 211
terrorism 61, 158–60
Till, Emmett 108
Till, Mamie 108
torture 89, 119, 125, 141, 146 n.29, 156, 159–60

transformation
  of individuals 20, 24, 30, 78, 80, 123, 144, 211
  of the world 46, 63, 80, 85–6, 89, 91–3, 98–9, 108–11, 145, 150, 163
transparency 77, 170, 174–5, 177–8, 180, 187, 200–1.
  See also truth-telling
trauma 56, 61, 108, 123, 135, 137, 154 n.3, 178, 181–4, 201, 205, 211.
  See also abuse, as trauma
Trump, Donald 21, 142 n.20, 144 n.24
truth-telling
  about abuse and suffering 2–3, 125, 128, 138–9, 149–50, 161, 183, 207
  institutional 170–83, 187
  as liberative practice 54, 56, 128, 133–4, 146, 183, 186, 197
  as witness 108, 139, 146–50, 157, 191, 207
Turner, Nat 101

Vesey, Denmark 101
victim 62, 119, 121, 126, 204, 210, 212. *See also* survivor
  of armed conflict 85, 93
  of John Howard Yoder 140, 170–80, 182, 187, 189, 198, 200, 202, 205–6, 210
  of sexual abuse 65–6, 133–50, 154–60, 162, 165–6, 170–84, 192, 197–8, 203, 210
  of slavery 109
violence 26, 28–9, 34–5, 54, 97–100, 119, 121, 126, 130–1, 133–4, 138–41, 144–50, 152, 157–9, 185, 198, 200–12.
  See also abuse
  military 83–4, 87, 100, 159–60, 205
  sexualized 35, 85, 109, 122, 133–44, 146–50, 152–66, 170–1, 181, 186–7, 189–90, 193–6, 198, 200–3, 205, 208–11
  of the state 61, 75, 89, 100, 155, 159–60, 163, 205, 212
  systemic 40, 54, 62, 66, 83–4, 87, 91, 100, 103–4, 108, 111, 158, 170, 194–6, 201, 204–6, 210

war viii, 3–4, 6, 26, 29, 85, 100, 102, 104, 117, 159
Weinstein, Harvey 142–3, 204
West, Traci 170, 203
whiteness. *See also* Jesus, coded as white; race
  deconstructing and decentering 24–5, 29, 32, 42, 44, 56–7, 79, 107–8, 110–11
  logic of 19–20, 22–3, 50–1, 106, 117, 196
  as normative 18–25, 29, 31–2, 41, 60, 97–9, 101–5, 108, 152 n.1, 194
  privilege 18–20, 24, 28, 60, 77, 104–6, 153
white nationalism 22
white racism 23–4, 41, 105, 109
white supremacy 20, 22, 70, 74–5, 97, 101, 103–4, 106, 109–10
wholeness 46–7, 62, 64, 116, 123, 128, 130. *See also* salvation

Wisdom. *See* Sofia
witness, Christian   3, 6, 62, 93,
    105, 117, 131, 134, 164,
    175, 185, 187, 206.
    See also bearing witness
womanist theology   41–3, 48, 52,
    57, 59–61, 64, 118, 157,
    201–2, 210
Women's Concerns Report
    34–50, 52. *See also*
    Committee on Women's
    Concerns
worship. *See also* prayer
    act of   13, 109, 157, 203
    liturgy   20, 24, 89, 99, 122,
        176–9, 185–7, 197, 203
    Lord's Prayer   28, 46–7, 66
    practice of   22, 34, 36, 47, 102,
        105, 123, 130, 193, 197–8

Yoder, John Howard
    abuse by   3, 60, 139–40, 166,
        170–9, 182–3, 189–91,
        198, 200–12

legacy of   xi, 3–5, 13, 140 n.14,
    170, 172–3, 175, 178,
    181, 189, 198, 200–4,
    206–11
responses to Yoder's abuse by
    Anabaptist Mennonite
        Biblical Seminary
        170–9, 181–7, 189–90,
        210
    Institute of Mennonite
        Studies   xi
    institutions   170, 176, 205,
        210
    MennoMedia   190 n.6
    Mennonite Church
        USA   140, 170–6,
        189–98, 208, 210
    Mennonite women   3–5,
        173, 176, 178–9, 184–5,
        200, 203–12
    Society of Christian Ethics
        170, 201–3
teaching works by   172–3,
    208–11